For A
New Liberty

FOR A NEW LIBERTY

Murray N. Rothbard

The Macmillan Company · New York · New York
Collier-Macmillan Publishers · London

The Macmillan Company
866 Third Avenue, New York, N.Y. 10022
Collier-Macmillan Canada Ltd., Toronto, Ontario

Library of Congress Catalog Card Number: 72–87165

First Printing

Printed in the United States of America

Contents

v

vi   *Contents*

For A
New Liberty

1

Introduction: The New Libertarian Movement

The New Libertarians

IN THE SPRING of 1971, a new and seemingly strange ideological movement burst upon the public consciousness. Centered, as are so many new movements, on the college campuses, but also including adult leaders, these new "libertarians" were suddenly everywhere, in issue after issue of *The New York Times, Newsweek, Time, Playboy, Esquire, The Wall Street Journal, The National Observer,* and the Washington *Post,* daily papers in Philadelphia and Boston, and countless appearances on radio and television, including the NBC–TV "Today" show. A host of major publishers hastened to schedule books on the new movement, a movement whose writings had previously been confined to privately printed leaflets and mimeographed "little" magazines.

Why this spate of publicity? The wave of publicity began after the 1970 elections, when the press began to observe that the previously formidable New Left movement on the campuses was suddenly dead and gone, to the extent that the only campus activity in the elections had been by groups of young conservatives. Apathy or disillusion on the left had suddenly replaced militant activism on campus after campus throughout the country, and what little political action remained was conservative. In particular, the major activists on New York campuses were a host of youths for the Conservative party's Jim Buckley for Senate. What particularly puzzled the media was that at influential Columbia University, a few short years earlier the bellwether of campus revolution, the "Buckley for Senate" movement was led by youths calling themselves "libertarian" who in many ways seemed the reverse of conservative. Furthermore, they found that the libertarian group at Columbia— "Freedom Conspiracy"—was, *mirabile dictu*, the largest ideological group on the campus. But what sort of "conservatives" were kids who opposed the war in Vietnam, fiercely favored civil liberties and the repeal of drug laws, and advocated total disobedience to the draft, which they considered slavery?

Reportage on the Freedom Conspiracy, the subsequent total break of this group and other libertarians from the conservative right, and an angry attempt by Bill Buckley to squelch the new movement generated the rest of the publicity. Nationwide attention came to this peculiar movement, which seemed "rightist" on some issues (free enterprise, private property, the welfare system), and "leftist" on others (the war, the draft, civil liberties), and also seemed to have the capacity to irritate *The National Review* conservatives beyond all measure. And even though many of the new libertarians had been youth leaders for Nixon in 1968, none of the factions and groups within this rapidly growing movement supported him for reelection in 1972. Some, indeed, supported anyone *but* Nixon, others formed a new Libertarian Party, while still others rejected political action altogether.

Interest in the new libertarianism has also been sparked by the fact that the movement emerged precisely at the time America suffers as never before from an ideological vacuum. For forty years, if not for the entire century, the dominant ideology in the United States has been liberalism; furthermore, liberalism has governed our political institutions for virtually the same length of time. But it has become increasingly obvious, even to liberals, that something has gone very wrong with the liberal dream, and that the accelerating crisis in America demonstrates that liberalism itself is flawed at its very core. In the 1930s and 1940s, Franklin D. Roosevelt was the god of the new liberalism; under the Rooseveltian aegis America would be led and prodded into a New Eden: an Eden of prosperity through the welfare state at home and peace through a "strong" foreign policy and collective security abroad. Yet, after four decades of New Deal and post-New Deal rule, four decades of being moulded in the Rooseveltian image, even liberals have found that the dream has turned to ashes. At home, Big Liberal Government has led to oppressive rule by oligarchic bureaucracies; the welfare state has become a State that subsidizes, controls, and pushes around the American public, and the poor more than most other groups. The welfare state has become the warfare state, the military-industrial garrison state, creating cartels, crippling individual and local initiative, and repressing the liberties of the citizenry. The liberal drive for racial integration by federal force has suddenly turned into a nightmare of race war; the vaunted democratization of America through the public school system has become a horror of crime, ignorance, and coercive oppression of the nation's school children—in fact, an America that has always prided itself on its educational system is helplessly seeing that system in grave and growing crisis: spiritual, educational, and financial. The cities are turning into jungles.

And last but not least, in foreign affairs the New Deal program of "internationalism" on behalf of freedom and democracy has become a morass of what Charles A. Beard perceptively warned would turn into "perpetual war for perpetual peace"; and the "liberation" of foreign peoples has patently meant their genocidal "liberation" from this earth by mass slaughter inflicted by American firepower.

Neither can anyone maintain any longer that the trouble

comes from the abandonment of liberalism by "reactionary" successors to Franklin Roosevelt. For it has become increasingly clear that FDR's successors were truly his heirs in every way. If Lyndon Baines Johnson has always referred to Franklin Roosevelt as his "Big Daddy," the patrimony should by now be evident to everyone. We are reaping the fruits of four decades of Big, Unlimited, Government at home and abroad; Vietnam is the fruit of collective security, just as the military-industrial complex and the educational jungles are the fruits of the welfare state and the "mixed economy" at home.

It was, in fact, the growing realization of the abject failure of liberalism at home and abroad that generated the New Left in the late 1960s. But the New Left had burned itself out not simply in the futility of random violence, but still more in the knowledge that it had totally alienated itself from the great bulk of the American people, middle and working class alike. For a group that attempted to speak in the name of "The People," this was a certain path to oblivion.

With liberalism failing and the New Left dead, where could the growing number of dissidents turn? Certainly not to conservatism—*National Review*—Bill Buckley, Strom Thurmond—conservatism, which only promised a more intensified form of the evils of liberalism. For if the liberals were implicated and tied to the Vietnam horror, the modern conservatives had always led the way in calling for ever greater and wider war. Superhawks yearning with only thinly veiled secrecy for the "nuking" of Moscow and Peking, loud admirers of the military and therefore of the military-industrial economy, apostles of repression and the outlawing of "immorality," the conservatives could only meet each vital problem with a call for all out force by the State—the army or the police, depending on the theater of operations. Ridden and oppressed by a Leviathan State increasingly out of control in its depredations against the citizenry, how could restive Americans or disillusioned liberals turn to a conservatism that only promised them a great deal more of their current malady of statism? To many, then, the new libertarianism seemed to be a new and refreshing alternative, an alternative with ideas and rhetoric capable of appealing to left and right alike, and to a broad range of Americans from campus hippies to conservative Middle Americans. To a growing number of Americans, libertarianism sounded attractive and appealing; could it work in practice?

The Movement

The current libertarian movement came of age at the biennial convention of the Young Americans for Freedom at St. Louis at the end of August 1969. There had developed within this outstanding organization of conservative youth a strong heretical libertarian minority, which had formed itself into the "Libertarian Caucus." Virtually the youth political-action arm of William F. Buckley and *The National Review*, YAF had been founded at Buckley's estate at Sharon, Connecticut, in 1959. While paying brief homage to individualist and libertarian rhetoric in its founding statement, YAF's action programs have been quite the opposite, being confined to anticommunism at home and abroad, supplemented in recent years by collaborating with the police in suppressing student rebellions. In short, while some of its rhetoric was anti-State, YAF's actual policies consisted of calling upon the State (whether the army or the police) to use its coercive weapons more forcefully.

The growing body of "libertarians" within YAF had taken its individualist rhetoric more seriously. Many had joined YAF attracted by the individualistic rhetoric of the Goldwater campaign. They had by now arrived at the view that the government should confine its power strictly to defense of the individual and his property against attack, but they found increasingly that the ruling elite and the bulk of the membership of YAF had no (or even negative) interest in laissez-faire. And they found the YAF leadership less than anxious to repeal laws, such as laws against drug use, that invaded personal liberty.

The sticking point came on the explosive issue of the draft, an issue that is obviously intensely personal and relevant to the nation's youth. The YAF leadership had grudgingly come around to the view that the draft should be replaced by a volunteer army, but their reasons were strictly pragmatic: a volunteer army would be more efficient and more dedicated, and the cost to the taxpayers would be minimal. But to the libertarians the draft is not a matter of technical efficiency. To them, the draft is slavery pure and simple; slavery, moreover, in which the slave has a good chance of killing or being killed. For the libertarians, then, opposition to conscription is total and absolute. Therefore, while YAF officially suggested the replacement of the draft by a volunteer army, the Libertarian Caucus was ready to advocate draft resistance, including escape to Canada or outright refusal to obey the law. To the conservatives of YAF, dedicated to "law and order" and obedience to all law, the libertarian call for civil disobedience to the draft was anathema.

At the 1969 YAF convention in St. Louis, the libertarians were rebuffed and defeated at every turn, giving increasing point to the position of the small Anarchist Caucus, which had been urging the far larger group of libertarians to split off openly from the organization. Not only had the Anarchist Caucus gone a step beyond the Libertarians to advocate anarchism, but it had also proceeded to denounce the war in Vietnam as a manifestation of American imperialism; in contrast, YAF itself was, of course, in favor of the war, while the libertarians had been moving to an "isolationist" position of opposing the war as an unjustified extension of government into the affairs of other nations.[1] The crisis point of the convention came when one of the anarchists came to the floor and dramatically set fire to his draft card. The conservative ranks erupted into the cry,

---

[1] The statement of the Anarchist Caucus can be found in Henry J. Silverman, ed., *American Radical Thought: The Libertarian Tradition* (Lexington, Mass.: D. C. Heath and Co., 1970), pp. 266–73. An account of the YAF convention can be found in Jerome Tuccille, *Radical Libertarianism: A Right Wing Alternative* (Indianapolis: Bobbs Merrill, 1970), pp. 96–109.

"Kill the commie," and a virtual riot ensued, with the conservatives escalating their cries to "Kill the libertarians!" Even the libertarian chant of "laissez-faire!" was countered by the conservatives' "lazy fairies!"

The hysterical gut reaction of the conservatives to even the most fundamental pleas for individual liberty served to radicalize and polarize the Libertarian Caucus. Systematically, both during and after the convention, the YAF national leadership angrily purged the grass roots state officers who were either anarchists or libertarians; the remainder resigned from the organization. The great libertarian split from YAF, and, by extension, from the conservative movement in America, had finally taken place. In the process, YAF lost the bulk of its leaders and membership in California, Pennsylvania, New Jersey, and Virginia.

Having been ejected from the conservative movement, and being activists by nature, the libertarians decided to form their own organizations rather than fragment and dissipate their activity. The cohesive California movement, centered in the Los Angeles area, formed its own California Libertarian Alliance, numbering about 1,000 members. The remainder of the Libertarian Caucus decided to merge with a small, Maryland-based group called the Society for Rational Individualism, which had been issuing a monthly magazine, *The Rational Individualist*. The two groups formed, in late 1969, the Society for Individual Liberty, with approximately 3,000 members. SIL is the largest and best-established libertarian organization in the country. It has two major centers: Maryland, where the monthly *Individualist* is published; and Philadelphia, which issues leaflets and organizes chapters on college campuses and other locations throughout the country.

SIL, however, is by no means the only organization or tendency within the libertarian movement. The movement has grown so large that it contains within itself numerous factions, splits, tendencies, and variations ranging through a wide ideological spectrum. In one sense, we can say that libertarians have already succumbed to the factional and destructive tendencies of older ideological movements, notably the Marxists; but in another sense, the diversity is a sign of growth and vitality, and a sign also of a developing intellectual concern with the subtle and advanced doctrinal issues, as well as increasing attention to tactical and strategic differences that are inevitable in even the most cohesive movement. When a movement consists of only a handful of people, the very idea of worrying about strategy and tactics seems grotesquely unreal; it is only when a movement begins to have a palpable impact on society that a concern over strategy will develop.

Throughout the numerous factions and splinters of the movement, however, there is agreement on the central core of the libertarian creed. The crucial axiom of that creed is: no man or group of men have the right to aggress against the person or property of anyone else. This might be called the "non-aggression" axiom. "Aggression" is defined as the initiation of the use or threat of physical violence against the person or property of someone else. Aggression is therefore synonymous with "invasion." How this axiom may be arrived at will be discussed below, and the paths toward attaining the axiom vary among different groups of libertarians. But all libertarians agree on nonaggression as the central axiom of their doctrine.

If no man may aggress against—invade—the person or property of another, this means that every man is free to do whatever he wishes, except commit such aggression. The great nineteenth-century libertarian theorist Herbert Spencer formulated a similar axiom: "Law of Equal Liberty." "Freedom" or "liberty" is therefore rigorously defined in such a credo as: the absence of invasion. A man is free when he is not being aggressed against; and all men, or "society," is free when no aggression or invasion is being committed.

If no man may aggress against another; if, in short, everyone has the absolute right to be "free" from aggression, then this at once implies that the libertarian stands foursquare for what are generally known as "civil liberties": the freedom to speak, publish, assemble, and to engage in such "victimless crimes" as pornography, sexual deviation, and prostitution (which the libertarian does not regard as "crimes" at all, since he defines a "crime" as violent invasion of someone else's person or property). Furthermore, he regards conscription as slavery on a massive scale. And since war, especially modern war, entails the mass slaughter of civilians, the libertarian regards such conflicts as mass murder and therefore totally illegitimate.

All of these positions are now considered "leftist" on the contemporary ideological scale. On the other hand, since the libertarian also opposes invasion of the rights of private property, this also means that he just as emphatically opposes government interference with property rights or with the free-market economy through controls, regulations, subsidies, or prohibitions. For if every individual has the right to his own property without having to suffer aggressive depredation, then he also has the right to give away his property (bequest and inheritance) and to exchange it for the property of others (free contract and the free market economy) without interference. The libertarian favors the right to unrestricted private property and free-exchange; hence, a system of "laissez-faire capitalism."

In current terminology again, the libertarian position on property and economics would be called "extreme right wing." But the libertarian sees no inconsistency in being "leftist" on some issues and "rightist" on others. On the contrary, he sees his own position as virtually the *only* consistent one, consistent on behalf of the liberty of every individual. For how can the leftist be opposed to the violence of war and conscription while at the same time supporting the violence of taxation and government control? And how can the rightist trumpet his devotion to private property and free enterprise while at the same time favoring war, conscription, and the outlawing of non-invasive activities and practices that he deems immoral? And how can the rightist favor a free market while seeing nothing amiss in the vast subsidies, distortions, and unproductive inefficiencies involved in the military-industrial complex?

While opposing any and all private or group aggression against the rights of person and property, the libertarian sees that throughout history and into the present day, there has been one central, dominant, and overriding aggressor upon all of these rights: the State. In contrast to all other thinkers, left, right, or in-between, the libertarian refuses to give the State the moral sanction to commit actions that almost everyone agrees would be immoral, illegal, and criminal if committed by any person or group in society. The libertarian, in short, insists on applying the general moral law to everyone, and makes no special exemptions for any person or group. But if we look at the State naked, as it were, we see that it is universally allowed, and even encouraged, to commit all the acts which even nonlibertarians concede are reprehensible crimes. The State habitually commits mass murder, which it calls "war," or sometimes "suppression of subversion"; the State engages in enslavement into its military forces, which it calls "conscription"; and it lives and has its being in the practice of forcible theft, which it calls "taxation." The libertarian insists that whether or not such practices are supported by the majority of the population is not germane to their nature: that, regardless of popular sanction, War is Mass Murder, Conscription is Slavery, and Taxation is Robbery. The libertarian, in short, is almost completely the child in the fable, pointing out insistently that the emperor has no clothes.

Throughout the ages, the emperor has had a series of pseudo-clothes provided for him by the nation's intellectual caste. In past centuries, the intellectuals informed the public that the State or its rulers were divine, or at least clothed in divine authority, and therefore what might *look* to the naïve and untutored eye as despotism, mass murder, and theft on a grand scale was only the divine working its benign and mysterious ways in the body politic. In recent decades, as the divine sanction has worn a bit threadbare, the emperor's "court intellectuals" have spun ever more sophisticated apologia: informing the public that what the government does is for the "common good" and the "public welfare," that the process of taxation-and-spending works through the mysterious process of the "multiplier" to keep the economy on an even keel, and that, in any case, a wide variety of governmental "services" could not possibly be performed by citizens acting voluntarily on the market or in society. All of this the libertarian denies: he sees the various apologia as fraudulent means of obtaining public support for the State's rule, and he insists that whatever services the government actually performs could be supplied far more efficiently and far more morally by private and cooperative enterprise.

The libertarian therefore considers one of his prime educational tasks is to spread the demystification and desanctification of the State among its hapless subjects. His task is to demonstrate repeatedly and in depth that not only the emperor but even the "democratic" state has no clothes; that all governments subsist by exploitive rule over the public; and that such rule is the reverse of objective necessity. He strives to show that the very existence of taxation and the State necessarily sets up a class division between the exploiting rulers and the exploited ruled. He seeks to show that the task of the court intellectuals who have always supported the State has ever been to weave mystification in order to induce the public to accept State rule, and that these intellectuals obtain, in return, a share in the power and pelf extracted by the rulers from their deluded subjects.

Take, for example, the institution of taxation, which statists have claimed is in some sense really "voluntary." Anyone who truly believes in the "voluntary" nature of taxation is invited to refuse to pay taxes and to see what then happens to him. If we analyze taxation, we find that, among all the persons and institutions in society, only the government acquires its revenues through coercive violence. Everyone else in society acquires income *either* through voluntary gift (lodge, charitable society, chess club) *or* through the sale of goods or services voluntarily purchased by consumers. If anyone *but* the government proceeded to "tax," this would clearly be considered coercion and thinly disguised banditry. Yet the mystical trappings of "sovereignty" have so veiled the process that only libertarians are prepared to call taxation what it is: legalized and organized theft on a grand scale.

The Spectrum

Having examined the central core of libertarian thought and attitude, let us explore the numerous factions and tendencies within the current libertarian movement, all of which at least pay homage to the central doctrine. While the terms "left" and "right" have become hopelessly muddled through shifting and inconsistent use over the years, it still remains convenient to align the various tendencies and factions of the libertarian movement along its own particular "left-right" spectrum.[2]

At the extreme right-wing fringe of the movement and, as with all fringe groups, at times scarcely discernible as being within the spectrum, are those who believe in old-fashioned laissez-faire. The major laissez-faire group is the Foundation for Economic Education of Irvington-on-Hudson, New York, for which many middle-aged members of the libertarian movement have worked at one time or another. President and dominant figure at FEE is Leonard E. Read, who established the organization in 1946. Formerly, he had been an official with the Los Angeles Chamber of Commerce and the National Industrial Conference Board. Prominent people associated with FEE include Ludwig von Mises, the doyen of laissez-faire economics; Henry Hazlitt, former editorial writer for *The New York Times* and economic columnist for *Newsweek*; and John Chamberlain, syndicated columnist and once a prominent radical writer of the 1930s.

Laissez-fairists classically believe that a central government

[2] A more detailed analysis of the libertarian spectrum may be found in Murray N. Rothbard, "Know Your Rights," *WIN* (March 1, 1971).

must exist, and therefore that taxes too must exist, but insist that taxation be confined to the prime "governmental" function of defending person and property against violent attack. Any pressing of government beyond this function is considered illegitimate. In its early years, the FEE staff was far more "anarchistic," friendly to such classical nonviolent anarchists as Tolstoy and Thoreau, and willing at least to consider the more extreme, anarchist position. Thus, in 1950, Mr. Read, after proclaiming the necessity for keeping the violence of government strictly limited to the defense of person and property, questioned whether even those limits were sufficient. He confessed that even such limits left him with two critical questions to which he had not been able to find satisfactory answers. First, "Can violence be instituted, regardless of how official or how limited in intention, without begetting violence outside officialdom and beyond the prescribed limitation?" Second, and more important, "Is not limitation of government, except for relatively short periods, impossible? Will not the predatory instincts of some men, which government is designed to suppress, eventually appear in the agents selected to do the suppressing? These instincts, perhaps, are inseparable companions of power . . . If there be criminals among us, what is to keep them from gaining and using the power of government?" [3]

In recent years, however, particularly since the rise of the idea of civil disobedience on the New Left, FEE has moved sharply "rightward" (i.e., "State-ward"). All hints of flirtation with anarchism have been dropped, and FEE publications have been ringing with stern injunctions for obedience to law-and-order. In fact, Read and FEE have taken the position that it is immoral and illegitimate to disobey the laws of the American State—no matter how admittedly unjust any of these laws or

[3] Leonard E. Read, *Students of Liberty* (Irvington-on-Hudson: Foundation for Economic Education, 1950), p. 14. Strong Tolstoyan influence may also be found in Read, "On That Day Began Lies," *Essays on Liberty*, Vol. I (Irvington-on-Hudson: Foundation for Economic Education, 1952), pp. 231–52.

edicts might be. Influencing legislators to amend or repeal these laws is considered the only morally permissible form of political action against unjust acts of government. The only exception Mr. Read would grant to this call for civil obedience is the unlikely event that his freedom to protest and argue against unjust laws should ever be curtailed by government.

Despite its former prominence among libertarians, the great bulk of today's libertarians, especially among the youth, have totally rejected FEE's classical laissez-faire position. For one thing, they have seen its basic inconsistency: if taxation for building dams or steel mills is robbery, then it is also robbery for *whatever* government activity it may finance, including such supposedly legitimate "governmental" functions as the police, the armed forces, and the courts. If it is legitimate for the State to coerce the taxpayer into financing the police, then why is it not equally legitimate to coerce the taxpayer for many other activities, including building steel factories, subsidizing favored groups, etc? If taxation is robbery, then surely it is robbery no matter the *ends*, benevolent or malevolent, for which the State employs these stolen funds.

Most libertarians also reject the laissez-fairist position of FEE that it is morally imperative to obey *all* laws, no matter how despotic, as well as FEE's patriotic devotion—held by most American laissez-fairists—to the United States Constitution and to the American State. If a law or edict is unjust and despotic, and therefore invades the rights of the individual, libertarians find it hard to justify any moral command to obey that law, although, of course, it may well be tactically prudent to do so. Furthermore, most libertarians today find the American Constitution (even as originally construed and framed) scarcely a libertarian document. In fact, the Constitution was itself an illegal and statist *coup d'état* against the far more libertarian Articles of Confederation.

Finally, most libertarians also find current laissez-fairists—in stark contrast to their nineteenth-century forebears—conspicuously silent on the heavy responsibility of big business for the accelerated growth of statism in twentieth-century America; instead, the blame is almost always placed on unions, politicians, and leftish intellectuals. Moreover, there is almost never any criticism of the greatest single force propelling the growth of the Leviathan State in America—the military-industrial complex, and the American Empire fueled by that complex. For all these reasons, the FEE-laissez-fairist position has virtually no influence on today's libertarian youth, who now constitute the vast bulk of the libertarian movement.

One degree to the left of FEE, but still on the right of the libertarian spectrum, is the Randian and neo-Randian movements, those who follow or have been influenced by the novelist Ayn Rand. Since the publication of Rand's novel *Atlas Shrugged* in 1957, the emotional impact of this and other Rand novels attracted a large following of young people into her "Objectivist" movement. In addition to the emotional drawing-power of the novels, Randianism provided the eager acolyte with an attempt at an integrated philosophical system, grounded on Aristotelian epistemology, and blended with a Nietzschean egoism, pretentious hero-worship, laissez-faire economics, and a natural rights political philosophy grounded on the libertarian axiom of nonaggression. Since the dramatic and irrevocable split between Rand and her appointed "intellectual heir" and chief organizer, Nathanial Branden, in 1968, Randianism has virtually collapsed as an organized movement, but her philosophical influence remains prodigious on the great bulk of libertarian youth.

Politically, Ayn Rand is to the left of the laissez-fairists in at least formally rejecting taxation as robbery, and therefore as illegitimate. However, instead of proceeding logically from a rejection of taxation to outright "anarcho-capitalism," Randian political doctrine wants to preserve the existing unitary State, with its crucial monopoly over the means of coercion and over ultimate arbitration and decision-making; it wishes to define its "government" as a utopian institution which retains its State

monopoly of coercion and decision-making and yet gains its
revenue only by voluntary contributions from its citizens. Still
worse, while Randians agree that taxation is robbery, they stub-
bornly refuse to regard the existing tax-subsisting government
as a band of robbers. Hence, Rand illogically infuses into the
political outlook of herself and her charges an emotional devotion to the *existing* American government and the American
Constitution which totally negates her own libertarian axioms.
While Rand opposes the war in Vietnam, for example, she does
so purely on tactical grounds as a mistake not in our "national
interest" rather than as a gigantic antilibertarian exercise in
mass murder and destruction of Vietnamese property. As a result, she is far more passionate in her hostility to the un-
patriotic *protesters* against the war than she is to the war itself.
Thus, she advocated the firing of Professor Eugene Genovese
from Rutgers University, on the surprisingly *anti*individualist
ground that "no man may support the victory of the enemies
of his country." And even though Rand passionately opposes
the draft as slavery, she also believes with Read and the laissez-
fairists that it is illegitimate to disobey the laws of the American State, including the draft, no matter how unjust—so long
as her freedom to protest such laws remains.

Along with FEE, Rand also moved "rightward" during the
1960s, particularly in her implacable hostility to the New Left
and the campus rebellions, so much so as to ignore the vital
role of the draft and the Vietnam war in igniting this massive
protest. This "rightward" move has gone so far as to lead her
to support the multibillion-dollar American space program, despite its evident violation of even the most elementary laissez-
faire principles, and to defend air pollution as either nonexistent or essential to modern technology and industrial civilization.

Part of the reason for Rand's increasing superpatriotism is
her simplistic attitude toward the "international communist
conspiracy." While Randians are not exactly champions of war,
they are prevented by their simplistic diabolism from absorbing

the revisionist insights into American foreign policy—from realizing that the Cold War and American interventions overseas
were caused by the expanding aggressions of American imperialism rather than by a noble response to "communist expansionism" by the "freest nation on earth." Randians persist
in the general conservative myth that the antipode of individualism is communism, failing to realize that the *real* antipode to liberty in America today is the existing Corporate
Monopoly Welfare-Warfare State.

A corollary attitude of Rand's is her view of Big Business.
While pro forma opposing probusiness as well as antibusiness
interventions by government, Rand is too committed emo-
tionally to worship of the Big Businessman-as-Hero to concede
that it is precisely Big Business that is largely responsible for
the twentieth-century march into aggressive statism that she
abhors. In her superpatriotism, her misty devotion to the Big
Businessman, and her stern adherence to civil obedience, Ayn
Rand takes her place with the orthodox laissez-fairists on the
extreme right fringe of the libertarian spectrum.

With the decline of organized Randianism since the split of
1968, however, the great bulk of Randians have been cast adrift
to think for themselves, and large numbers of them have been
moving steadily "leftward" into the mainstream of the libertarian movement. Ayn Rand herself continues to set forth her
official "line" in her fortnightly *Ayn Rand Letter*; and orthodox
Randian economists, in particular Alan Greenspan and Dr.
Martin Anderson, were influential in the early years of the Nixon
administration. Among the neo-Randians the full panoply of
Randian political attitudes continues to be held by such persons as Nathanial Branden himself, who has organized his own
schismatic movement in California, largely confined to his
psychological theories and activities; by radio commentator
Jeffrey St. John; and by Robert M. Bleiberg, editor of the financial weekly, *Barron's*.

The Libertarian Caucus of YAF and the old Society of Rational Individualists, the constituents of the merged Society for

Individual Liberty, were originally Randian in outlook. But since 1968, SIL, the California Libertarian Alliance, and other youthful libertarians have moved rapidly and surefootedly into the central mainstream of the libertarian movement. This mainstream consists of two major positions: (1) "anarcho-capitalism" in basic political philosophy, and (2) an abandonment of superpatriotism and its replacement by a genuinely individualist and libertarian outlook toward the state, civil obedience, and American foreign policy.

In the first place, most neo-Randians, devoted as they are to philosophy and logical analysis, have perceived the great logical flaw in Randian political theory: that if no man may aggress upon another, then neither may any outfit calling itself "government" presume to exert a coercive monopoly of force and the making of ultimate judicial decisions (e.g., as in the Supreme Court). Hence, they saw that no government may legitimately use coercion to preserve itself, and hence they took the next crucial logical step: they became what has been termed "anarcho-capitalists." In short, while retaining their devotion to the free market and to the rights of private property, this legion of youthful neo-Randians concluded that *all* services, including defense, the police, and the courts, must become freely marketable. Not only is taxation morally illegitimate as robbery; so too is it morally illegitimate to establish a coercive monopoly of such "defense" or "protection" functions, and then to revere it as "our government." Hence they have become "free-market anarchists" or "anarcho-capitalists," people who believe that defense, like any other service, must only be provided on the free market and not through monopoly or tax coercion.

Further, if taxation is robbery, then it becomes clear that a tax or monopoly-coercing government is a robber band, and deserves not reverence but abolition—or, if abolition cannot be achieved, at the least there should be a relentless whittling down of governmental power and activity. Civil disobedience to unjust laws and decrees—including not only the draft but taxation itself—becomes morally legitimate if not always strategically or tactically prudent.

Superpatriotism is at the least very difficult for any anarchist, so the great bulk of anarcho-capitalists have abandoned their former rightist devotion to the Cold War and to American foreign policy. Generally, they have adopted an "ultra-isolationist" foreign policy as the external corollary to their opposition to domestic statism. Hence they staunchly oppose the war in Southeast Asia, and call for immediate withdrawal from the conflict.

Particularly influential among "adult" leaders of the anarcho-capitalist mainstream have been the writings of the present author; Jerome Tuccille, ex-YAFer and ex-Randian author of *Radical Libertarianism* and the novelized nonfiction *It Usually Begins with Ayn Rand*; and Morris and Linda Tannehill, authors of *The Market for Liberty*. Robert D. Kephart, publisher of the conservative *Human Events*, has recently founded the monthly *Libertarian Review*, which bids fair to become the major intellectual organ for the libertarian movement. Youth leaders are literally too numerous to do justice to, but we might mention particularly Jarret B. Wollstein, co-leader of the Society for Individual Liberty; James D. Davidson, head of the National Taxpayers Union; and Roy A. Childs, Jr., of SIL and now editor of the *Libertarian Review*, who has been particularly effective in persuading SIL's neo-Randians to adopt the anarcho-capitalist position.

Particularly influential over the years and now a center for the California movement has been Robert LeFevre, head of Rampart College and leader of the absolute pacifist variant within the anarcho-capitalist mainstream. Calling his viewpoint "autarchism" rather than anarchism, LeFevre holds to absolute pacifism, believing it immoral not only to aggress against the person or property of anyone else, but also to defend that person or property by means of violence. This view contrasts with all the other groups of libertarians, who hold it perfectly legitimate to use violence only to defend oneself against violent attack. Heavily influenced by LeFevre have been Wichita businessmen Charles G. Koch and Robert D. Love, as well as numerous other libertarian businessmen.

On the left-wing fringe of the spectrum are libertarians who, as former rightists and Randians, had become deeply impressed by the libertarian elements of the New Left during the late '60s, particularly in opposition to the draft, the Vietnam war, and American imperialism. Calling themselves "radical libertarians," the left-libertarian youth formed the Radical Libertarian Alliance and the Anarchist Caucus of YAF in early 1969. Plunging into a tactical and strategic alliance with the New Left, the left-libertarians soon abandoned the central mainstream in two ways: (1) by becoming enamored of ultrarevolutionary tactics, including violence and street fighting; and (2) by progressing from an attitude of never criticizing New Left allies to actually embracing, on the extreme left fringe, of outright anarcho-syndicalism or anarcho-communism. By thus proceeding to classical nineteenth-century left-anarchism, by weakening or abandoning adherence to free-market capitalism or the rights of private property, the left fringe effectively moved toward taking itself out of the current libertarian movement. The left-tendency is now grouped in several minuscule organizations, none of which compare to SIL or CLA in size or influence. The main adult leader of the extreme left fringe is former Goldwater speech writer Karl Hess, who had gone through a neo-Randian phase—reflected in his *Playboy* article, "The Death of Politics," in mid-1969—and had passed through the mainstream and on to an extreme left position by the fall of 1969.

PART I:

The Libertarian Creed

2

Property and Exchange

Property Rights

IF THE CENTRAL AXIOM of the libertarian creed is nonaggression against anyone's person and property, how is this axiom arrived at? What is its groundwork or support? Here, libertarians, past and present, have differed considerably. Roughly, there are three broad types of foundation for the libertarian axiom, corresponding to three kinds of ethical philosophy: the emotivist, the utilitarian, and the natural rights viewpoint. The emotivists assert that they take liberty or nonaggression as their premise purely on subjective, emotional grounds. While their own intense emotion might seem a valid basis for their own political philosophy, this can scarcely serve to convince anyone else. By ultimately taking themselves outside the realm of rational discourse, the emotivists thereby insure the lack of general success of their own cherished doctrine.

The utilitarians declare, from their study of the consequences of liberty as opposed to alternative systems, that liberty will lead more surely to widely approved goals: harmony, peace, prosperity, etc. Now no one disputes that relative consequences should be studied in assessing the merits or demerits of respective creeds. But there are many problems in confining ourselves to a utilitarian ethic. For one thing, utilitarianism assumes that we can weigh alternatives, and decide upon policies, on the basis of their good or bad *consequences*. But if it is legitimate to apply value judgments to the *consequences* of X, why is it not equally legitimate to apply such judgments to X *itself?* May there not be something about an act itself which, in its very nature, can be considered good or evil?

Another problem with the utilitarian is that he will rarely adopt a principle as an absolute and consistent yardstick to apply to the varied concrete situations of the real world. He will only use a principle, at best, as a vague guideline or aspiration, as a *tendency* which he may choose to override at any time. This was the major defect of the nineteenth-century English Radicals, who had adopted the laissez-faire view of the eighteenth-century liberals but had substituted a supposedly "scientific" utilitarianism for the supposedly "mystical" concept of natural rights as the groundwork for that philosophy. Hence the nineteenth-century laissez-faire liberals came to use laissez-faire as a vague tendency rather than as an unblemished yardstick, and therefore increasingly and fatally compromised the libertarian creed. To say that a utilitarian cannot be "trusted" to maintain libertarian principle in every specific application may sound harsh, but it puts the case fairly. A notable contemporary example is the free market economist Professor Milton Friedman who, like his classical economics forebears, holds to freedom as against state intervention as a general tendency, but in practice allows a myriad of damaging exceptions, exceptions which serve to vitiate the principle almost completely, notably in the fields of police and military affairs, education, taxation, welfare, "neighborhood effects," antitrust laws, and money and banking.

Let us consider a stark example: Suppose a society which fervently considers all redheads to be agents of the Devil and therefore to be executed whenever found. Let us further assume that only a small number of redheads exist in any generation—so few as to be statistically insignificant. The utilitarian-libertarian might well reason: "While the murder of isolated redheads is deplorable, the executions are small in number; the vast majority of the public, as non-redheads, achieves enormous psychic satisfaction from the public execution of redheads. The social cost is negligible, the social, psychic benefit to the rest of society is great; therefore, it is right and proper for society to execute the redheads." The natural-rights libertarian, overwhelmingly concerned as he is for the *justice* of the act, will react in horror and staunchly and unequivocally oppose the executions as totally unjustified murder and aggression upon nonaggressive persons. The *consequence* of stopping the murders—depriving the bulk of society of great psychic pleasure—would not influence such a libertarian, the "absolutist" libertarian, in the slightest. Dedicated to justice and to logical consistency, the natural-rights libertarian cheerfully admits to being "doctrinaire," to being, in short, an unabashed follower of his own doctrines.

Let us turn then to the natural-rights basis for the libertarian creed, a basis which, in one form or another, has been adopted by most of the libertarians, past and present. "Natural rights" is the cornerstone of a political philosophy which, in turn, is embedded in a greater structure of "natural law." Natural law theory rests on the insight that we live in a world of more than one—in fact, a vast number—of entities, and that each entity has distinct and specific properties, a distinct "nature," which can be investigated by man's reason, by his sense perception and mental faculties. Copper has a distinct nature and behaves in a certain way, and so does iron, salt, etc. The species man, therefore, has a specifiable nature, as does the world around him and the ways of interaction between them. To put it with undue brevity, the activity of each inorganic and organic entity is determined by its own nature and by the nature of the other entities with which it comes in contact. Specifically, while the behavior of plants and at least the lower animals is determined by their biological nature or perhaps by their "instincts," the nature of man is such that each individual person must, in order to act, choose his own ends and employ his own means in order to attain them. Possessing no automatic instincts, each man must learn about himself and the world, use his mind to select values, learn about cause and effect, and act purposively to maintain himself and advance his life. Since men can think, feel, evaluate, and act only as individuals, it becomes vitally necessary for each man's survival and prosperity that he be free to learn, choose, develop his faculties, and act upon his knowledge and values. This is the necessary path of human nature; to interfere with and cripple this process by using violence goes profoundly against what is necessary by man's nature for his life and prosperity. Violent interference with a man's learning and choices is therefore profoundly "antihuman"; it violates the natural law of man's needs.

Individualists have always been accused by their enemies of being "atomistic"—of postulating that each individual lives in a kind of vacuum, thinking and choosing without relation to anyone else in society. This, however, is an authoritarian straw man; few, if any, individualists have ever been "atomists." On the contrary, it is evident that individuals always learn from each other, cooperate and interact with each other; and that this, too, is required for man's survival. But the point is that each individual makes the final choice of which influences to adopt and which to reject, or of which to adopt first and which afterwards. The libertarian welcomes the process of voluntary exchange and cooperation between freely acting individuals; what he abhors is the use of violence to cripple such voluntary cooperation and force someone to choose and act in ways different from what his own mind dictates.

The most viable method of elaborating the natural rights statement of the libertarian position is to divide it into parts, and to begin with the basic axiom of the "right to self-ownership." The right to self-ownership asserts the absolute right of each man, by virtue of his (or her) being a human being, to "own" his or her own body; that is, to control that body free of coercive interference. Since each individual must think, learn, value, and choose his or her ends and means in order to survive and flourish, the right to self-ownership gives man the right to perform these vital activities without being hampered and restricted by coercive molestation.

Consider, too, the consequences of *denying* each man the right to own his own person. There are then only two alternatives: either (1) a certain class of people, A, have the right to own another class, B; or (2) everyone has the right to own his own equal quotal share of everyone else. The first alternative implies that while Class A deserves the rights of being human, Class B is in reality subhuman and therefore deserves no such rights. But since they *are* indeed human beings, the first alternative contradicts itself in denying natural human rights to one set of humans. Moreover, as we shall see, allowing Class A to own Class B means that the former is allowed to exploit, and therefore to live parasitically, *at the expense* of the latter. But this parasitism itself violates the basic economic requirement for life: production and exchange.

The second alternative, what we might call "participatory communalism" or "communism," holds that every man should have the right to own his equal quotal share of everyone else. If there are two billion people in the world, then everyone has the right to own one two-billionth of every other person. In the first place, we can state that this ideal rests on an absurdity: proclaiming that every man is entitled to own a part of everyone else, yet is not entitled *to own himself*. Secondly, we can picture the viability of such a world: a world in which *no* man is free to take *any* action whatever without prior approval or indeed command by *everyone* else in society. It should be clear that in that sort of "communist" world, no one would be able to do anything, and the human race would quickly perish. But if a world of zero self-ownership and one hundred percent other ownership spells death for the human race, then any steps in that direction also contravene the natural law of what is best for man and his life on earth.

Finally, however, the participatory communist world *cannot* be put into practice. For it is physically impossible for everyone to keep continual tabs on everyone else, and thereby to exercise his equal quotal share of partial ownership over every other man. In practice, then, the concept of universal and equal other-ownership is utopian and impossible, and supervision and therefore control and ownership of others necessarily devolves upon a specialized group of people, who thereby become a ruling class. Hence, in practice, any attempt at communist rule will automatically become class rule, and we would be back at our first alternative.

The libertarian therefore rejects these alternatives and concludes by adopting as his primary axiom the universal right of self-ownership, a right held by everyone by virtue of being a human being. A more difficult task is to settle on a theory of property in nonhuman objects, in the things of this earth. It is comparatively easy to recognize the practice when someone is aggressing against the property right of another's person: If A assaults B, he is violating the property right of B in his own body. But with nonhuman objects the problem is more complex. If, for example, we see X seizing a watch in the possession of Y, we cannot automatically assume that X is aggressing against Y's right of property in the watch; for may not X have been the original, "true" owner of the watch who can therefore be said to be repossessing his own legitimate property? In order to decide, we need a theory of justice in property, a theory that will tell us whether X or Y or indeed someone else is the legitimate owner.

A great many libertarians, mostly those in the right wing of the libertarian spectrum, attempt to resolve the problem by asserting that whoever the existing government decrees has the property title should be considered the just owner of the property. At this point, we have not yet delved deeply into the nature of government, but the anomaly here should be glaring enough: it is surely odd to find a group eternally suspicious of virtually any and all functions of government suddenly leaving it to government to define and apply the precious concept of property, the base and groundwork of the entire social order. It is particularly the utilitarian laissez-fairists who believe it most feasible to begin the new libertarian world by confirming all existing property titles; that is, property titles and rights as decreed by the very government that is condemned as a chronic aggressor.

Let us illustrate with a hypothetical example. Suppose that libertarian agitation and pressure has escalated to such a point that the government and its various branches are ready to abdicate. But they engineer a cunning ruse. Just before the government of New York State abdicates it passes a law turning over the entire territorial area of New York to become the private property of the Rockefeller family. The Massachusetts legislature does the same for the Kennedy family. And so on for each state. The government could then abdicate and decree the abolition of taxes and coercive legislation, but the victorious libertarians would now be confronted with a dilemma. Do they recognize the new property titles as legitimately private property? The utilitarians, who have no theory of justice in property rights, would, if they were consistent with their acceptance of given property titles as decreed by government, have to accept a new social order in which 50 new satraps would be collecting taxes in the form of unilaterally imposed "rent." The point is that *only* natural-rights libertarians, only those libertarians who have a theory of justice in property titles that does not depend on government decree, could be in a position to scoff at the new rulers' claims to have private property in the territory of the country, and to rebuff these claims as invalid. As the great nineteenth-century liberal Lord Acton saw clearly, the natural law provides the only sure ground for a continuing critique of governmental laws and decrees.[1] What, specifically, the natural rights position on property titles may be is the question to which we now turn.

We have established each individual's right to self-ownership,

---

[1] See Gertrude Himmelfarb, *Lord Acton; A Study in Conscience and Politics* (Chicago: Phoenix Books, 1962), pp. 204–05. Compare also John Wild, *Plato's Modern Enemies and the Theory of Natural Law* (Chicago: University of Chicago Press, 1953), p. 176.

to a property right in his own body and person. But people are not floating wraiths; they are not self-subsistent entities; they can only survive and flourish by grappling with the earth around them. They must, for example, *stand* on land areas; they must also, in order to survive and maintain themselves, transform the resources given by nature into "consumer goods," into objects more suitable for their use and consumption. Food must be grown and eaten; minerals must be mined and then transformed into capital and then useful consumer goods, etc. Man, in other words, must own not only his own person, but also material objects for his control and use. How, then, should the property titles in these objects be allocated?

Let us take, as our first example, a sculptor fashioning a work of art out of clay and other materials; and let us waive, for the moment, the question of original property rights in the clay and the sculptor's tools. The question then becomes: *who* owns the work of art as it emerges from the sculptor's fashioning? It is, in fact, the sculptor's "creation," not in the sense that he has created matter, but in the sense that he has transformed nature-given matter—the clay—into another form dictated by his own ideas and fashioned by his own hands and energy. Surely, it is a rare person who, with the case put thus, would say that the sculptor does *not* have the property right in his own product. Surely, if every man has the right to own his own body, and if he must grapple with the material objects of the world in order to survive, then the sculptor has the right to own the product he has made, by his energy and effort, a veritable *extension* of his own personality. He has placed the stamp of his person upon the raw material, by "mixing his labor" with the clay, in the phrase of the great property theorist John Locke. And the product transformed by his own energy has become the material embodiment of the sculptor's ideas and vision. John Locke put the case this way:

. . . every man has a *property* in his own *person*. This nobody has any right to but himself. The *labour* of his body and the *work* of his hands, we may say, are properly his. Whatsoever, then, he removes out of the state that nature hath provided and left it in, he hath mixed his labour with it, and joined it to something that is his own, and thereby makes it his property. It being by him removed from the common state nature placed it in, it hath by this labour something annexed to it that excludes the common right of other men. For this labour being the unquestionable property of the labourer, no man but he can have a right to what that is once joined to . . .[2]

As in the case of the ownership of people's bodies, we again have three logical alternatives: (1) either the transformer, or "creator," has the property right in his creation; or (2) another man or set of men have the right in that creation, i.e., have the right to appropriate it by force without the sculptor's consent; or (3)—the "communal" solution—every individual in the world has an equal, quotal share in the ownership of the sculpture. Again, put baldly, there are very few who would not concede the monstrous injustice of confiscating the sculptor's property, either by one or more others, or on behalf of the world as a whole. By what right do they do so? By what right do they appropriate to themselves the product of the creator's mind and energy? In this clear-cut case, the right of the creator to own what he has mixed his person and labor with would be generally conceded. (Once again, as in the case of communal ownership of persons, the world communal solution would, in practice, be reduced to an oligarchy of a *few* others expropriating the creator's work *in the name* of "world public" ownership.)

The main point, however, is that the case of the sculptor is not qualitatively different from *all* cases of "production." The man or men who had extracted the clay from the ground and had sold it to the sculptor may not be as "creative" as the sculptor, but they too are "producers," they too have mixed their ideas and their technological know-how with the nature-given soil to emerge with a useful product. They, too, are "pro-

[2] John Locke, *An Essay Concerning the True Original, Extent and End of Civil Government*, in E. Barker, ed., *Social Contract* (New York: Oxford University Press, 1948), pp. 17–18.

ducers," and they too have mixed their labor with natural materials to transform those materials into more useful goods and services. These persons, too, are entitled to the ownership of their products. Where then does the process begin? Again, let us turn to Locke:

He that is nourished by the acorns he picked up under an oak, or the apples he gathered from the trees in the wood, has certainly appropriated them to himself. Nobody can deny but the nourishment is his. I ask then, when did they begin to be his? When he digested? or when he ate? or when he boiled? or when he brought them home? or when he picked them up? And 'tis plain, if the first gathering made them not his, nothing else could. That labour put a distinction between them and common. That added something to them more than Nature, the common mother of all, had done, and so they became his private right. And will any one say he had no right to those acorns or apples he thus appropriated because he had not the consent of all mankind to make them his? Was it a robbery thus to assume to himself what belonged to all in common? If such a consent as that was necessary, man had starved, notwithstanding the plenty God had given him. . . . Thus, the grass my horse has bit, the turfs my servant has cut, and the ore I have digged in my place, where I have a right to them in common with others, become my property without the assignation or consent of any body. The labour that was mine, removing them out of that common state they were in, hath fixed my property in them.

By making an explicit consent of every commoner necessary to any one's appropriating to himself any part of what is given in common, children or servants could not cut the meat which their father or master had provided for them in common without assigning to every one his peculiar part. Though the water running in the fountain be every one's, yet who can doubt but that in the pitcher is his only who drew it out? His labour hath taken it out of the hands of Nature where it was common . . . and hath thereby appropriated it to himself.

Thus the law of reason makes the deer that Indian's who killed it; 'tis allowed to be his goods who hath bestowed his labour upon it, though, before, it was the common right of every one. And amongst those who are counted the civilized part of mankind . . . this original law of nature for the beginning of property, in what was before common, still takes place, and by virtue thereof, what fish any one catches in the ocean, that great and still remaining common of mankind; or what ambergris any one takes up here is by the labour that removes it out of that common state nature left it in, made his property who takes that pains about it.[3]

If every man owns his own person and therefore his own labor, and if by extension he owns whatever property he has "created" or gathered out of the previously unused, unowned, "state of nature," then what of the last great question: the right to own or control the earth *itself*? In short, if the gatherer has the right to own the acorns or berries he picks, or the farmer the right to own his crop of wheat or peaches, *who* has the right to own the land on which these things have grown? It is at this point that Henry George and his followers, who have gone all the way so far with the libertarians, leave the track and deny the individual's right to own the piece of land itself, the *ground* on which these activities have taken place. The Georgists argue that, while every man should own the goods which he produces or creates, since Nature or God created the land itself, no individual has the right to assume ownership of that land. Yet, if the land is to be used at all as a resource in any sort of efficient manner, it must be owned or controlled by *someone* or some group, and we are again faced with our three alternatives: either the land belongs to the first user, the man who first brings it into production; *or* it belongs to a group of others; *or* it belongs to the world as a whole, with every individual owning a quotal part of every acre of land. George's option for the last solution hardly solves his moral problem: if the land itself should belong to God or Nature, then why is it more moral for every acre in the world to be owned by the world as a whole, than to concede individual ownership? In practice, again, it is obviously impossible for every person in

---

[3] Locke, *Civil Government*, pp. 18–19. While Locke was a brilliant property theorist, we are not claiming that he developed and applied his theory with anything like complete consistency.

the world to exercise effective ownership of his four-billionth portion (if the world population is, say, four billion) of every piece of the world's land surface. In practice, of course, a small oligarchy would do the controlling and owning, and not the world as a whole.

But apart from these difficulties in the Georgist position, the natural-rights justification for the ownership of ground land is the same as the justification for the original ownership of all other property. For, as we have seen, no producer *really* "creates" matter; he takes nature-given matter and transforms it by his labor energy in accordance with his ideas and vision. But *this* is precisely what the pioneer—the "homesteader"—does when he brings previously unused land into his own private ownership. Just as the man who makes steel out of iron ore transforms that ore out of his know-how and with his energy, and just as the man who takes the iron out of the ground does the same, so does the homesteader who clears, fences, cultivates or builds upon the land. The homesteader, too, has transformed the character of the nature-given soil by his labor and his personality. The homesteader is just as legitimately the owner of the property as the sculptor or the manufacturer; he is just as much a "producer" as the others.

Furthermore, if the original land is nature- or God-given then so are the people's talents, health, and beauty. And just as all these attributes are given to specific individuals and not to "society," so then are land and natural resources. All of these resources are given to individuals and not to "society," which is an abstraction that does not actually exist. There is no existing entity called "society"; there are only interacting individuals. To say that "society" should own land or any other property in common, then, must mean that a group of oligarchs—in practice, government bureaucrats—should own the property, and at the expense of expropriating the creator or the homesteader who had originally brought this product into existence.

Moreover, no one can produce *anything* without the cooperation of original land, if only as standing room. No man can produce or create anything by his labor alone; he must have the cooperation of land and other natural raw materials.

Man comes into the world with just himself and the world around him—the land and natural resources given him by nature. He takes these resources and transforms them by his labor and mind and energy into goods more useful to man. Therefore, if an individual cannot own original land, neither can he in the full sense own any of the fruits of his labor. The farmer cannot own his wheat crop if he cannot own the land on which the wheat grows. Now that his labor has been inextricably mixed with the land, he cannot be deprived of one without being deprived of the other.

Moreover, if a producer is *not* entitled to the fruits of his labor, who is? It is difficult to see why a newborn Pakistani baby should have a moral claim to a quotal share of ownership of a piece of Iowa land that someone has just transformed into a wheatfield—and vice versa of course for an Iowan baby and a Pakistani farm. Land in its original state is unused and unowned. Georgists and other land communalists may claim that the whole world population *really* "owns" it, but if no one has yet used it, it is in the real sense owned and controlled by no one. The pioneer, the homesteader, the first user and transformer of this land, is the man who first brings this simple valueless thing into production and social use. It is difficult to see the morality of depriving him of ownership in favor of people who have never gotten within a thousand miles of the land, and who may not even know of the existence of the property over which they are supposed to have a claim.

The moral, natural rights issue involved here is even clearer if we consider the case of animals. Animals are "economic land," since they are original nature-given resources. Yet will anyone deny full title to a horse to the man who finds and domesticates it—is this any different from the acorns and berries that are generally conceded to the gatherer? Yet in land, too, some homesteader takes the previously "wild," undomesticated land, and "tames" it by putting it to productive use. Mixing his labor with land sites should give him just as clear a title as in the case of animals. As Locke declared: "As much land as a man tills, plants, improves, cultivates, and can use the product of, so much is his property. He by his labour does, as it were, enclose it from the common." [4]

The libertarian theory of property was eloquently summed up by two nineteenth-century laissez-faire French economists:

If man acquires rights over things, it is because he is at once active, intelligent and free; by his activity he spreads over external nature; by his intelligence he governs it, and bends it to his use; by his liberty, he establishes between himself and it the relation of cause and effect and makes it his own. . . .

Where is there, in a civilized country, a clod of earth, a leaf, which does not bear this impress of the personality of man? In the town, we are surrounded by the works of man; we walk upon a level pavement or a beaten road; it is man who made healthy the formerly muddy soil, who took from the side of a far-away hill the flint or stone which covers it. We live in houses; it is man who has dug the stone from the quarry, who has hewn it, who has planed the woods; it is the thought of man which has arranged the materials properly and made a building of what was before rock and wood. And in the country, the action of man is still everywhere present; men have cultivated the soil and generations of laborers have mellowed and enriched it; the works of man have dammed the rivers and created fertility where the waters had brought only desolation. . . . Everywhere a powerful hand is divined which has moulded matter, and an intelligent will which has adapted it . . . to the satisfaction of the wants of one same being. Nature has recognized her master, and man feels that he is at home in nature. Nature has been *appropriated* by him for his use; she has become his *own*; she is his *property*. This property is legitimate; it constitutes a right as sacred for man as is the free exercise of his faculties. It is his because it has come entirely from himself, and is in no way anything but an emanation from his being. Before him, there was scarcely anything but matter; since him, and by him, there is interchangeable wealth, that is to say, articles having acquired a value by some industry, by manufacture, by handling, by extraction, or

---

[4] Locke, *Civil Government*, p. 20.

simply by transportation. From the picture of a great master, which is perhaps of all material production that in which matter plays the smallest part, to the pail of water which the carrier draws from the river and takes to the consumer, wealth, whatever it may be, acquires its value only by communicated qualities, and these qualities are part of human activity, intelligence, strength. The producer has left a fragment of his own person in the thing which has thus become valuable, and may hence be regarded as a prolongation of the faculties of man acting upon external nature. As a free being he belongs to himself; now the cause, that is to say, the productive force, is himself; the effect, that is to say, the wealth produced, is still himself. Who shall dare contest his title of ownership so clearly marked by the seal of his personality? . . .

It is then, to the human being, the creator of all wealth, that we must come back . . . it is by labor that man impresses his personality on matter. It is labor which cultivates the earth and makes of an unoccupied waste an appropriated field; it is labor which makes of an untrodden forest a regularly ordered wood; it is labor, or rather, a series of labors often executed by a very numerous succession of workmen, which brings hemp from seed, thread from hemp, cloth from thread, clothing from cloth; which transforms the shapeless pyrite, picked up in the mine, into an elegant bronze which adorns some public place, and repeats to an entire people the thought of an artist. . . .

Property, made manifest by labor, participates in the rights of the person whose emanation it is; like him, it is inviolable so long as it does not extend so far as to come into collision with another right; like him, it is individual, because it has origin in the independence of the individual, and because, when several persons have cooperated in its formation, the latest possessor has purchased with a value, the fruit of his personal labor, the work of all the fellow-laborers who have preceded him: this is what is usually the case with manufactured articles. When property has passed, by sale or by inheritance, from one hand to another, its conditions have not changed; it is still the fruit of human liberty manifested by labor, and the holder has the rights as the producer who took possession of it by right.[5]

[5] Leon Wolowski and Émile Levasseur, "Property," in *Lalor's Cyclopedia of Political Science* . . . (Chicago: M. B. Cary & Co., 1884), III, 392–93.

Society and the Individual

We have talked at length of individual rights; but what, it may be asked, of the "rights of society"? Don't they supersede the rights of the mere individual? The libertarian, however, is an individualist; he believes that one of the prime errors in social theory is to treat "society" as if it were an actually existing entity. "Society" is sometimes treated as a superior or quasi-divine figure with overriding "rights" of its own; at other times as an existing evil which can be blamed for all the ills of the world. The individualist holds that only individuals exist, think, feel, choose, and act; and that "society" is not a living entity but simply a label for a set of interacting individuals. Treating society as a thing that chooses and acts, then, serves to obscure the real forces at work. If, in a small community, ten people band together to rob and expropriate three others, then this is clearly and evidently a case of a group of individuals acting in concert against another group. In this situation, if the ten people presumed to refer to themselves as "society" acting in "its" interest, the rationale would be laughed out of court; even the ten robbers would probably be too shamefaced to use this sort of argument. But let their size increase, and this kind of obfuscation becomes rife and succeeds in duping the public.

The fallacious use of a collective noun like "nation," similar in this respect to "society," has been trenchantly pointed out by the historian Parker T. Moon:

When one uses the simple monosyllable "France" one thinks of France as a unit, an entity. When . . . we say "France sent *her* troops to conquer Tunis"—we impute not only unity but personality to the country. The very words conceal the facts and make international relations a glamorous drama in which personalized nations are the actors, and all too easily we forget the flesh-and-blood men and women who are the true actors . . . if we had no such word as "France". . . then we should more accurately describe the Tunis expedition in some such way as this: "A few of these thirty-eight million persons sent thirty thousand others to conquer Tunis." This way of putting the fact immediately suggests a question, or rather a series of questions. Who were the "few"? Why did they send the thirty thousand to Tunis? And why did these obey? Empire-building is done not by "nations," but by men. The problem before us is to discover the men, the active, interested minorities in each nation, who are directly interested in imperialism and then to analyze the reasons why the majorities pay the expense and fight the wars necessitated by imperialist expansion.[6]

The individualist view of "society" has been summed up in the phrase: *"Society" is everyone but yourself*. Put thus bluntly, this analysis can be used to consider those cases where "society" is treated, not only as a superhero with superrights, but as a supervillain on whose shoulders massive blame is placed. Consider the typical view that not the individual criminal, but "society," is responsible for his crime. Take, for example, the case where Smith robs or murders Jones. The "old-fashioned" view is that Smith is responsible for his act. The modern liberal counters that "society" is responsible. This sounds both sophisticated and humanitarian, until we apply the individualist perspective. Then we see that what liberals are *really* saying is that *everyone but* Smith, including of course the victim Jones, is responsible for the crime. Put this baldly, almost everyone would recognize the absurdity of this position. But conjuring up the fictive entity "society" obfuscates this process. As the sociologist Arnold W. Green puts it: "It would follow, then, that if society is responsible for crime, and criminals are not responsible for crime, only those members of society who do not commit crime can be held responsible for crime. Nonsense this obvious can be circumvented only by conjuring up society as devil, as evil being apart from people and what they do."[7]

The great American libertarian writer Frank Chodorov stressed this view of society when he wrote that "Society Are People."

[6] Parker Thomas Moon, *Imperialism and World Politics* (New York: Macmillan, 1930), p. 58.

[7] Arnold W. Green, "The Reified Villain," *Social Research* (Winter, 1968), p. 656.

Society is a collective concept and nothing else; it is a convenience for designating a number of people. So, too, is family or crowd or gang, or any other name we give to an agglomeration of persons. Society . . . is not an extra "person"; if the census totals a hundred million, that's all there are, not one more, for there cannot be any accretion to Society except by procreation. The concept of Society as a metaphysical person falls flat when we observe that Society disappears when the component parts disperse; as in the case of a "ghost town" or of a civilization we learn about by the artifacts they left behind. When the individuals disappear so does the whole. The whole has no separate existence. Using the collective noun with a singular verb leads us into a trap of the imagination; we are prone to personalize the collectivity and to think of it as having a body and a psyche of its own.[8]

Free Exchange and Free Contract

The central core of the libertarian creed, then, is to establish the absolute right to private property of every man: first, in his own body, and second, in the previously unused natural resources which he first transforms by his labor. These two axioms, the right of self-ownership and the right to "homestead," establish the complete set of principles of the libertarian system. The entire libertarian doctrine then becomes the spinning out and the application of all the implications of this central doctrine. For example, a man, X, owns his own person and labor, and the farm he clears on which he grows wheat. Another man, Y, owns the fish he catches; A third man, Z, owns the cabbages he has grown and the land under it. But if a man owns anything, he then has the right to *give away* or *exchange* these property titles to someone else, after which point the other person also has absolute property title. From this corollary right to private property stems the basic justification for free contract and for the free-market economy. Thus, if X grows wheat, he may and probably will agree to exchange some of that wheat

[8] Frank Chodorov, *The Rise and Fall of Society* (New York: Devin-Adair, 1959), pp. 29–30.

for some of the fish caught by Y or for some of the cabbages grown by Z. With both X and Y making voluntary agreements to exchange property titles (or Y and Z, or X and Z) the property then becomes with equal legitimacy the property of the other person. If X exchanges wheat for Y's fish, then that fish becomes X's property to do with as he wishes, and the wheat becomes Y's property in precisely the same way.

Further, a man may exchange not only the tangible objects he owns but also his own labor, which of course he owns as well. Thus, Z may sell his labor services of teaching farmer X's children in return for some of the farmer's produce.

It so happens that the free-market economy, and the specialization and division of labor it implies, is by far the most productive form of economy known to man, and has been responsible for industrialization and for the modern economy on which civilization has been built. This is a fortunate utilitarian result of the free market, but it is not, to the libertarian, the *prime* reason for his support of this system. That prime reason is moral, and is rooted in the natural rights defense of private property we have developed above. Even if a society of despotism and systematic invasion of rights could be shown to be more productive than what Adam Smith called "the system of natural liberty," the libertarian would support this system. Fortunately, as in so many other areas, the utilitarian and the moral, natural rights and general prosperity, go hand in hand.

The developed-market economy, as complex as the system appears to be on the surface, is nothing more than a vast network of voluntary and mutually agreed-upon two-person exchanges such as we have shown to occur between wheat and cabbage farmers, or between the farmer and the teacher. Thus, when I buy a newspaper for a dime, a mutually beneficial two-person exchange takes place: I transfer my ownership of the dime to the news dealer and he transfers ownership of the paper to me. We do this because, under the division of labor, I calculate that the paper is worth more to me than the dime, while the news dealer prefers the dime to keeping the paper. Or, when

I teach at a university, I estimate that I prefer my salary to not expending my labor of teaching, while the university authorities calculate that they prefer gaining my teaching services to not paying me the money. If the newsdealer insisted on charging 50¢ for the paper, I might well decide that it isn't worth the price; similarly, if I should insist on triple my present salary, the university might well decide to dispense with my services.

Many people are willing to concede the justice and propriety of property rights and the free-market economy, to concede that the farmer should be able to charge whatever his wheat will bring from consumers or the worker to reap whatever others are willing to pay for his services. But they balk at one point: inheritance. If Willie Stargell is ten times as good and "productive" a ball player as Joe Jack, they are willing to concede the justice of Stargell's earning ten times the amount; but what, they ask, is the justification for someone whose only merit is being born a Rockefeller inheriting far more wealth than someone born a Rothbard? The libertarian answer is to concentrate *not* on the recipient, the child Rockefeller or the child Rothbard, but to concentrate on the *giver*, the man who bestows the inheritance. For if Smith and Jones and Stargell have the right to their labor and property and to exchange the titles to this property for the similar property of others, they also have the right to *give* their property to whomever they wish. And of course most such gifts consist of the gifts of the property owners to their children—in short, inheritance. If Willie Stargell owns his labor and the money he earns from it, then he has the right to give that money to the baby Stargell.

In the developed free-market economy, then, the farmer exchanges the wheat for money; the wheat is bought by the miller who processes and transforms the wheat into flour; the miller sells the flour to the baker who produces bread; the baker sells the bread to the wholesaler, who in turn sells it to the retailer, who finally sells it to the consumer. And at each step of the way, the producer may hire the labor services of the workers in exchange for money. How "money" enters the equation is a complex process; but it should be clear that *conceptually* the use of money is equivalent to any single or group of useful commodities that are exchanged for the wheat, flour, etc. Instead of money, the commodity exchanged could be cloth, iron, or whatever. At each step of the way, mutually beneficial exchanges of property titles are agreed upon and transacted.

We are now in a position to see how the libertarian defines the concept of "freedom" or "liberty." Freedom is a condition in which a person's ownership rights in his own body and his legitimate material property are *not* invaded, are not aggressed against. A man who steals another man's property is invading and restricting the victim's freedom, as does the man who beats another over the head. Freedom and unrestricted property right go hand in hand. On the other hand, to the libertarian, "crime" is an act of aggression against a man's property right, either in his own person or his materially owned objects. Crime is an invasion, by the use of violence, against a man's property and therefore against his liberty. "Slavery"—the opposite of freedom —is a condition in which the slave has little or no right of self-ownership; his person and his produce are systematically expropriated by his master by the use of violence.

The libertarian, then, is clearly an individualist but *not* an egalitarian. The only "equality" he would advocate is the equal right of every man to the property in his own person, to the property in the unused resources he "homesteads," and to the property of others he has acquired either through voluntary exchange or gift.

Property Rights and "Human Rights"

Liberals will generally concede the right of every individual to his "personal liberty," to his freedom to think, speak, write, and engage in such personal "exchanges" as sexual activity between "consenting adults." In short, the liberal attempts to uphold the individual's right to the ownership of his own body, but then denies his right to "property," i.e., to the ownership of material objects. Hence, the typical liberal dichotomy between "human rights," which he upholds, and "property rights," which he rejects. Yet the two, according to the libertarian, are inextricably intertwined; they stand or fall together.

Take, for example, the liberal socialist who advocates government ownership of all the "means of production" while upholding the "human" right of freedom of speech or press. How is this "human" right to be exercised if the individuals constituting the public are denied their right to ownership of property? If, for example, the government owns all the newsprint and all the printing shops, how is the right to a free press to be exercised? If the government owns all the newsprint, it then necessarily has the right and the power to allocate that newsprint, and someone's "right to a free press" becomes a mockery if the government decides not to allocate newsprint in his direction. And since the government must allocate scarce newsprint in *some* way, the right to a free press of, say, minorities or "subversive" antisocialists will get short shrift indeed. The same is true for the "right to free speech" if the government owns all the assembly halls, and therefore allocates those halls as it sees fit. Or, for example, if the government of Soviet Russia, being atheistic, decides not to allocate many scarce resources to the production of matzohs, for Orthodox Jews the "freedom of religion" becomes a mockery; but again, the Soviet government can always rebut that Orthodox Jews are a small minority and that capital equipment should not be diverted to matzoh production.

The basic flaw in the liberal separation of "human rights" and "property rights" is that people are treated as ethereal abstractions. If a man has the right to self-ownership, to the control of his life, then in the real world he must also have the right to sustain his life by grappling with and transforming resources; he must be able to own the ground and the resources on which he stands and which he must use. In short, to sustain his "human right"—or his property rights in his own person—he must also have the property right in the material world, in the objects which he produces. Property rights *are* human rights, and are essential to the human rights which liberals attempt to maintain. The human right of a free press depends upon the human right of private property in newsprint.

In fact, there *are no* human rights that are separable from property rights. The human right of free speech is simply the property right to hire an assembly hall from the owners, or to own one oneself; the human right of a free press is the property right to buy materials and then print leaflets or books and to sell them to those who are willing to buy. There is no extra "right of free speech" or free press beyond the property rights we can enumerate in any given case. And furthermore, discovering and identifying the property rights involved will resolve any apparent conflicts of rights that may crop up.

Consider, for example, the classic example where liberals generally concede that a person's "right of freedom of speech" must be curbed in the name of the "public interest": Justice Holmes' famous dictum that no one has the right to cry "fire" falsely in a crowded theater. Holmes and his followers have used this illustration again and again to prove the supposed necessity for all rights to be relative and tentative rather than precise and absolute.

But the problem here is *not* that rights cannot be pushed too far, but that the whole case is discussed in terms of a vague and woolly "freedom of speech" rather than in terms of the rights of private property. Suppose we analyze the problem under the aspect of property rights. The fellow who brings on a riot by falsely shouting "fire" in a crowded theater is, necessarily, either the owner of the theater (or the owner's agent) or a paying patron. If he is the owner, then he has committed fraud on his customers. He has taken their money in exchange for a promise to put on a movie or play: and now, instead, he disrupts the show by falsely shouting "fire" and breaking up the performance. He has thus welshed on his contractual obligation, and has thereby stolen the property—the money—of his patrons and has violated their property rights.

Suppose, on the other hand, that the shouter is a patron and not the owner. In that case, he is violating the property right of the owner—as well as of the other guests to their paid-for performance. As a guest, he has gained access to the property on certain terms, including an obligation not to violate the owner's property or to disrupt the performance the owner is putting on. His malicious act, therefore, violates the property rights of the theater owner and of all the other patrons.

There is no need, therefore, for individual rights to be restricted in the case of the false shouter of "fire." The rights of the individual are *still* absolute; but they are *property* rights. The fellow who maliciously cried "fire" in a crowded theater is indeed a criminal, but *not* because his so-called "right of free speech" must be pragmatically restricted on behalf of the "public good"; he is a criminal because he has clearly and obviously violated the property rights of another person.

3

The State

The State as Aggressor

THE CENTRAL THRUST of libertarian thought, then, is to oppose any and all aggression against the property rights of individuals in their own persons and in the material objects they have voluntarily acquired. While individual and gangs of criminals are of course opposed, there is nothing unique here to the libertarian creed, since almost all persons and schools of thought oppose the exercise of random violence against persons and property.

There is, however, a difference of emphasis on the part of libertarians even in this universally accepted area of defending people against crime. In the libertarian society there would be no "district attorney" who prosecutes criminals in the name of a nonexistent "society," even against the wishes of the victim of crime. The victim would himself decide whether to press charges. Furthermore, as another side to the same coin, in a libertarian world the victim would be able to press suit against a wrongdoer without having to convince the same district attorney that he should proceed. Moreover, in the system of crimi-

47

nal punishment in the libertarian world, the emphasis would never be, as it is now, on "society's" jailing the criminal; the emphasis would necessarily be on compelling the criminal to make restitution to the victim of his crime. The present system, in which the victim is not recompensed but instead has to pay taxes to support the incarceration of his own attacker—would be evident nonsense in a world that focuses on the defense of property rights and therefore on the victim of crime.

Furthermore, while most libertarians are not pacifists, they would not join the present system in interfering with people's *right* to be pacifists. Thus, suppose that Jones, a pacifist, is aggressed against by Smith, a criminal. If Jones, as the result of his beliefs, is against defending himself by the use of violence and is therefore opposed to any prosecution of crime, then Jones will simply fail to prosecute, and that will be the end of it. There will be no governmental machinery that pursues and tries criminals even against the wishes of the victim.

But the critical difference between libertarians and other people is not in the area of private crime; the critical difference is their view of the role of the State—the government. For libertarians regard the State as the supreme, the eternal, the best organized, aggressor against the persons and property of the mass of the public. *All* States everywhere, whether democratic, dictatorial, or monarchical, whether red, white, blue, or brown.

The State! Always and ever the government and its rulers and operators have been considered above the general moral law. The "Pentagon Papers" are only one recent instance among innumerable instances in history, of men, most of whom are perfectly honorable in their private lives, who lie in their teeth before the public. Why? For "reasons of State." Service to the State is supposed to excuse all actions that would be considered immoral or criminal if committed by "private" citizens. The distinctive feature of libertarians is that they coolly and uncompromisingly apply the general moral law to people acting in their roles as members of the State apparatus. Libertarians make no exceptions. For centuries, the State (or more strictly, individuals acting in their roles as "members of the government") has cloaked its criminal activity in high-sounding rhetoric. For centuries the State has committed mass murder and called it "war"; then ennobled the mass slaughter that "war" involves. For centuries the State has enslaved people into its armed battalions and called it "conscription" in the "national service." For centuries the State has robbed people at bayonet point and called it "taxation." In fact, if you wish to know how libertarians regard the State and any of its acts, simply think of the State as a criminal band, and all of the libertarian attitudes will logically fall into place.

Let us consider, for example, what it is that sharply distinguishes government from all other organizations in society. Many political scientists and sociologists have blurred this vital distinction, and refer to all organizations and groups as hierarchical, structured, "governmental," etc. Left-wing anarchists, for example, will oppose equally government *and* private organizations such as corporations on the ground that each is equally "elitist" and "coercive." But the "rightist" libertarian is not opposed to inequality, and his concept of "coercion" applies only to the use of violence. The libertarian sees a crucial distinction between government, whether central, state, or local, and all other institutions in society. Or rather, two crucial distinctions. First, every other person or group receives its income by voluntary payment: either by voluntary contribution or gift (such as the local community chest or bridge club), *or* by voluntary purchase of its goods or services on the market (i.e., grocery store owner, baseball player, steel manufacturer, etc.) *Only* the government obtains its income by coercion and violence—i.e., by the direct threat of confiscation or imprisonment if payment is not forthcoming. This coerced levy is "taxation." A second distinction is that, apart from criminal outlaws, *only* the government can use its funds to commit violence against its own or any other subjects; only the government can prohibit pornography, compel a religious observance, or put people in jail for selling goods at a higher price than the government deems fit. Both distinctions, of course, can be summed up as: *only* the government, in society, is empowered to aggress against the property rights of its subjects, whether to extract revenue, to impose its moral code, or to kill those with whom it disagrees. Furthermore, any and all governments, even the least despotic, have always obtained the bulk of their income from the coercive taxing power. And historically, by far the overwhelming portion of all enslavement and murder in the history of the world have come from the hands of government. And since we have seen that the central thrust of the libertarian is to oppose all aggression against the rights of person and property, the libertarian necessarily opposes the institution of the State as the inherent and overwhelmingly the most important enemy of those precious rights.

There is another reason why State aggression has been far more important than private, a reason apart from the greater organization and central mobilizing of resources that the rulers of the State can impose. The reason is the absence of any check upon State depredation, a check that does exist when we have to worry about muggers or the Mafia. To guard against private criminals we have been able to turn to the State and its police; but who can guard us against the State itself? No one. For another critical distinction of the State is that it compels the monopolization of the service of protection; the State arrogates to itself a virtual monopoly of violence and of ultimate decision-making in society. If we don't like the decisions of the State courts, for example, there are no other agencies of protection to which we may turn.

It is true that, in the United States, at least, we have a constitution that imposes strict limits on some powers of government. But, as we have discovered in the past century, no constitution can interpret or enforce itself; it must be interpreted by *men*. And if the ultimate power to interpret a constitution is given to the government's own Supreme Court, then the inevitable tendency is for the Court to continue to place its imprimatur on ever-broader powers for its own government. Furthermore, the highly touted "checks and balances" and "separation of powers" in the American government are flimsy indeed, since in the final analysis all of these divisions are part of the same government and are governed by the same set of rulers.

One of America's most brilliant political theorists, John C. Calhoun, wrote prophetically of the inherent tendency of a State to break through the limits of its written constitution:

A written constitution certainly has many and considerable advantages, but it is a great mistake to suppose that the mere insertion of provisions to restrict and limit the powers of the government, without investing those for whose protection they are inserted with the means of enforcing their observance, will be sufficient to prevent the major and dominant party from abusing its powers. Being the party in possession of the government, they will . . . be in favor of the powers granted by the constitution and opposed to the restrictions intended to limit them. As the major and dominant parties, they will have no need of these restrictions for their protection. . . .

The minor or weaker party, on the contrary, would take the opposite direction and regard them as essential to their protection against the dominant party. . . . But where there are no means by which they could compel the major party to observe the restrictions, the only resort left them would be a strict construction of the constitution. . . . To this the major party would oppose a liberal construction—one which would give to the words of the grant the broadest meaning of which they were susceptible. It would then be construction against construction—the one to contract and the other to enlarge the powers of the government to the utmost. But of what possible avail could the strict construction of the minor party be, against the liberal interpretation of the major, when the one would have all the powers of the government to carry its construction into effect and the other be deprived of all means of enforcing its construction? In a contest so unequal, the result would not be doubtful. The party in favor of the restrictions would be overpowered. . . . The end of the contest would be the subversion of the constitution . . . the restrictions would ultimately be annulled and the government be converted into one of unlimited powers.

Nor would the division of government into separate and, as it regards each other, independent departments prevent this result . . . as each and all the departments—and, of course, the entire government—would be under the control of the numerical majority, it is too clear to require explanation that a mere distribution of its powers among its agents or representatives could do little or nothing to counteract its tendency to oppression and abuse of power.[1]

But why worry about the weakness of limits on governmental power? Especially in a "democracy," in the phrase so often used by American liberals in their heyday before the mid-1960s when doubts began to creep into the liberal utopia: "Are *we* not the government?" In the phrase "we are the government," the useful collective term "we" has enabled an ideological camouflage to be thrown over the naked exploitative reality of political life. For if *we* truly *are* the government, then *anything* a government does to an individual is not only just and not tyrannical; it is also "voluntary" on the part of the individual concerned. If the government has incurred a huge public debt which must be paid by taxing one group on behalf of another, this reality of burden is conveniently obscured by blithely saying that "we owe it to ourselves" (but *who* are the "we" and *who* the "ourselves"?). If the government drafts a man, or even throws him into jail for dissident opinions, then he is only "doing it to himself" and therefore nothing improper has occurred. Under this reasoning, then, Jews murdered by the Nazi government were *not* murdered; they must have "committed suicide," since they *were* the government (which was democratically chosen), and therefore anything the government did to them was only voluntary on their part. But there is no way out of such grotesqueries for those supporters of government who see the State merely as a benevolent and voluntary agent of the public.

And so we must conclude that "we" are *not* the government; the government is *not* "us." The government does not in any accurate sense "represent" the majority of the people, but even

[1] John C. Calhoun, *A Disquisition on Government* (New York: Liberal Arts Press, 1953), pp. 25–27.

if it did, even if 90 percent of the people decided to murder or enslave the other 10 percent, this would *still* be murder and slavery, and would not be voluntary suicide or enslavement on the part of the oppressed minority. Crime is crime, aggression against rights is aggression, no matter how many citizens agree to the oppression. There is nothing sacrosanct about the majority; the lynch mob, too, is the majority in its own domain.

But while, as in the lynch mob, the majority can become actively tyrannical and aggressive, the normal and continuing condition of the State is *oligarchic* rule: rule by a coercive elite which has managed to gain control of the State machinery. There are two basic reasons for this: one is the inequality and division of labor inherent in the nature of man, which gives rise to an "Iron Law of Oligarchy" in all of man's activities; and second is the parasitic nature of the State enterprise itself.

We have said that the individualist is not an egalitarian. Part of the reason for this is the individualist's insight into the vast diversity and individuality within mankind, a diversity that has the chance to flower and expand as civilization and living standards progress. Individuals differ in ability and in interest both within and between occupations; and hence, in all occupations and walks of life, whether it be steel production or the organization of a bridge club, leadership in the activity will inevitably be assumed by a relative handful of the most able and energetic, while the remaining majority will form themselves into rank-and-file followers. This truth applies to all activities, whether they are beneficial or malevolent (as in criminal organizations). Indeed, the discovery of the Iron Law of Oligarchy was made by the Italian sociologist Robert Michels, who found that the Social Democratic Party of Germany, despite its rhetorical commitment to egalitarianism, was rigidly oligarchical and hierarchical in its actual functioning.

A second basic reason for the oligarchic rule of the State is its parasitic nature—the fact that it lives coercively off the production of the citizenry. To be successful to its practitioners, the fruits of parasitic exploitation must be confined to a relative minority, otherwise a meaningless plunder of all by all would result in no gains for anyone. Nowhere has the coercive and parasitic nature of the State been more clearly limned than by the great late nineteenth-century German sociologist, Franz Oppenheimer. Oppenheimer pointed out that there are two and only two mutually exclusive means for man to obtain wealth. One, the method of production and voluntary exchange, the method of the free market, Oppenheimer termed the "economic means"; the other, the method of robbery by the use of violence, he called the "political means." The political means is clearly parasitic, for it requires previous production for the exploiters to confiscate, and it subtracts from instead of adding to the total production in society. Oppenheimer then proceeded to define the State as the "organization of the political means" —the systematization of the predatory process over a given territorial area.[2]

In short, private crime is, at best, sporadic and uncertain; the parasitism is ephemeral, and the coercive, parasitic lifeline can be cut at any time by the resistance of the victims. The State provides a legal, orderly, systematic channel for predation on the property of the producers; it makes certain, secure, and relatively "peaceful" the lifeline of the parasitic caste in society. The great libertarian writer Albert Jay Nock wrote vividly that "the State claims and exercises the monopoly of crime. . . . It forbids private murder, but itself organizes murder on a colossal scale. It punishes private theft, but itself lays unscrupulous hands on anything it wants, whether the property of citizen or of alien." [3]

At first, of course, it is startling for someone to consider taxation as robbery, and therefore government as a band of robbers. But anyone who persists in thinking of taxation as in some sense a "voluntary" payment can see what happens if he chooses

[2] Franz Oppenheimer, *The State* (New York: Vanguard Press, 1926), pp. 24–27 and passim.

[3] Albert Jay Nock, *On Doing the Right Thing, and Other Essays* (New York: Harper & Bros., 1928), p. 145.

not to pay. The great economist Joseph Schumpeter, himself by no means a libertarian, wrote that "the state has been living on a revenue which was being produced in the private sphere for private purposes and had to be deflected from these purposes by political force. The theory which construes taxes on the analogy of club dues or of the purchase of the services of, say, a doctor only proves how far removed this part of the social sciences is from scientific habits of mind." [4] The eminent Viennese "legal positivist" Hans Kelsen attempted, in his treatise, *The General Theory of Law and the State*, to establish a political theory and justification of the State, on a strictly "scientific" and value-free basis. What happened is that early in the book, he came to the crucial sticking-point, the *pons asinorum* of political philosophy: *What* distinguishes the edicts of the State from the commands of a bandit gang? Kelsen's answer was simply to say that the decrees of the State are "valid," and to proceed happily from there, without bothering to define or explain this concept of "validity." Indeed, it would be a useful exercise for nonlibertarians to ponder this question: *How* can you define taxation in a way which makes it different from robbery?

To the great nineteenth-century individualist anarchist—and constitutional lawyer—Lysander Spooner, there was no problem in finding the answer. Spooner's analysis of the State as robber group is perhaps the most devastating ever written:

It is true that the *theory* of our Constitution is, that all taxes are paid voluntarily; that our government is a mutual insurance company, voluntarily entered into by the people with each other. . . .

But this theory of our government is wholly different from the practical fact. The fact is that the government, like a highwayman, say to a man: "Your money, or your life." And many, if not most, taxes are paid under the compulsion of that threat.

The government does not, indeed, waylay a man in a lonely place, spring upon him from the roadside, and holding a pistol to his head, proceed to rifle his pockets. But the robbery is none the less a robbery on that account; and it is far more dastardly and shameful.

The highwayman takes solely upon himself the responsibility, danger, and crime of his own act. He does not pretend that he has any rightful claim to your money, or that he intends to use it for your own benefit. He does not pretend to be anything but a robber. He has not acquired impudence enough to profess to be merely a "protector," and that he takes men's money against their will, merely to enable him to "protect" those infatuated travellers, who feel perfectly able to protect themselves, or do not appreciate his peculiar system of protection. He is too sensible a man to make such professions as these. Furthermore, having taken your money, he leaves you, as you wish him to do. He does not persist in following you on the road, against your will; assuming to be your rightful "sovereign," on account of the "protection" he affords you. He does not keep "protecting" you, by commanding you to bow down and serve him; by requiring you to do this, and forbidding you to do that; by robbing you of more money as often as he finds it for his interest or pleasure to do so; and by branding you as a rebel, a traitor, and an enemy to your country, and shooting you down without mercy, if you dispute his authority, or resist his demands. He is too much of a gentleman to be guilty of such impostures, and insults, and villainies as these. In short, he does not, in addition to robbing you, attempt to make you either his dupe or his slave.[5]

If the State is a group of plunderers, *who* then constitutes the State? Clearly, the ruling elite consists at any time of (a) the full-time *apparatus*—the kings, politicians, and bureaucrats who man and operate the State; and (b) the groups who have maneuvered to gain privileges, subsidies, and benefices from the State. The remainder of society constitutes the ruled. It was, again, John C. Calhoun who saw with crystal clarity that, no matter how small the power of government, no matter how low the tax burden or how equal its distribution, the very nature of government creates two unequal and inherently con-

---

[5] Lysander Spooner, *No Treason, No. VI: The Constitution of No Authority* (1870, reprinted in Larkspur, Colo.: Pine Tree Press, 1966), p. 17.

flicting classes in society: those who, on net, *pay* the taxes (the "tax-payers"), and those who, on net, *live off* taxes (the "tax-consumers"). Suppose that the government imposes a low and seemingly equally-distributed tax to pay for building a dam. This very act takes money from most of the public to pay it out to net "tax-consumers": the bureaucrats who run the operation, the contractors and workers who build the dam, etc. And the greater the scope of government decision-making, the greater its fiscal burdens, Calhoun went on, the greater the burden and the artificial inequality it imposes between these two classes:

Few, comparatively, as they are, the agents and employees of the government constitute that portion of the community who are the exclusive recipients of the proceeds of the taxes. Whatever amount is taken from the community in the form of taxes, if not lost, goes to them in the shape of expenditures or disbursements. The two—disbursement and taxation—constitute the fiscal action of the government. They are correlatives. What the one takes from the community under the name of taxes is transferred to the portion of the community who are the recipients under that of disbursements. But as the recipients constitute only a portion of the community, it follows, taking the two parts of the fiscal process together, that its action must be unequal between the payers of the taxes and the recipients of their proceeds. Nor can it be otherwise; unless what is collected from each individual in the shape of taxes shall be returned to him in that of disbursements, which would make the process nugatory and absurd. . . .

The necessary result, then, of the unequal fiscal action of the government is to divide the community into two great classes: one consisting of those who, in reality, pay the taxes and, of course, bear exclusively the burden of supporting the government; and the other, of those who are the recipients of their proceeds through disbursements, and who are, in fact, supported by the government; or, in fewer words, to divide it into tax-payers and tax-consumers.

But the effect of this is to place them in antagonistic relations in reference to the fiscal action of the government—and the entire course of policy therewith connected. For the greater the taxes and disbursements, the greater the gain of the one and the loss of the other, and vice versa. . . . The effect, then, of every increase is to enrich and strengthen the one, and impoverish and weaken the other.[6]

If states have everywhere been run by an oligarchic group of predators, how have they been able to maintain their rule over the mass of the population? The answer, as the philosopher David Hume pointed out over two centuries ago, is that in the long run *every* government, no matter how dictatorial, rests on the support of the majority of its subjects. Now this does not of course render these governments "voluntary," since the very existence of the tax and other coercive powers show how much compulsion the State must exercise. Nor does the majority support have to be eager and enthusiastic approval; it could well be mere passive acquiescence and resignation. The conjunction in the famous phrase "death and taxes" implies a passive and resigned acceptance to the assumed inevitability of the State and its taxation.

The tax-consumers, the groups that benefit from the operations of the State, will of course be eager rather than passive followers of the State mechanism. But these are only a minority. How is the compliance and acquiescence of the mass of the population to be secured? Here we come to the central problem of political philosophy—that branch of philosophy that deals with politics, the exercise of regularized violence: the mystery of civil obedience. Why do people obey the edicts and depredations of the ruling elite? Conservative writer James Burnham, who is the reverse of libertarian, put the problem very clearly, admitting that there is no rational justification for civil obedience: "Neither the source nor the justification of government can be put in wholly rational terms . . . why should I accept the hereditary or democratic or any other principle of legitimacy? Why should a principle justify the rule of that man over me?" His own answer is hardly calculated to convince

[6] Calhoun, *Disquisition on Government,* pp. 16–18.

many others: "I accept the principle, well . . . because I do, because that is the way it is and has been." ⁷ But suppose that one does *not* accept the principle; what will the "way" be then? And why have the bulk of subjects agreed to accept it?

The State and the Intellectuals

The answer is that, since the early origins of the State, its rulers have always turned, as a necessary bolster to their rule, to an alliance with society's class of intellectuals. The masses do not create their own abstract ideas, or indeed think through these ideas independently; they follow passively the ideas adopted and promulgated by the body of intellectuals, who become the effective "opinion-moulders" in society. And since it is precisely a moulding of opinion on behalf of the rulers that the State almost desperately needs, this forms a firm basis for the age-old alliance of the intellectuals and the ruling classes of the State. The alliance is based on a *quid pro quo*: on the one hand, the intellectuals spread among the masses the idea that the State and its rulers are wise, good, sometimes divine, and at the very least inevitable and better than any conceivable alternatives. In return for this panoply of ideology, the State incorporates the intellectuals as part of the ruling elite, granting them power, status, prestige, and material security. Furthermore, intellectuals are needed to staff the bureaucracy and to "plan" the economy and society.

Before the modern era, particularly potent among the intellectual handmaidens of the State was the priestly caste, cementing the powerful and terrible alliance of warrior chief and medicine man, of Throne and Altar. The State "established" the Church, and conferred upon it power, prestige, and wealth extracted from its subjects. In return, the Church anointed the State with divine sanction and inculcated this sanction into the populace. In the modern era, when theocratic arguments have

⁷ James Burnham, *Congress and the American Tradition* (Chicago: Henry Regnery, 1959), pp. 6–8.

lost much of their lustre among the public, the intellectuals have posed as the scientific cadre of "experts," and have been busy informing the hapless public that political affairs, foreign and domestic, are much too complex for the average person to bother his head about. Only the State and its corps of intellectual experts, planners, scientists, economists, and "national security managers" can possibly hope to deal with these problems. The role of the masses, even in "democracies," is to ratify and assent to the decisions of their knowledgeable rulers.

Historically, the union of Church and State, of Throne and Altar, has been the most effective device for inducing obedience and support among the subjects. Burnham attests to the power of myth and mystery in inducing support when he writes that "In ancient times, before the illusions of science had corrupted traditional wisdom, the founders of Cities were known to be gods or demi-gods." [8] To the established priestcraft, the ruler was either anointed by God or, in the case of the absolute rule of many Oriental despotisms, was even himself God; hence, any questioning or resistance to his rule would be blasphemy.

Many and subtle are the ideological weapons the State and its intellectuals have used over the centuries to induce their subjects to accept their rule. One excellent weapon has been the power of *tradition*. The longer lasting the rule of any given State, the more powerful this weapon; for then the X-Dynasty or the Y-State has the seeming weight of centuries of tradition behind it. Worship of one's ancestors then becomes a non-too-subtle means of cultivating worship of one's ancestral rulers. The force of tradition is, of course, bolstered by ancient *habit*, which confirms the subjects in the seeming propriety and legitimacy of the rule under which they live. Thus, the political theorist Bertrand De Jouvenel has written:

The essential reason for obedience is that it has become a habit of the species. . . . Power is for us a fact of nature. From the earliest days of recorded history it has always presided over human desti-

8 Burnham, *op. cit.*, p. 3.

nies . . . the authorities which ruled . . . in former times did not disappear without bequeathing to their successors their privilege nor without leaving in men's minds imprints which are cumulative in their effect. The succession of governments which, in the course of centuries, rule the same society may be looked on as one underlying government which takes on continuous accretions.[9]

Another potent ideological force is for the State to deprecate the *individual* and exalt either the past or the present collectivity of society. Any isolated voice, any raiser of new doubts, can then be attacked as a profane violator of the wisdom of his ancestors. Moreover, any new idea, much less any new *critical* idea, must necessarily *begin* as a small minority opinion. Therefore, in order to ward off any potentially dangerous idea from threatening majority acceptance of its rule, the State will try to nip the new idea in the bud by ridiculing any view that sets itself against mass opinion. The ways in which the State rulers in ancient Chinese despotisms used religion as a method of binding the individual to the State-run society were summarized by Norman Jacobs:

Chinese religion is a social religion, seeking to solve the problems of social interests, not individual interests. . . . Religion is essentially a force of impersonal social adjustment and control—rather than a medium for the personal solutions of the individual—and social adjustment and control are effected through education and reverence for superiors. . . . Reverence for superiors—superior in age and hence in education and experience—is the ethical foundation of social adjustment and control. . . . In China, the inter-relationship of political authority with orthodox religion equated heterodoxy with political error. The orthodox religion was particularly active in persecuting and destroying heterodox sects; in this it was backed by the secular power.[10]

[9] Bertrand De Jouvenel, *On Power* (New York: Viking Press, 1949), p. 22.
[10] Norman Jacobs, *The Origin of Modern Capitalism and Eastern Asia* (Hong Kong: Hong Kong University Press, 1958), pp. 161–63, 185. The great work on all aspects of Oriental despotism is Karl A. Wittfogel, *Oriental Despotism: A Comparative Study of Total Power* (New Haven: Yale University Press, 1957).

The general tendency of government to seek out and thwart any heterodox views was outlined, in typically witty and delightful style, by the libertarian writer H. L. Mencken:

All [that government] can see in an original idea is potential change, and hence an invasion of its prerogatives. The most dangerous man, to any government, is the man who is able to think things out for himself, without regard to the prevailing superstitions and taboos. Almost inevitably he comes to the conclusion that the government he lives under is dishonest, insane and intolerable, and so, if he is romantic, he tries to change it. And even if he is not romantic personally he is very apt to spread discontent among those who are.[11]

It is also particularly important for the State to make its rule seem *inevitable*: even if its reign is disliked, as it often is, it will then be met with the passive resignation expressed in the familiar coupling of "death and taxes." One method is to bring to its side historical determinism: if X-State rules us, then this has been inevitably decreed for us by the Inexorable Laws of History (or the Divine Will, or the Absolute, or the Material Productive Forces), and nothing that any puny individuals may do can change the inevitable. It is also important for the State to inculcate in its subjects an aversion to any outcropping of what is now called "a conspiracy theory of history." For a search for "conspiracies," as misguided as the results often are, means a search for motives, and an attribution of individual responsibility for the historical misdeeds of ruling elites. If, however, any tyranny or venality, or aggressive war imposed by the State was brought about *not* by particular State rulers but by mysterious and arcane "social forces," or by the imperfect state of the world—or if, in some way, *everyone* was guilty ("We are *all* murderers," proclaims a common slogan), then there is no point in anyone's becoming indignant or rising up against such misdeeds. Furthermore, a discrediting of "conspiracy theories" —or indeed, of anything smacking of "economic determinism"

[11] H. L. Mencken, *A Mencken Crestomathy* (New York: Alfred A. Knopf, 1949), p. 145.

—will make the subjects more likely to believe the "general welfare" reasons that are invariably put forth by the modern State for engaging in any aggressive actions.

The rule of the State is thus made to seem inevitable. Furthermore, any alternative to the existing State is encased in an aura of fear. Neglecting its own monopoly of theft and predation, the State raises the spectre among its subjects of the chaos that would supposedly ensue if the State should disappear. The people on their own, it is maintained, could not possibly supply their own protection against sporadic criminals and marauders. Furthermore, each State has been particularly successful over the centuries in instilling fear among its subjects of *other* State rulers. With the land area of the globe now parcelled out among particular States, one of the basic doctrines and tactics of the rulers of each State has been to identify *itself* with the territory it governs. Since most men tend to love their homeland, the identification of that land and its population with the State is a means of making natural patriotism work to the State's advantage. If, then, "Ruritania" is attacked by "Walldavia," the first task of the Ruritanian State and its intellectuals is to convince the people of Ruritania that the attack is really upon *them*, and not simply upon their ruling class. In this way, a war between *rulers* is converted into a war between *peoples*, with each people rushing to the defense of their rulers in the mistaken belief that the rulers are busily defending *them*. This device of nationalism has been particularly successful in recent centuries; it was not very long ago, at least in Western Europe, when the mass of subjects regarded wars as irrelevant battles between various sets of nobles and their retinues.

Another tried and true method for bending subjects to one's will is the infusion of guilt. Any increase in private well-being can be attacked as "unconscionable greed," "materialism," or "excessive affluence"; and mutually beneficial exchanges in the market can be denounced as "selfish." Somehow the conclusion always drawn is that more resources should be expropriated from the private sector and siphoned into the parasitic "public," or State, sector. Often the call upon the public to yield more resources is couched in a stern call by the ruling elite for more "sacrifices" for the national or the common weal. Somehow, however, while the public is supposed to sacrifice and curtail its "materialistic greed," the sacrifices are always one way. The *State* does not sacrifice; the State eagerly grabs more and more of the public's material resources. Indeed, it is a useful rule of thumb: when your ruler calls aloud for "sacrifices," look to your own life and pocketbook!

This sort of argumentation reflects a general double standard of morality that is always applied to State rulers but not to anyone else. No one, for example, is surprised or horrified to learn that businessmen are seeking higher profits. No one is horrified if workers leave lower-paying for higher-paying jobs. All this is considered proper and normal behavior. But if anyone should dare assert that politicians and bureaucrats are motivated by the desire to maximize *their* incomes, the hue and cry of "conspiracy theorist" or "economic determinist" spreads throughout the land. The general opinion—carefully cultivated, of course, by the State itself—is that men enter politics or government purely out of devoted concern for the common good and the public weal. What gives the gentlemen of the State apparatus their superior moral patina? Perhaps it is the dim and instinctive knowledge of the populace that the State *is* engaged in systematic theft and predation, and they may feel that only a dedication to altruism on the part of the State makes these actions tolerable. To consider politicians and bureaucrats subject to the same monetary aims as everyone else would strip the Robin Hood veil from State predation. For it would then be clear that, in the Oppenheimer phrasing, ordinary citizens were pursuing the peaceful, productive "economic means" to wealth, while the State apparatus was devoting itself to the coercive and exploitative organized "political means." The emperor's clothes of supposed altruistic concern for the common weal would then be stripped from him.

The intellectual arguments used by the State throughout

history to "engineer consent" by the public can be classified into two parts: (1) that rule by the existing government is inevitable, absolutely necessary, and far better than the indescribable evils that would ensue upon its downfall; and (2) that the State rulers are especially great, wise, and altruistic men—far greater, wiser, and better than their simple subjects. In former times, the latter argument took the form of rule by "divine right" or by the "divine ruler" himself, or by an "aristocracy" of men. In modern times, as we indicated earlier, this argument stresses not so much divine approval as rule by a wise guild of "scientific experts" especially endowed in knowledge of statesmanship and the arcane facts of the world. The increasing use of scientific jargon, especially in the social sciences, has permitted intellectuals to weave apologia for State rule which rival the ancient priestcraft in obscurantism. For example, a thief who presumed to justify his theft by saying that he was really helping his victims by his spending, thus giving retail trade a needed boost would be hooted down without delay. But when this same theory is clothed in Keynesian mathematical equations and impressive references to the "multiplier effect," it carries far more conviction with a bamboozled public.

In recent years, we have seen the development in the United States of a profession of "national security managers," of bureaucrats who never face electoral procedures, but who continue, through administration after administration, secretly using their supposed special expertise to plan wars, interventions, and military adventures. Only their egregious blunders in the Vietnam war have called their activities into any sort of public question; before that, they were able to ride high, wide, and handsome over the public they saw mostly as cannon fodder for their own purposes.

A public debate between "isolationist" Senator Robert A. Taft and one of the leading national security intellectuals, McGeorge Bundy, was instructive in demarking both the issues at stake and the attitude of the intellectual ruling elite. Bundy attacked Taft in early 1951 for opening a public debate on the

waging of the Korean war. Bundy insisted that only the executive policy leaders were equipped to manipulate diplomatic and
military force in a lengthy decades-long period of limited war
against the communist nations. It was important, Bundy maintained, that public opinion and public debate be excluded from
promulgating any policy role in this area. For, he warned, the
public was unfortunately not committed to the rigid national
purposes discerned by the policy managers; it merely responded
to the *ad hoc* realities of given situations. Bundy also maintained that there should be no recriminations or even examinations of the decisions of the policy managers, because it was
important that the public accept their decisions without question. Taft, in contrast, denounced the secret decision-making
by military advisers and specialists in the executive branch, decisions effectively sealed off from public scrutiny. Furthermore,
he complained, "If anyone dared to suggest criticism or even a
thorough debate, he was at once branded as an isolationist and
a saboteur of unity and the bipartisan foreign policy." [12]

Similarly, at a time when President Eisenhower and Secretary
of State Dulles were privately contemplating going to war in
Indochina, another prominent national security manager,
George F. Kennan, was advising the public that "There are
times when, having elected a government, we will be best ad-
vised to let it govern and let it speak for us as it will in the
councils of the nations." [13]

We see clearly why the State needs the intellectuals; but why
do the intellectuals need the State? Put simply, the intellectual's
livelihood in the free market is generally none too secure; for
the intellectual, like everyone else on the market, must depend
on the values and choices of the masses of his fellowmen, and
it is characteristic of these masses that they are generally unin-

[12] See Leonard P. Liggio, "Why the Futile Crusade?," *Left and Right*
(Spring, 1965), pp. 59–60 (reprinted in *Left and Right: Selected Essays*
(New York: Arno Press, 1972).

[13] George F. Kennan, *Realities of American Foreign Policy* (Princeton:
Princeton University Press, 1954), pp. 95–96.

terested in intellectual concerns. The State, on the other hand, is willing to offer the intellectuals a warm, secure, and permanent berth in its apparatus, a secure income, and the panoply of prestige.

The eager alliance between the State and the intellectuals was symbolized by the avid desire of the professors at the University of Berlin, in the nineteenth century, to form themselves into what they themselves proclaimed as the "intellectual body-guard of the House of Hohenzollern." From a superficially different ideological perspective, it can be seen in the revealingly outraged reaction of the eminent Marxist scholar of ancient China, Joseph Needham, to Karl Wittfogel's acidulous critique of ancient Chinese despotism. Wittfogel had shown the importance for bolstering the system of the Confucian glorification of the gentleman-scholar officials who manned the ruling bureaucracy of despotic China. Needham charged indignantly that the "civilization which Professor Wittfogel is so bitterly attacking was one which could make poets and scholars into officials." [14] What matter the totalitarianism so long as the ruling class is abundantly staffed by certified intellectuals!

The worshipful and fawning attitude of intellectuals toward their rulers has been illustrated many times throughout history. A contemporary American counterpart to the "intellectual bodyguard of the House of Hohenzollern" is the attitude of so many liberal intellectuals toward the office and person of the President. Thus, to political scientist Professor Richard Neustadt, the President is the "sole crown-like symbol of the Union." And policy manager Townsend Hoopes, in the winter of 1960, wrote that "under our system the people can look only to the President to define the nature of our foreign policy problem and the national programs and sacrifices required to

---

[14] Joseph Needham, "Review of Karl A. Wittfogel, *Oriental Despotism,*" *Science and Society* (1958), p. 65. For an attitude in contrast to Needham's, see John Lukacs, "Intellectual Class or Intellectual Profession?," in George B. deHuszar, ed., *The Intellectuals* (Glencoe, Ill.: The Free Press, 1960), p. 522.

meet it with effectiveness." [15] After generations of such rhetoric, it is no wonder that Richard Nixon, on the eve of his election as President, should thus describe his role: "He [the President] must articulate the nation's values, define its goals and marshall its will." Nixon's conception of his role is hauntingly similar to Ernst Huber's articulation, in the Germany of the 1930s, of the *Constitutional Law of the Greater German Reich.* Huber wrote that the head of State "sets up the great ends which are to be attained and draws up the plans for the utilization of all national powers in the achievement of the common goals . . . he gives the national life its true purpose and value." [16]

The attitude and motivation of the contemporary national security intellectual bodyguard of the State has been caustically described by Marcus Raskin, who was a staff member of the National Security Council during the Kennedy administration. Calling them "megadeath intellectuals," Raskin writes that:

. . . their most important function is to justify and extend the existence of their employers. . . . In order to justify the continued large-scale production of these [thermonuclear] bombs and missiles, military and industrial leaders needed some kind of theory to rationalize their use. . . . This became particularly urgent during the late 1950's, when economy-minded members of the Eisenhower Administration began to wonder why so much money, thought, and resources were being spent on weapons if their use could not be justified. And so began a series of rationalizations by the "defense intellectuals" in and out of the universities. . . . Military procurement will continue to flourish, and they will continue to demonstrate why it must. In this respect they are no different from the great majority of modern specialists who accept the assumptions of the organizations which employ them because of the rewards in

[15] Richard Neustadt, "Presidency at Mid-Century," *Law and Contemporary Problems* (Autumn, 1956), pp. 609–45; Townsend Hoopes, "The Persistence of Illusion: The Soviet Economic Drive and American National Interest," *Yale Review* (March 1960), p. 336.

[16] Quoted in Thomas Reeves and Karl Hess, *The End of the Draft* (New York: Vintage Books, 1970), pp. 64–65.

money and power and prestige. . . . They know enough not to question their employers' right to exist.[17]

This is not to say that all intellectuals everywhere have been "court intellectuals," servitors and junior partners of power. But this has been the ruling condition in the history of civilizations —generally in the form of a priestcraft—just as the ruling condition in those civilizations has been one or another form of despotism. There have been glorious exceptions, however, particularly in the history of Western civilization, where intellectuals have often been trenchant critics and opponents of State power, and have used their intellectual gifts to fashion theoretical systems which could be used in the struggle for liberation from that power. But invariably, these intellectuals have only been able to arise as a significant force when they have been able to operate from an independent power base—an independent property base—separate from the apparatus of the State. For wherever the State controls all property, wealth, and employment, everyone is economically dependent on it, and it becomes difficult, if not impossible, for such independent criticism to arise. It has been in the West, with its decentralized foci of power, its independent sources of property and employment, and therefore of bases from which to criticize the State, where a body of intellectual critics has been able to flourish. In the middle ages, the Roman Catholic Church, which was at least separate if not independent from the State, and the new free towns were able to serve as centers of intellectual and also of substantive opposition. In later centuries, teachers, ministers, and pamphleteers in a relatively free society were able to use their independence from the State to agitate for further expansion of freedom. In contrast, one of the first libertarian philosophers, Lao-tse, living in the midst of ancient Chinese despotism, saw no hope for achieving liberty in that totalitarian society

[17] Marcus Raskin, "The Megadeath Intellectuals," *The New York Review of Books* (November 14, 1963), pp. 6–7. Also see Martin Nicolaus, "The Professor, the Policeman, and the Peasant," *Viet-Report* (June–July 1966), pp. 15–19.

except by counseling quietism, to the point of the individual's dropping out of social life altogether.

With decentralized power, with a church separate from the State, with flourishing towns and cities able to develop outside the feudal power structure, and freedom in society, the economy was able to develop in Western Europe in a way that transcended all previous civilizations. Furthermore, the Germanic —and particularly the Celtic—tribal structure which succeeded the disintegrating Roman Empire had strong libertarian elements. Instead of a mighty State apparatus exerting a monopoly of violence, disputes were solved by contending tribesmen consulting the elders of the tribe on the nature and application of the tribe's customary and common law. The "chief" was generally merely a war leader who was only called into his warrior role whenever war with other tribes was underway. There was no permanent war or military bureaucracy in the tribes. In Western Europe, as in many other civilizations, the typical model of the origin of the State was not via a voluntary "social contract" but by the conquest of one tribe by another. The original liberty of the tribe or the peasantry thus falls victim to the conquerors. At first, the conquering tribe killed and looted the victims and rode on. But at some time the conquerors decided that it would be more profitable to settle down among the conquered peasantry and rule and loot them on a permanent and systematic basis. The periodic tribute exacted from the conquered subjects eventually came to be called "taxation." And, with equal generality, the conquering chieftains parcelled out the land of the peasantry to the various warlords, who were then able to settle down and collect feudal "rent" from the peasantry. The peasants were often enslaved, or rather enserfed, to the land itself to provide a continuing source of exploited labor for the feudal lords.[18]

---

[18] On the typical genesis of the State, see Oppenheimer, *op. cit.*, Chapter II. While scholars such as Lowie and Wittfogel (*op. cit.*, pp. 324–25) dispute the Gumplowicz-Oppenheimer-Rüstow thesis that the State *always* originated in conquest, they concede that conquest often entered into the

We may note a few prominent instances of the birth of a modern State through conquest. One was the military conquest of the Indian peasantry in Latin America by the Spaniards. The conquering Spanish not only established a new State over the Indians, but the land of the peasantry was parcelled out among the conquering warlords, who were ever after to collect rent from the tillers of the land. Another instance was the new political form imposed upon the Saxons of England after their conquest by the Normans in 1066. The land of England was parcelled out among the Norman warrior lords, who thereby formed a State and feudal-land apparatus of rule over the subject population. For the libertarian, the most interesting and certainly the most poignant example of the creation of a State through conquest was the destruction of the libertarian society of ancient Ireland by England in the seventeenth century, a conquest which established an imperial State and ejected numerous Irish from their cherished land. The libertarian society of Ireland, which lasted for a thousand years—and which will be described further below—was able to resist English conquest for hundreds of years because of the absence of a State which could be conquered easily and then used by the conquerors to rule over the native population.

But while throughout Western history, intellectuals have formulated theories designed to check and limit State power, each State has been able to use its own intellectuals to turn those ideas around into further legitimations of its own advance of power. Thus, originally, in Western Europe the concept of the "divine right of kings" was a doctrine promoted by the Church to *limit* State power. The idea was that the king could not just impose his arbitrary will. His edicts were limited to

---

alleged internal development of States. Furthermore, there is evidence that in the first great civilization, Sumer, a prosperous, free and Stateless society existed until military *defense* against conquest induced the development of a permanent military and State bureaucracy. Cf. Samual Noah Kramer, *The Sumerians* (Chicago: University of Chicago Press, 1963), pp. 73ff.

conforming with the divine law. As absolute monarchy advanced, however, the kings were able to turn the concept around to the idea that God put his stamp of approval on any of the king's actions; that he ruled by "divine right."

Similarly, the concept of parliamentary democracy began as a popular check on the absolute rule of the monarch. The king was limited by the power of parliament to grant him tax revenues. Gradually, however, as parliament displaced the king as head of State, the parliament itself became the unchecked State sovereign. In the early nineteenth century, English utilitarians, who advocated additional individual liberty in the name of social utility and the general welfare, were to see these concepts turned into sanctions for expanding the power of the State.

As De Jouvenel writes:

Many writers on theories of sovereignty have worked out one or the other of these restrictive devices. But in the end every single such theory has, sooner or later, lost its original purpose, and come to act merely as a springboard to Power, by providing it with the powerful aid of an invisible sovereign with whom it could in time successfully identify itself.[19]

Certainly, the most ambitious attempt in history to impose limits on the State was the Bill of Rights and other restrictive parts of the United States Constitution. Here, written limits on government became the fundamental law, to be interpreted by a judiciary supposedly independent of the other branches of government. All Americans are familiar with the process by which John C. Calhoun's prophetic analysis has been vindicated; the State's own monopoly judiciary has inexorably broadened the construction of State power over the last century and a half. But few have been as keen as liberal Professor Charles Black—who hails the process—in seeing that the State has been able to transform judicial review itself from a limiting device into a powerful instrument for gaining legitimacy for its ac-

---

[19] De Jouvenel, *op. cit.*, p. 27.

tions in the minds of the public. If a judicial decree of "unconstitutional" is a mighty check on governmental power, so too a verdict of "constitutional" is an equally mighty weapon for fostering public acceptance of ever greater governmental power.

Professor Black begins his analysis by pointing out the crucial necessity for "legitimacy" of any government in order to endure; that is, basic majority acceptance of the government and its actions. Acceptance of legitimacy, however, becomes a real problem in a country like the United States, where "substantive limitations are built into the theory on which the government rests." What is needed, adds Black, is a method by which the government can assure the public that its expanding powers are indeed "constitutional." And this, he concludes, has been the major historic function of judicial review. Let Black illustrate the problem:

The supreme risk [to the government] is that of disaffection and a feeling of outrage widely disseminated throughout the population, and loss of moral authority by the government as such, however long it may be propped up by force or inertia or the lack of an appealing and immediately available alternative. Almost everybody living under a government of limited powers, must sooner or later be subjected to some governmental action which as a matter of private opinion he regards as outside the power of government or positively forbidden to government. A man is drafted, though he finds nothing in the Constitution about being drafted. . . . A farmer is told how much wheat he can raise; he believes, and he discovers that some respectable lawyers believe with him, that the government has no more right to tell him how much wheat he can grow than it has to tell his daughter whom she can marry. A man goes to the federal penitentiary for saying what he wants to, and he paces his cell reciting . . . "Congress shall make no laws abridging the freedom of speech.". . . A businessman is told what he can ask, and must ask, for buttermilk.

The danger is real enough that each of these people (and who is not of their number?) will confront the concept of governmental limitation with the reality (as he sees it) of the flagrant overstepping of actual limits, and draw the obvious conclusion as to the status of his government with respect to legitimacy.[20]

This danger is averted, Black adds, by the State's propounding the doctrine that *some one* agency must have the ultimate decision on constitutionality, and that this agency must be part of the federal government itself. For while the seeming independence of the federal judiciary has played a vital role in making its actions virtual Holy Writ for the bulk of the population, it is also true that the judiciary is part and parcel of the government apparatus and is appointed by the executive and legislative branches. Professor Black concedes that the government has thereby set itself up as a judge in its own case, and has thus violated a basic juridical principle for arriving at any kind of just decision. But Black is remarkably lighthearted about this fundamental breach: "The final power of the State . . . must stop where the law stops it. And who shall set the limit, and who shall enforce the stopping, against the mightiest power? Why, the State itself, of course, through its judges and its laws. Who controls the temperate? Who teaches the wise? . . ." [21] And so Black admits that when we have a State, we hand over all our weapons and means of coercion to the State apparatus, we turn over all of our powers of ultimate decision-making to this deified group, and *then* we must jolly well sit back quietly and await the unending stream of justice that will pour forth from these institutions—even though they are basically judging their own case. Black sees no conceivable alternative to this coercive monopoly of judicial decisions enforced by the State, but here is precisely where our new movement challenges this conventional view and asserts that there *is* a viable alternative: libertarianism.

Seeing no such alternative, Professor Black falls back on mysticism in his defense of the State, for in the final analysis he finds the achievement of justice and legitimacy from the State's

[20] Charles L. Black, Jr., *The People and the Court* (New York: Macmillan, 1960), pp. 42–43.
[21] *Ibid.*, pp. 32–33.

perpetual judging of its own cause to be "something of a miracle." In this way, the liberal Black joins the conservative Burnham in falling back on the miraculous and thereby admitting that there is no satisfactory rational argument in support of the State.[22]

Applying his realistic view of the Supreme Court to the famous conflict between the Court and the New Deal in the 1930s, Professor Black chides his liberal colleagues for their shortsightedness in denouncing judicial obstructionism:

. . . the standard version of the story of the New Deal and the Court, though accurate in its way, displaces the emphasis. . . . It concentrates on the difficulties; it almost forgets how the whole thing turned out. The upshot of the matter was (and this is what I like to emphasize) that after some twenty-four months of balking . . . the Supreme Court, without a single change in the law of its composition, or, indeed, in its actual manning, *placed the affirmative stamp of legitimacy on the New Deal, and on the whole new conception of government in America.* [*Italics the author's.*] [23]

In this way, the Supreme Court was able to put the quietus to the large body of Americans who had strong constitutional objections to the expanded powers of the New Deal:

Of course, not everyone was satisfied. The Bonnie Prince Charlie of constitutionally commanded laissez-faire still stirs the hearts of a few zealots in the Highlands of choleric unreality. But there is no longer any significant or dangerous public doubt as to the constitutional power of Congress to deal as it does with the national economy. . . . We had no means, other than the Supreme Court, for imparting legitimacy to the New Deal." [24]

---

[22] In contrast to the complacency of Black was the trenchant critique of the Constitution and the powers of the Supreme Court by the political scientist J. Allen Smith. Smith wrote that "Clearly, common sense required that no organ of the government should be able to determine its own powers." J. Allen Smith, *The Growth and Decadence of Constitutional Government* (New York: Henry Holt and Co., 1930), p. 87. Clearly, common sense and "miracles" dictate very different views of government.

[23] *Ibid.*, p. 64.

[24] *Ibid.*, p. 65.

Thus, even in the United States, unique among governments in having a Constitution, parts of which at least were meant to impose strict and solemn limits upon its actions, even here the Constitution has proved to be an instrument for ratifying the expansion of State power rather than the opposite. As Calhoun saw, any written limits that leave it to government to interpret its own powers are bound to be interpreted as sanctions for expanding and not binding those powers. In a profound sense, the idea of binding down power with the chains of a written Constitution has proved to be a noble experiment that failed. The idea of a strictly limited government has proved to be utopian; some other, more radical means must be found to prevent the growth of the aggressive State. The libertarian system would meet this problem by scrapping the entire notion of creating a government—an institution with a coercive monopoly of force over a given territory—and *then* hoping to find ways to keep that government from expanding. The libertarian alternative is to abstain from such a monopoly government to begin with.

We will explore the entire notion of a State-less society, a society without formal government, in later chapters. But one instructive exercise is to try to abandon the habitual ways of seeing things, and to consider the argument for the State *de novo*. Let us try to transcend the fact that for as long as we can remember, the State has monopolized police and judicial services in society. Suppose that we were all starting completely from scratch, and that millions of us had been dropped down upon the earth, fully grown and developed, from some other planet. Debate begins as to how protection (police and judicial services) will be provided. Someone says: "Let's all give all of our weapons to Joe Jones over there, and to his relatives. And let Jones and his family decide all disputes among us. In that way, the Joneses will be able to protect all of us from any aggression or fraud that anyone else may commit. With all the power and all the ability to make ultimate decisions on disputes in the hands of Jones, we will all be protected from one another.

And then let us allow the Joneses to obtain their income from this great service by using their weapons, and by exacting as much revenue by coercion as they shall desire." Surely in that sort of situation, no one would treat this proposal with anything but ridicule. For it would be starkly evident that there would be no way, in that case, for any of us to protect ourselves from the aggressions, or the depredations, of the Joneses themselves. No one would then have the total folly to respond to that long-standing and most perceptive query: "Who shall guard the guardians?" by answering with Professor Black's blithe: "Who controls the temperate?" It is only because we have become accustomed over thousands of years to the existence of the State that we now give precisely this kind of absurd answer to the problem of social protection and defense.

And, of course, the State never really did begin with this sort of "social contract." As Oppenheimer pointed out, the State generally began in violence and conquest; even if at times internal processes gave rise to the State, it was certainly never by general consensus or contract.

The libertarian creed can now be summed up as (1) the absolute right of every man to the ownership of his own body; (2) the equally absolute right to own and therefore to control the material resources he has found and transformed; and (3) therefore, the absolute right to exchange or give away the ownership to such titles to whoever is willing to exchange or receive them. As we have seen, each of these steps involves *property* rights, but even if we call step (1) "personal" rights, we shall see that problems about "personal liberty" inextricably involve the rights of material property or free exchange. Or, briefly, the rights of personal liberty and "freedom of enterprise" almost invariably intertwine and cannot really be separated.

We have seen that the exercise of personal "freedom of speech," for example, almost invariably involves the exercise of "economic freedom"—i.e., freedom to own and exchange material property. The holding of a meeting to exercise freedom of speech involves the hiring of a hall, traveling to the hall over roads, and using some form of transportation, etc. The closely related "freedom of the press" even more evidently involves the cost of printing and of using a press, the sale of leaflets to willing buyers—in short, all the ingredients of "economic freedom." Furthermore, our example of "shouting fire in a crowded theater" provides us with the clear guideline for deciding *whose* rights must be defended in any given situation— the guidelines being provided by our criterion: the rights of property.

PART II:

Libertarian Applications to Current Problems

4

The Problems

Let us take a brief look at the major problem areas of our society, and see if we can detect any red thread that runs through all of them.

The war in Vietnam. This is generally acknowledged to be our overriding problem. The war is an expression of our foreign policy, which is, of course, a monopoly of the federal government. The war is being waged by our armed forces which, again, is a compulsory monopoly of our federal government. And the forces are fed by the slavery of conscription, once again a monopoly of the government. So our government is wholly responsible for this problem, as a whole and in all of its aspects.

Crime in the streets. Consider: the crime in question is being committed, by definition, on the streets. The streets are owned, almost universally, by government, which thereby has a virtual monopoly of street-ownership. The police, who are supposed to guard us against this crime, are a compulsory monopoly of the government. And the courts, which are in the business of convicting and punishing criminals, are also a coercive monopoly of the government. So government has been in charge of every single aspect of the crime-in-the-streets problem. The failure here, just as the failure in Vietnam, must be chalked up solely to government.

Traffic congestion. Once again, this occurs solely on government-owned streets and roads.

The military-industrial complex. This complex is entirely a creature of the federal government. It is the government that decides to spend countless billions on overkill weaponry, it is the government that hands out contracts, the government that subsidizes inefficiency through cost-plus guarantees, the government that builds plants and leases or gives them outright to contractors. Of course, the businesses involved lobby for these privileges, but it is only through *government* that the mechanism for this privilege, and this wasteful misallocation of resources, can possibly exist.

Transportation. The crisis of transportation involves not only congested streets, but also decaying railroads, overpriced airlines, airport congestion at peak hours, and subways (e.g., New York City) that are suffering deficits and visibly heading toward collapse. Yet: the railroads were overbuilt from extensive government subsidies (federal, state, and local) during the nineteenth century, and have been the most heavily regulated industry for the longest period of time in American history. Airlines are cartellized through regulation by the Civil Aeronautics Board, and subsidized through such regulation, mail contracts, and virtually free airports. Airports for commercial lines are all owned by branches of the government, largely local. The New York City subways have been government-owned for decades.

River pollution. The rivers are, in effect, unowned, i.e., they have been kept as "public domain" owned by government. Furthermore, by far the biggest culprits in water pollution are the municipally owned sewage disposal systems. Again: government is at the same time the largest polluter, as well as the careless "owner" of the resource.

Water shortages. Water shortages are chronic in some areas of the country, and intermittent in others, such as New York City. Yet the government, (1) via its ownership of the public domain, owns the rivers from which much of the water comes, and (2) as virtually the only commercial *supplier* of water, the government owns the reservoirs and water conduits.

Air pollution. Again, the government, as owner of the public domain, "owns" the air. Furthermore, it has been the courts, owned solely by the government, which, as an act of deliberate policy, have for generations failed to protect our property rights in our bodies and orchards from the pollution generated by industry. Moreover, much of the direct pollution comes from government-owned plants.

Power shortages and blackouts. Throughout the land, state and local governments have created compulsory monopolies of gas and electric power and have granted these monopoly privileges to private utility companies, which are then regulated and have their rates set by government agencies to insure a permanent and fixed profit. Again, government has been the source of the monopoly and the regulation.

Telephone service. Increasingly failing telephone service comes, again, from a utility which receives a compulsory monopoly privilege from government, and which finds its rates set by government to guarantee a profit. As in the case of gas and electricity, no one is allowed to compete with the monopoly phone company.

Postal service. Suffering from heavy deficits throughout its existence, the postal service, in stark contrast to the goods and services produced by private industry on the free market, has become steadily higher in price and lower in quality. The mass of the public, using first-class mail, has been forced to subsidize businesses using second- and third-class services. Again, the Post Office has been, since the late nineteenth century, a compulsory monopoly of government. Whenever private firms have been allowed to compete, even illegally, in delivery of mail, they have invariably provided better service at a lower price.

Television. Television consists of bland programs and distorted news. Radio and television channels have been national-ized for half a century by the federal government, which grants channels as a gift to privileged licensees, and can and does withdraw these gifts when a station displeases the government's Federal Communications Commission. How can any genuine freedom of speech or of the press exist under such conditions?

Welfare system. Welfare, of course, is exclusively the prov-ince of government, largely state and local.

Urban housing. Along with traffic, one of our most conspicu-ous urban failures. Yet there are few other industries that have been so closely intertwined with government. Urban planning has controlled and regulated the cities. Zoning laws have ringed housing and land use with innumerable restrictions. Property taxes have crippled urban development and forced abandon-ment of houses. Building codes have restricted housing con-struction and made it more costly. Urban renewal has provided massive subsidies to real estate developers, forced the bulldoz-ing of apartments and rental stores, lowered the supply of hous-ing, and intensified racial discrimination. Extensive government loans have generated overbuilding in the suburbs. Rent controls have created apartment shortages and reduced the supply of residential housing.

Union strikes and restrictions. Unions have become a nui-sance with power to cripple the economy, but only as a result of numerous special privileges afforded by the government; especially various immunities accorded unions, particularly the Wagner Act of 1935, still in effect, which compels employers to bargain with unions which gain a majority vote of a "bargaining unit" arbitrarily defined by the government itself.

Education. The growing failure of our educational system, especially the public schools, has become all too evident in recent years. And yet the public schools, the site of the worst failure, are of course totally owned and operated by the govern-ment and are backed by compulsory attendance laws which force all children through high school age to attend school—either public or private schools certified by governmental authorities. Higher education, too, has become intertwined with government in recent decades: many universities are government-owned, and the others are systematic receivers of grants, subsidies, and contracts.

High taxes. High and rising taxes have crippled almost everyone, and are hampering productivity, incentives and thrift, as well as the free energies of the people. Taxes, of course, are exclusively the province of government.

If we look around, then, at the crucial problem areas of our society—the areas of crisis and failure—we find in each and every case a "red thread" marking and uniting them all: the thread of government. In every one of these cases, government either has totally run or heavily influenced the activity. John Kenneth Galbraith, in his best-selling *The Affluent Society*, recognized that the government sector was the focus of our social failure—but drew instead the odd lesson that therefore still more funds and resources must be diverted from the private to the public sector. He thereby ignored the fact that the role of government in America—federal, state, and local—has expanded enormously, both absolutely and proportionately, in this century and especially in recent decades. Unfortunately, Galbraith never once raised the question: Is there something inherent in government operation and activity, something which *creates* the very failures which we see abounding? In Part II we shall investigate some of the major problems of government and of liberty in this country, see where the failures came from, and propound the solutions of the new libertarianism.

5

Involuntary Servitude

IF THERE IS ANYTHING a libertarian must be squarely and totally against, it is *involuntary servitude*—forced labor—an act which denies the most elemental right of self-ownership. "Liberty" and "slavery" have ever been recognized to be polar opposites. The libertarian, therefore, is totally opposed to slavery.[1] An academic question nowadays, one might object? But is it really? For what *is* slavery but (a) forcing people to work at tasks the slave-master wishes, and (b) paying them either pure subsistence or, at any rate, less than the slave would have accepted voluntarily. In short, forced labor at below free-market wages.

Thus, are we really free of "slavery," of involuntary servitude in present-day America? Is the prohibition against involuntary servitude of the Thirteenth Amendment really being obeyed? [2]

---

[1] There is one exception: the punishment of criminals who had themselves aggressed against or enslaved their victims. Such punishment in a libertarian system would at least involve forcing the criminal to work in order to pay restitution to his victim.

[2] Significantly, the Thirteenth Amendment's only exception is the punishment of convicted criminals mentioned in the previous note: "Neither

86

Conscription

Surely, for one example, there can be no more blatant case of involuntary servitude than our entire system of *conscription*. Every youth is forced to register with the selective service system when he turns eighteen. He is compelled to carry his draft card at all times, and, at whatever time the federal government deems fit, he is seized by the authorities and inducted into the armed forces. There his body and will are no longer his own; he is subject to the dictates of the government; and he can be forced to kill and to place his own life in jeopardy if the authorities so decree. What else is involuntary servitude if not the draft?

The utilitarian aspect permeates the argument for the conscription system. Thus the government uses the argument: *Who* will defend us against foreign attack if we do not employ coercion and conscript our defenders? There are several rebuttals for a libertarian to make to this line of reasoning. In the first place, if you and I and our next-door neighbor think that we need defending, we have no moral right to use coercion—the bayonet or the revolver—to force someone else to defend us. This act of conscripting is just as much a deed of unjustifiable aggression—of kidnapping and possibly murder—as the alleged aggression we are trying to guard ourselves against in the first place. If we add that the draftees owe their bodies and their lives, if necessary, to "society" or to "their country," then we must retort: *Who is* this "society" or this "country" that is being used as a talisman to justify enslavement? It is simply all individuals in the territorial area *except* the youths being conscripted. "Society" and "country" are in this case mythical abstractions that are being used to cloak the naked use of coercion to promote the interests of specific individuals.

Secondly, to move to the utilitarian plane, *why* is it consid-

slavery nor involuntary servitude except as a punishment for crime whereof the party shall have been duly convicted, shall exist within the United States, or any place subject to their jurisdiction."

ered necessary to conscript defenders? No one is conscripted on the free market, yet on that market people obtain, through voluntary purchase and sale, every conceivable manner of goods and services, even the most necessary ones. On the market, people can and do obtain food, shelter, clothing, medical care, etc. Why can't they hire defenders as well? Indeed, there are plenty of people being hired every day to perform dangerous services: forest firefighters, rangers, test pilots, and . . . police and private guards and watchmen. Why can't soldiers be hired in the same way?

Or, to put it another way, the government employs countless thousands of people for all sorts of services, from truck drivers to scientists to typists; how is it that none of these people have to be conscripted? Why is there no "shortage" of these occupations to supposedly force the government to resort to compulsion to obtain them? To go a step further, even within the army there is no "shortage" of officers and no need to draft them; no one conscripts generals or admirals. The answer to these questions is simple: there is no shortage of government typists because the government goes out on the market and hires them at the market wage; there is no shortage of generals because they are paid handsomely, in salaries, perquisites, and pensions. There *is* a shortage of buck privates because their pay is—or was, until very recently—abysmally below the market wage. For years, even including the monetary value of the free food, shelter, and other services supplied the GI's, the earnings of the buck private were something like one-half the salary he could have earned in civilian life. Is it any wonder that there has been a chronic shortage of enlistees? For years it has been known that the way to induce people to volunteer for hazardous jobs is to pay them extra as a compensation. But the government has been paying the men half of what they could earn in private life.[3]

There is also the special disgrace of the doctors' draft, in

[3] Cf. James C. Miller III, ed., *Why the Draft?* (Baltimore: Penguin Books, 1968).

which physicians are subject to the draft at ages far beyond anyone else. Are doctors, then, to be penalized for their entry into the profession of medicine? What is the moral justification for onerous burdens placed on this particular, and vitally important, profession? Is this the way to cure the shortage of doctors—to put every man on notice that if he becomes a physician he will be sure to be drafted, and at a specially late age? Once again, the armed forces' need for doctors could easily be satisfied if the government were willing to pay physicians the market salary, plus enough to compensate them for the hazardous labor. If the government wishes to hire nuclear physicists or "think-tank" strategists, it finds ways of doing so at extremely handsome salaries. Are doctors lower forms of humanity?

The Army

While conscription into the armed forces is a blatant and aggravated form of involuntary servitude, there is another, far more subtle and therefore less detectable form: the structure of the army itself. Consider this: in what other occupation in the country are there severe penalties, including prison and in some cases execution, for "desertion," i.e., for quitting the particular employment? If someone quits General Motors, is he shot at sunrise?

It might be objected that, in the case of enlistees, the soldier or officer has voluntarily agreed to serve for a certain term, and he is therefore obligated to continue in service for that term of years. But the whole concept of "term of service" is part of the problem. Suppose, for example, that an engineer signs a contract with ARAMCO to serve for three years in Saudi Arabia. After a few months he decides that the life is not for him and he quits. This may well be a *moral* default on his part—a breach of moral obligation. But is it a legally enforceable obligation? In short, can he or should he be forced by the monopoly of weaponry of government to keep working for the remainder of his term? If so, that would be forced labor and enslavement.

For while it is true that he made a promise of future work, his body continues, in a free society, to be owned by himself alone. In practice and in libertarian theory as well, then, the engineer might be morally criticized for the breach, he may be black-listed by other oil firms, he may be forced to return any advance pay tendered to him by the company, but he will *not* be enslaved to ARAMCO for the three-year period.

But if this is true of ARAMCO, or of any other occupation or job in private life, why should it be different in the army? If a man signs up for seven years and then quits, he should be allowed to leave. He will lose pension rights, he will be morally criticized, he may be blacklisted from similar occupations, but he cannot, as a self-owner, be enslaved against his will.

It may be protested that the armed forces is a peculiarly important occupation that needs this sort of coercive sanction that other jobs do not have. Setting aside the importance of such occupations as medicine, agriculture, transportation, etc., that need not resort to such methods, let us consider a comparable defense occupation in civilian life—the police. Surely the police perform an equally, and perhaps more vital, service —and yet every year people join the police and quit the force, and there is no coercive attempt to bind their labor through years of enlistment. In addition to demanding the end of conscription, then, the libertarian also proposes to do away with the entire concept of a *term* of enlistment and the practice of slavery this implies. Let the armed forces operate in ways similar to police, firemen, rangers, private guards, etc.—free of the blight and the moral crime of involuntary servitude.

But there is more to be said about the army as an institution, even if it were made completely voluntary. Americans have almost totally forgotten one of the noblest and strongest elements in the original American heritage: determined opposition to the entire institution of a "standing army." A government that has a permanent standing army at its disposal will always be tempted to use it, and to use it in an aggressive, interventionist, and warlike manner. While foreign policy will be dealt with

below, it is clear that a permanent army is a standing temptation to the State to enlarge its power, to push around other
people as well as other countries, and to dominate the internal
life of the nation. The original aim of the Jeffersonian movement—a largely libertarian factor in American political life—
was to abolish the standing army and navy altogether. The
original American principle was that if the nation was attacked,
then the citizens would hasten to join to repel the invader. A
standing armed force, then, could only lead to trouble and to
the aggrandizement of State power. In the course of his trenchant and prophetic attack on the proposed Constitution in
the Virginia ratifying convention, Patrick Henry warned of a
standing army: "Congress, by the power of taxation, by that of
raising an army, and by their control over the militia, have the
sword in one hand, and the purse in the other. Shall we be safe
without either?" [4]

Any standing army, then, poses a standing threat to liberty.
Its monopoly of coercive weapons, its modern tendency toward
creating and supporting a "military-industrial complex" to supply that army, and last, but not least, as Patrick Henry notes,
the taxing power to finance that army, pose a continuing threat
of the army's perpetual expansion in size and power. *Any* tax-
supported institution, of course, is opposed by the libertarian as
coercive, but an army is uniquely menacing for its amassing
and collecting into one set of hands the massive power of modern weaponry.

[4] Arthur A. Ekirch, Jr., *The Civilian and the Military* (New York: Oxford University Press, 1956), p. 28. For a trenchant attack by a Jeffersonian theorist on the American executive as commander-in-chief of the armed
forces, see John Taylor of Caroline, *An Inquiry into the Principles and Policy of the Government of the United States* (1814, rep. New Haven: Yale
University Press, 1950), pp. 175ff. On the important influence of seven-
teenth-century English libertarian theorists and their hostility to a standing
army upon the American Revolution, see Bernard Bailyn, *The Ideological
Origins of the American Revolution* (Cambridge: Harvard Univ. Press,
1967), pp. 61–64. Also see Don Higgenbotham, *The War of American Independence* (New York: Macmillan, 1971), pp. 14–16.

Anti-Strike Laws

On October 4, 1971, President Nixon invoked the Taft-Hartley Act to obtain a court injunction forcing the suspension of a dock strike for eighty days; this was the ninth time the federal government had used the Act in a dock strike. Months earlier, the head of the New York City teachers' union went to jail for several days for defying a law prohibiting public employees from striking. It is no doubt convenient for a long-suffering public to be spared the disruptions of a strike. Yet the "solution" imposed was forced labor, pure and simple; the workers were coerced, against their will, into going back to work. There is no moral excuse, in a society claiming to be opposed to slavery and in a country which has outlawed involuntary servitude, for any legal or judicial action prohibiting strikes—or jailing union leaders who fail to comply. Slavery is all too often more convenient for the slave-masters.

It is true that the strike is a peculiar form of work stoppage. The strikers do not merely quit their jobs; they also assert that somehow, in some metaphysical sense, they still "own" their jobs and are entitled to them, and intend to return to them when the issues are resolved. But the remedy for this self-contradictory policy, as well as for the disruptive power of labor unions, is not to pass laws outlawing strikes; the remedy is to remove the substantial body of law, federal, state, and local, that confers special governmental privileges on labor unions. All that is needed, both for libertarian principle and for a healthy economy, is to remove and abolish these special privileges.

These privileges have been enshrined in federal law—especially in the Wagner-Taft-Hartley Act, passed originally in 1935, and the Norris-LaGuardia Act of 1931. The latter prohibits the courts from issuing injunctions in cases of imminent union violence; the former compels employers to bargain "in good faith" with any union that wins the votes of the majority of a work unit arbitrarily defined by the federal government—and also prohibits employers from discriminating against union organizers. It was only after the Wagner Act—and its predecessor, the NIRA in 1933—that labor unions were able to become a powerful force in American life. It was then that unions skyrocketed from something like five percent to over twenty percent of the labor force. Furthermore, local and state laws often protect unions from being sued, and they place restrictions on the employers' hiring of strikebreaking labor; and police are often instructed not to interfere in the use of violence against strikebreakers by union pickets. Take away these special privileges and immunities, and labor unions would sink back to their previous negligible role in the American economy.

It is characteristic of our statist trend that, when general indignation against unions led to the Taft-Hartley Act of 1947, the government did not repeal any of these special privileges. Instead, it added special restrictions upon unions to limit the power which the government itself had created. Given a choice, the natural tendency of the State is to add to its power, not to cut it down; and so we have the peculiar situation of the government first building up unions and then howling for restrictions against their power. This is reminiscent of the American farm programs, in which one branch of the Department of Agriculture pays farmers to *restrict* their production, while another branch of the same agency pays them to increase their productivity. Irrational, surely, from the point of view of the consumers and the taxpayers, but perfectly rational from the point of view of the subsidized farmers *and* of the growing power of the bureaucracy. Similarly, the government's seemingly contradictory policy on unions serves, first, to aggrandize the power of government over labor relations, and second, to foster a suitably integrated and Establishment-minded unionism as junior partner in government's role over the economy.

The Tax System

In a sense, the entire system of taxation is a form of involuntary servitude. Take, in particular, the *income tax*. The high levels of income tax mean that all of us work a large part of

the year—several months—for *nothing* for Uncle Sam before
being allowed to enjoy our incomes on the market. Part of the
essence of slavery, after all, is forced work for someone at little
or no pay. But the income tax means that we sweat and earn
income, only to see the government extract a large chunk of it
by coercion for its own purposes. What is this but forced labor
at no pay?

The *withholding* feature of the income tax is a still more
clear-cut instance of involuntary servitude. For as the intrepid
Connecticut industrialist Vivien Kellems argued years ago, the
employer is forced to expend time, labor, and money in the
business of deducting and transmitting his employees' taxes to
the federal and state governments—yet the employer is not
recompensed for this expenditure. What moral principle justifies the government's forcing employers to act as its unpaid tax
collectors?

The withholding principle, of course, is the linchpin of the
whole federal income tax system. Without the steady and relatively painless process of deducting the tax from the worker's
pay check, the government could never hope to raise the high
levels of tax from the workers in one lump sum. Few people
remember that the withholding system was only instituted during World War II, and was supposed to be a wartime expedi-
ent. Like so many other features of State despotism, however,
the wartime emergency measure soon became a hallowed part
of the American system.

It is perhaps significant that the federal government, chal-
lenged by Vivien Kellems to test the constitutionality of the
withholding system, failed to take up the challenge. In February 1948 Miss Kellems, a small manufacturer in Westport,
Connecticut, announced that she was defying the withholding
law and was refusing to deduct the tax from her employees. She
demanded that the federal government indict her, so that the
courts would be able to rule on the constitutionality of the
withholding system. The government refused to do so, but instead seized the amount due from her bank account. Miss
Kellems then sued in federal court for the government to re-

turn her funds. When the suit finally came to trial in February 1951, the jury ordered the government to refund her money. But the test of constitutionality never came.[5]

To add insult to injury, the individual taxpayer, in filling out his tax form, is also forced by the government to work at no pay on the laborious and thankless task of reckoning how much he owes the government. Here again, he cannot charge the government for the cost and labor expended in making out his return. Furthermore, the law requiring everyone to fill out his tax form is a clear violation of the Fifth Amendment of the Constitution, prohibiting the government from forcing anyone to incriminate himself. Yet the courts, often zealous in protecting Fifth Amendment rights in less sensitive areas, have done nothing here, in a case where the entire existence of the swollen federal government structure is at stake. The repeal of either the income tax or the withholding or self-incriminating provisions would force the government back to the relatively minor levels of power that the country enjoyed before the twentieth century.

Retail sales, excise, and admission taxes also compel unpaid labor—in these cases, the unpaid labor of the retailer in collecting and forwarding the taxes to the government.

The high costs of tax collecting for the government have another unfortunate effect—perhaps not unintended by the powers-that-be. These costs, readily undertaken by large businesses, impose a disproportionately heavy and often crippling cost upon the small employer. The large employer can then cheerfully shoulder the cost knowing that his small competitor bears far more of the burden.

The Courts

Compulsory labor permeates our legal and judicial structure. Thus, much venerated judicial procedure rests upon *coerced*

[5] On the Kellems case, see Vivien Kellems, *Toil, Taxes and Trouble* (New York: E. P. Dutton, 1952).

testimony. Since it is axiomatic to libertarianism that all coercion—in this case, all coerced labor—against everyone except convicted criminals be eliminated, this means that compulsory testimony must be abolished as well. In recent years, it is true, the courts have been alive to the Fifth Amendment protection that no alleged criminal be forced to testify against himself—to provide the material for his own conviction. The legislatures have been significantly weakening this protection by passing immunity laws, offering immunity from prosecution if someone will testify against his fellows—and, furthermore, compelling the witness to accept the offer and testify against his associates. But compelling testimony from anyone for any reason is forced labor—and, furthermore, is akin to kidnapping, since the person is forced to appear at the hearing or trial and is then forced to perform the labor of giving testimony. The problem is not only the recent immunity laws; the problem is to eliminate *all* coerced testimony, including the universal subpoenaing of witnesses to a crime, and then forcing them to testify. In the case of witnesses, there is no question whatever of their being guilty of a crime, so the use of compulsion against them—a use that no one has questioned until now—has even less justification than compelling testimony from accused criminals.

In fact, the entire power to *subpoena* should be abolished, because the *subpoena* power compels attendance at a trial. Even the accused criminal or tortfeasor should not be forced to attend his own trial, since he has not yet been convicted. If he is indeed—according to the excellent and libertarian principle of Anglo-Saxon law—innocent until proved guilty, then the courts have no right to compel the defendant to attend his trial. For remember, the *only* exemption to the Thirteenth Amendment's prohibition of involuntary servitude is "except as a punishment for crime whereof the party shall have been duly convicted"; an accused party has not yet been convicted. The most the court should be able to do, then, is to notify the defendant that he is going to be tried, and *invite* him or his lawyer to attend; otherwise, if they choose not to, the trial will proceed *in absentia*. Then, of course, the defendant will not enjoy the best presentation of his case.

Both the Thirteenth Amendment and the libertarian creed make the exception for the convicted criminal. The libertarian believes that a criminal loses his rights to the extent that he has aggressed upon the rights of another, and therefore that it is permissible to incarcerate the convicted criminal and subject him to involuntary servitude to that degree. In the libertarian world, however, the *purpose* of imprisonment and punishment will undoubtedly be different; there will be no "district attorney" who presumes to try a case on behalf of a nonexistent "society," and then punishes the criminal on "society's" behalf. In that world the prosecutor will always represent the *individual victim*, and punishment will be exacted to redound to the benefit of that victim. Thus, a crucial focus of punishment will be to force the criminal to repay, make restitution to, the victim. One such model was a practice in colonial America. Instead of incarcerating, say, a man who had robbed a farmer in the district, the criminal was coercively indentured out to the farmer —in effect, "enslaved" for a term—there to work for the farmer until his debt was repaid. Indeed, during the Middle Ages, restitution to the victim was the dominant concept of punishment; only as the State grew more powerful did the governmental authorities—the kings and the barons—encroach more and more into the compensation process, increasingly confiscating more of the criminal's property for themselves and neglecting the hapless victim. And as the emphasis shifted from restitution to punishment for abstract crimes "committed against the State," the punishments exacted by the State upon the wrongdoer became more severe.

As Professor Schafer writes, "As the state monopolized the institution of punishment, so the rights of the injured were slowly separated from penal law." Or, in the words of the turn-of-the-century criminologist William Tallack, "It was chiefly owing to the violent greed of feudal barons and medieval ecclesiastical

powers that the rights of the injured party were gradually infringed upon, and finally, to a large extent, appropriated by
these authorities, who exacted a double vengeance, indeed,
upon the offender, by forfeiting his property to themselves instead of to his victim, and then punishing him by the dungeon,
the torture, the stake or the gibbet. But the original victim of
wrong was practically ignored." [6]

At any rate, while the libertarian does not object to prisons
per se, he does balk at several practices common to the present
judicial and penal system. One is the lengthy jail term imposed
upon the defendant while awaiting trial. The constitutional
right to a "speedy trial" is not arbitrary but a way of minimiz-
ing the length of involuntary servitude *before* conviction for a
crime. In fact, except in those cases where the criminal has been
caught red-handed and where a certain presumption of guilt
therefore exists, it is impossible to justify *any* imprisonment
before conviction, let alone before trial. And even when someone is caught red-handed, there is an important reform that
needs to be instituted to keep the system honest: subjecting
the police and the other authorities to the same law as everyone
else. As will be discussed further below, if everyone is supposed
to be subject to the same criminal law, then exempting the
authorities from that law gives them a legal license to commit
continual aggression. The policeman who apprehends a criminal and arrests him, and the judicial and penal authorities who
incarcerate him before trial and conviction—all should be subject to the universal law. In short, if they have committed
an error and the defendant turns out to be innocent, then
these authorities should be subjected to the same penalties as
anyone else who kidnaps and incarcerates an innocent man.
Immunity in pursuit of their trade should no more serve
as an excuse than Lieutenant Calley was excused for com-

---

[6] Stephen Schafer, *Restitution to Victims of Crime* (Chicago: Quadrangle Books, 1960), pp. 7–8; William Tallack, *Reparation to the Injured and
the Rights of the Victims of Crime to Compensation* (London, 1900),
pp. 11–12.

mitting atrocities at My Lai in the course of the Vietnam war.[7]

The granting of *bail* is a halfhearted attempt to ease the problem of incarceration before trial, but it is clear that the practice of bail discriminates against the poor. The discrimination persists even though the rise of the business of bail-bonding has permitted many more people to raise bail. The rebuttal that the courts are clogged with cases and therefore cannot grant a speedy trial is, of course, no defense of the system; on the contrary, this built-in inefficiency is an excellent argument for the abolition of government courts.

Furthermore, the setting of bail is arbitrarily in the hands of the judge, who has excessive and little-checked power to incarcerate people before they are convicted. This is particularly menacing in the case of citations for *contempt of court*, because judges have almost unlimited power to slap someone into prison, after the judge himself has acted as a one-man prosecutor, judge, and jury in accusing, "convicting," and sentencing the culprit completely free from the ordinary rules of evidence and trial, and in violation of the fundamental legal principle of not being a judge in one's own case.

Finally, there is another cornerstone of the judicial system which has unaccountably gone unchallenged, even by libertarians, for far too long. This is *compulsory jury service*. There is little difference in kind, though obviously a great difference in degree, between compulsory jury duty and conscription; both are enslavement, both compel the individual to perform tasks on the State's behalf and at the State's bidding. And both are a function of pay at slave wages. Just as the shortage of voluntary enlistees in the army is a function of a pay scale far below the market wage, so the abysmally low pay for jury service insures that, even if jury "enlistments" were possible, not many would be forthcoming. Furthermore, not only are jurors co-

---

[7] For a hilarious critique of the immunities of the arresting and penal authorities, see H. L. Mencken, "The Nature of Liberty," *Prejudices: A Selection* (New York: Vintage Books, 1958), pp. 138–43.

erced into attending and serving on juries, but sometimes they are locked behind closed doors for many weeks, and prohibited from reading newspapers. What is this but prison and involuntary servitude for noncriminals?

It will be objected that jury service is a highly important civic function, and insures a fair trial which a defendant may not obtain from the judge, especially since the judge is part of the State system and therefore liable to be partial to the prosecutor's case. Very true, but precisely because the service is so vital, it is particularly important that it be performed by people who do it gladly, and voluntarily. Have we forgotten that free labor is happier and more efficient than slave labor? The abolition of jury-slavery should be a vital plank in any libertarian platform. The judges are not conscripted; neither are the opposing lawyers; and neither should the jurors.

It is perhaps not a coincidence that, throughout the United States, lawyers are everywhere exempt from jury service. Since it is almost always lawyers who write the laws, can we detect class legislation and class privilege at work?

Compulsory Commitment

One of the most shameful areas of involuntary servitude in our society is the widespread practice of compulsory commitment, or involuntary hospitalization, of mental patients. In former generations this incarceration of noncriminals was frankly carried out as a measure against mental patients, to remove them from society. The practice of twentieth-century liberalism has been superficially more humane, but actually far more insidious: now physicians and psychiatrists help incarcerate these unfortunates "for their own good." The humanitarian rhetoric has permitted a far more widespread use of the practice and, for one thing, has allowed disgruntled relatives to put away their loved ones without suffering a guilty conscience.

In the last decade, the libertarian psychiatrist and psychoanalyst Dr. Thomas S. Szasz has carried on a one-man crusade, at first seemingly hopeless but now increasingly influential in the psychiatric field, against compulsory commitment. In numerous books and articles, Dr. Szasz has delivered a comprehensive and systematic attack on this practice. He has insisted, for example, that involuntary commitment is a profound violation of medical ethics. Instead of serving the patient, the physician here serves others—the family, the state—to act against, and tyrannize over completely, the person he is supposed to be helping. Compulsory commitment and compulsory "therapy," moreover, are far more likely to aggravate and perpetuate "mental illness" than to cure it. All too often, Szasz points out, commitment is a device for incarcerating and thereby disposing of disagreeable relatives rather than a genuine aid to the patient.

The guiding rationale for compulsory commitment is that the patient might well be "dangerous to himself or to others." The first grave flaw in this approach is that the police, or the law, is stepping in, *not* when an overt aggressive act is in the process of occurring, but on someone's judgment that such an act *might* someday take place. But this provides an open sesame for unlimited tyranny. Anyone might be adjudged to be capable of or likely to commit a crime someday, and therefore on such grounds anyone may legitimately be locked up—not for a crime, but because someone *thinks* he *might* commit one. This sort of thinking justifies not only incarceration, but *permanent* incarceration, of *anyone* under suspicion. But the fundamental libertarian creed holds that every individual is capable of free will and free choice; that no one, however likely to commit a crime in the future based on a statistical or any other judgment, is inevitably determined to do so; and that, in any case, it is immoral, and itself invasive and criminal, to coerce anyone who is not an *overt* and present, rather than a suspected, criminal.

Recently Dr. Szasz was asked, "But don't you think that society has the right and the duty to care for those individuals adjudged to be 'dangerous to themselves and others'?" Szasz cogently replied:

I think the idea of "helping" people by imprisoning them and doing terrible things to them is a religious concept, as the idea of "saving" witches by torture and burning once was. As far as "dangerousness to self" is concerned, I believe, as did John Stuart Mill, that a man's body and soul are his own, not the state's. And furthermore, that each individual has the "right," if you will, to do with his body as he pleases—so long as he doesn't harm anyone else, or infringe on someone else's right.

As far as "dangerousness to others" goes, most psychiatrists working with hospitalized patients would admit this is pure fantasy. . . . There have in fact been statistical studies made which show that mental patients are much more law-abiding than the normal population.

And civil liberties lawyer Bruce Ennis adds that:

We know that 85 percent of all ex-convicts will commit more crimes in the future and that ghetto residents and teen-age males are far more likely to commit crime than the average member of the population. We also know, from recent studies, that mental patients are statistically *less* dangerous than the average guy. So if what we're really worried about is danger, why don't we, first, lock up all former convicts, and then lock up all ghetto residents, and then why don't we lock up all teen-age males? . . . The question Szasz has been asking is: If a person hasn't broken a law, what right has society to lock him up? [8]

The involuntarily committed may be divided into two classes: those who have committed no crime, and those who have. For the former, the libertarian calls unconditionally for their release. But what of the latter, what of criminals who, through insanity or other pleas, supposedly escape the "brutality" of prison punishment and instead receive medical care at the hands of the State? Here again, Dr. Szasz has pioneered in a vigorous and devastating critique of the despotism of liberal "humanitarianism." First, it is grotesque to claim that incar-

[8] Quoted in Maggie Scarf, "Dr. Thomas Szasz . . . ," *New York Times Magazine* (October 3, 1971), pp. 42, 45. Among other works, see Thomas S. Szasz, *Law, Liberty, and Psychiatry* (New York: Macmillan, 1963).

ceration in a state mental hospital is somehow "more humane" than equivalent incarceration in prison. On the contrary, the despotism of the authorities is likely to be more severe, and the prisoner is likely to have far less recourse in defense of his rights, for as someone certified as "mentally ill" he is placed into the category of a "nonperson" whom no one feels obliged to take seriously any longer. As Dr. Szasz has jocularly said: "Being in a state mental hospital would drive anyone crazy!"

But furthermore, we must question the entire notion of taking *anyone* out from under the rule of objective law. To do so is far more likely to be damaging than helpful to the people thus singled out. Suppose, for example, that two men, A and B, commit an equivalent robbery, and that the usual punishment for this crime is five years in prison. Suppose that B "gets off" this punishment by being declared mentally ill, and is transferred to a state mental institution. The liberal focusses on the possibility, say, that B may be released in two years by the state psychiatrist through being adjudged "cured" or "rehabilitated." But what if the psychiatrist *never* considers him cured, or does so only after a very long time? Then B, for the simple crime of theft, may face the horror of lifelong incarceration in a mental institution. Hence, the "liberal" concept of *indeterminate sentence*—of sentencing someone not for his objective crime but on the State's judgment of his psyche or spirit of cooperation—constitutes tyranny and dehumanization in its worst form. It is a tyranny, furthermore, which encourages the prisoner into deceptive behavior to try to fool the state psychiatrist—whom he perceives quite correctly as his enemy—into thinking that he is "cured" so that he can get out of this incarceration. To call this process "therapy" or "rehabilitation" is surely cruel mockery of these terms. It is far more principled, as well as more truly humane, to treat every prisoner in accordance with objective criminal law.

6

Personal Liberty

Freedom of Speech

THERE ARE, OF COURSE, many problems of personal liberty which cannot be subsumed under the category of "involuntary servitude." Freedom of speech and press have long been treasured by those who confine themselves to being "civil libertarians"—"civil" meaning that economic freedom and the rights of private property are left out of the equation. But we have already seen that "freedom of speech" cannot be upheld as an absolute except as it is subsumed under the general rights of property of the individual (emphatically *including* property right in his own person). Thus, the man who shouts "fire" in a crowded theater has no right to do so because he is aggressing against the contractual property rights of the theater owner and of the patrons of the performance.

Aside from invasions of property, however, freedom of speech will necessarily be upheld to the uttermost by every libertarian. Freedom to say, print, and sell any utterance becomes an absolute right, in whatever area the speech or expression chooses to cover. Here, civil libertarians have a generally good record, and in the judiciary the late Justice Hugo Black was particularly notable in defending freedom of speech from government restriction on the basis of the First Amendment of the Constitution.

But there are areas in which even the most ardent civil libertarians have been unfortunately fuzzy. What, for example, of "incitement to riot," in which the speaker is held guilty of a crime for whipping up a mob, which then riots and commits various actions and crimes against person and property? In our view, "incitement" can only be considered a crime if we deny every man's freedom of will and of choice, and assume that if A tells B and C: "You and him go ahead and riot!" that somehow B and C are then helplessly determined to proceed and commit the wrongful act. But the libertarian, who believes in freedom of the will, must insist that while it might be immoral or unfortunate for A to advocate a riot, that this is strictly in the realm of advocacy and should not be subject to legal penalty. Of course, if A also participates in the riot, then he himself becomes a rioter and is equally subject to punishment. Furthermore, if A is a boss in a criminal enterprise, and, as part of the crime, orders his henchmen: "You and him go and rob such and such a bank," then of course A, according to the law of accessories, becomes a participant or even leader in the criminal enterprise itself.

If advocacy should never be a crime, then neither should "conspiracy to advocate," for, in contrast to the unfortunate development of conspiracy law, "conspiring" (i.e., agreeing) to do something should never be more illegal than the act itself. (How, in fact, can "conspiracy" be defined except as an agreement by two or more people to do something that you, the definer, do not like?)[1]

---

[1] For a critique of the "clear and present danger" criterion as insufficient for drawing a clear line between advocacy and overt act, see Alexander Meiklejohn, *Political Freedom* (New York: Harper & Bros., 1960), pp. 29–50; and O. John Rogge, *The First and the Fifth* (New York: Thomas Nelson and Sons, 1960), pp. 88ff.

Another difficult zone is the law of libel and slander. It has generally been held legitimate to restrict freedom of speech if that speech has the effect of either falsely or maliciously damaging the reputation of another person. What the law of libel and slander does, in short, is to argue a "property right" of someone in his own reputation. Yet someone's "reputation" is not and cannot be "owned" by him, since it is purely a function of the subjective feelings and attitudes held by other people. But since no one can ever truly "own" the mind and attitude of another, this means that no one can literally have a property right in his "reputation." A person's reputation fluctuates all the time, in accordance with the attitudes and opinions of the rest of the population. Hence, speech attacking someone cannot be an invasion of his property right and therefore should not be subject to restriction or legal penalty.

It is, of course, immoral to level false charges against another person, but once again, the *moral* and the *legal* are, for the libertarian, two very different categories.

Furthermore, pragmatically, if there were no laws of libel or slander, people would be much less willing to credit charges without full documentation than they are now. Nowadays, if a man is charged with some flaw or misdeed, the general reaction is to believe it, since if the charge were false, "Why doesn't he sue for libel?" The law of libel, of course, discriminates in this way against the poor, since a person with few financial resources is scarcely as ready to carry on a costly libel suit as a person of affluent means. Furthermore, wealthy people can now use the libel laws as a club against poorer persons, restricting perfectly legitimate charges and utterances under the threat of sueing their poorer enemies for libel. Paradoxically, then, a person of limited resources is more apt to suffer from libel—and to have his own speech restricted—in the present system than he would in a world without any laws against libel or defamation.

Fortunately, in recent years the laws against libel have been progressively weakened, so that one can now deliver vigorous and trenchant criticisms of public officials and of people in the public eye without fear of being subject to costly legal action or legal punishment.

Another action that should be completely free of restriction is the boycott. In a boycott, one or more people use their right of speech to urge, for whatever reasons—important or trivial—that other people cease to buy someone else's product. If, for example, several people organize a campaign—for whatever reason—to urge consumers to stop buying XYZ Beer, this is again purely advocacy, and, furthermore, advocacy of a perfectly legitimate act—*not* purchasing the beer. A successful boycott might be unfortunate for the producers of XYZ Beer, but this, again, is strictly within the realm of free speech and the rights of private property. The makers of XYZ Beer take their chances with the free choices of consumers, and consumers are entitled to listen and to be swayed by anyone they choose. Yet our labor laws have infringed upon the right of labor unions to organize boycotts against business firms. It is also illegal, under our banking laws, to spread rumors about the insolvency of a bank—an obvious case of the government's extending special privileges to banks by outlawing freedom of speech in opposition to their use.

A particularly thorny question is the whole matter of picketing and demonstrations. Freedom of speech implies, of course, freedom of assembly—the freedom to gather together and express oneself in concert with others. But the situation becomes more complex when the use of the *streets* is involved. It is clear that picketing is illegitimate when it is used—as it often is—to block access to a private building or factory, or when the pickets threaten violence against those who cross the picket line. It is also clear that sit-ins are an illegitimate invasion of private property. But even "peaceful picketing" is not clearly legitimate, for it is part of a wider problem: Who decides on the use of the streets? The problem stems from the fact that the streets are almost universally owned by (local) government. But the government, not being a private owner, lacks any criterion for allocating the use of its streets, so that any decision it makes will be arbitrary.

Suppose, for example, that the Friends of Wisteria wish to demonstrate and parade on behalf of Wisteria in a public street. The police ban the demonstration, claiming that it will clog the streets and disrupt traffic. Civil libertarians will automatically protest and claim that the "right of free speech" of the Wisteria demonstrators is being unjustly abridged. But the police, too, may have a perfectly legitimate point: the streets may well be clogged, and it is the government's responsibility to maintain the flow of traffic. How then decide? Whichever way the government decides, *some* group of taxpayers will be injured by the decision. If the government decides to allow the demonstration, the motorists or pedestrians will be injured; if it does not, then the Friends of Wisteria will suffer a loss. In either case, the very fact of government decision-making generates inevitable conflict over who shall, and who shall not among the taxpayers and citizens, use the governmental resource.

It is only the universal fact of government ownership and control of the streets that makes this problem insoluble and cloaks the true solution to it. The point is that *whoever* owns a resource will decide on how that resource is to be used. The owner of a press will decide what will be printed on that press. And the owner of the streets will decide how to allocate their use. In short, if the streets were privately owned and the Friends of Wisteria asked for the use of Fifth Avenue to demonstrate, it will be up to the owner of Fifth Avenue to decide whether to rent the street for demonstration use or to keep it clear for traffic. In a purely libertarian world, where all streets are privately owned, the various street owners will decide, at any given time, whether to rent out the street for demonstrations, whom to rent it to, and what price to charge. It would then be clear that what is involved is not a "free speech" or "free assembly" question at all, but a question of property rights: of the right of a group to offer to rent a street, and of the right of the street-owner either to accept or reject the offer.

Freedom of Radio and Television

There is one important area of American life where no effective freedom of speech or the press does or can exist under the present system. That is the entire field of radio and television. In this area, the federal government, in the crucially important Radio Act of 1927, nationalized the airwaves. In effect, the federal government took title to ownership of all radio and television channels. It then presumed to grant licenses, at its will or pleasure, for use of the channels to various privately owned stations. On the one hand, the stations, since they receive the licenses gratis, do not have to pay for the use of the scarce airwaves, as they would on the free market. And so these stations receive a huge subsidy, which they are eager to maintain. But on the other hand, the federal government, as the licensor of the airwaves, asserts the right and the power to regulate the stations minutely and continuously. Thus, over the head of each station is the club of the threat of nonrenewal, or even suspension, of its license. In consequence, the idea of freedom of speech in radio and television is no more than a mockery. Every station is grievously restricted, and forced to fashion its programming to the dictates of the Federal Communications Commission. So every station must have "balanced" programming, broadcast a certain amount of "public service" announcements, grant equal time to every political candidate for the same office and to expressions of political opinion, censor "controversial" lyrics in the records it plays, etc. For many years, no station was allowed to broadcast any editorial opinion at all; now, every opinion must be balanced by "responsible" editorial rebuttals.

Because every station and every broadcaster must always look over its shoulder at the FCC, free expression in broadcasting is a sham. Is it any wonder that television opinion, when it is expressed at all on controversial issues, tends to be blandly in favor of the "Establishment"?

The public has only put up with this situation because it

has existed since the beginning of large-scale commercial radio. But what would we think, for example, if all newspapers were licensed, the licenses to be renewable by a Federal Press Commission, and with newspapers losing their licenses if they dare express an "unfair" editorial opinion, or if they don't give full weight to public service announcements? Would not this be an intolerable, not to say unconstitutional, destruction of the right to a free press? Or consider if all book publishers had to be licensed, and their licenses were not renewable if their book lists failed to suit a Federal Book Commission? Yet what we would all consider intolerable and totalitarian for the press and the book publishers is taken for granted in a medium which is now the most popular vehicle for expression and education: radio and television. Yet the principles in both cases are exactly the same.

Here we see, too, one of the fatal flaws in the idea of "democratic socialism", i.e., the idea that the government should own all resources and means of production yet preserve and maintain freedom of speech and the press for all its citizens. An abstract constitution guaranteeing "freedom of the press" is meaningless in a socialist society. The point is that where the government owns all the newsprint, the paper, the presses, etc., the government—as owner—*must* decide how to allocate the newsprint and the paper, and what to print on them. Just as the government as street owner must make a decision how the street will be used, so a socialist government will have to decide how to allocate newsprint and all other resources involved in the areas of speech and press: assembly halls, machines, trucks, etc. Any government may profess its devotion to freedom of the press, yet allocate all of its newsprint only to its defenders and supporters. A free press is again a mockery; furthermore, why *should* a socialist government allocate any considerable amount of its scarce resources to antisocialists? The problem of genuine freedom of the press then becomes insoluble.

The solution for radio and television? Simple: Treat these media precisely the same way the press and book publishers are treated. For both the libertarian and the believer in the American Constitution the government should withdraw completely from any role or interference in all media of expression. In short, the federal government should denationalize the airwaves and give or sell the individual channels to private ownership. When private stations genuinely own their channels, they will be truly free and independent; they will be able to put on any programs they wish to produce, or that they feel their listeners want to hear; and they will be able to express themselves in whichever way they wish without fear of government retaliation. They will also be able to sell or rent the airwaves to whomever they wish, and in that way the users of the channels will no longer be artificially subsidized.

Furthermore, if TV channels become free, privately owned, and independent, the big networks will no longer be able to put pressure upon the FCC to outlaw the effective competition of pay-television. It is only because the FCC has outlawed pay-TV that it has not been able to gain a foothold. "Free TV" is, of course, not truly "free"; the programs are paid for by the advertisers, and the consumer pays by covering the advertising costs in the price of the product he buys. One might ask what difference it makes to the consumer whether he pays the advertising costs indirectly or pays directly for each program he buys. The difference is that these are not the same consumers for the same products. The television advertiser, for example, is always interested in (a) gaining the widest possible viewing market; and (b) in gaining those *particular* viewers who will be most susceptible to his message. Hence, the programs will all be geared to the lowest common denominator in the audience, and particularly to those viewers most susceptible to the message; that is, those viewers who do not read newspapers or magazines, so that the message will not duplicate the ads he sees there. As a result, free-TV programs tend to be unimaginative, bland, and uniform. Pay-TV would mean that each program would search for its own market, and many specialized markets for specialized audiences would develop—just as highly lucrative specialized markets have developed in the magazine and book publishing fields. The quality of programs would be higher and the offerings far more diverse. In fact, the menace of potential pay-TV competition must be great for the networks to lobby for years to keep it suppressed. But, of course, in a truly free market, both forms of television, as well as cable-TV and other forms we cannot yet envision, could and would enter the competition.

One common argument against private ownership of TV annels is that these channels are "scarce," and therefore have be owned and parcelled out by the government. To an economist, this is a silly argument; *all* resources are scarce, in fact anything that has a price on the market commands that price precisely *because* it is scarce. We have to pay a certain amount for a loaf of bread, for shoes, for dresses *because* they are all sca ̀ce. If they were not scarce but superabundant like air, they would be free, and no one would have to worry about their production or allocation. In the press area, newsprint is scarce, paper is scarce, printing machinery and trucks are scarce, etc. The more scarce they are the higher the price they will command, and vice versa. Furthermore, and again pragmatically, there are far more television channels available than are now in use. The FCC's early decision to force stations into the VHF instead of the UHF zone created far more of a scarcity of channels than there needed to be.

Another common objection to private property in the broadcast media is that private stations would interfere with each other's broadcasts, and that such widespread interference would virtually prevent any programs from being heard or seen. But this is as absurd an argument for nationalizing the airwaves as claiming that since people *can* drive their cars over other people's land this means that all cars—or land—must be nationalized. The problem, in either case, is for the courts to demarcate property titles carefully enough so that any invasion of another's property will be clear-cut and subject to prosecution. In the case of land titles, this process is clear enough. But the point is that the courts can apply a similar process of staking out property rights in other areas—whether it be in airwaves, in water, or in oil pools. In the case of airwaves, the task is to find the technological unit—i.e., the place of transmission, the distance of the wave, and the technological width of a clear channel— and then to allocate property rights to this particular technological unit. If radio station WXYZ, for example, is assigned a property right in broadcasting on 1500 kilocycles, plus or minus a certain width of kilocycles, for 200 miles around Detroit, then any station which subsequently beams a program into the Detroit area on this wavelength would be subject to prosecution for interference with property rights. If the courts pursue their task of demarking and defending property rights, then there is no more reason to expect continual invasions of such rights in this area than anywhere else.

Most people believe that this is precisely the reason the airwaves were nationalized; that before the Radio Act of 1927, stations interfered with each other's signals and chaos ensued, and the federal government was finally forced to step in to bring order and make a radio industry feasible at last. But this is historical legend, not fact. The actual history is *precisely the opposite.* For when interference on the same channel began to occur, the injured party took the airwave aggressors into court, and the courts were beginning to bring order out of the chaos by very successfully applying the common law theory of property rights—in very many ways similar to the libertarian theory —to this new technological area. In short, the courts were beginning to assign property rights in the airwaves to their "homesteading" users. It was after the federal government saw the likelihood of this new extension of private property that it rushed in to nationalize the airwaves, using alleged chaos as the excuse.

To describe the picture a bit more fully, radio in the first years of the century was almost wholly a means of communication for ships—either ship-to-ship or ship-to shore messages. The Navy Department was interested in regulating radio as a means of ensuring safety at sea, and the initial federal regulation, a 1912 act, merely provided that any radio station had to have a license issued by the Secretary of Commerce. No powers to regulate or to decide not to renew licenses were written into the law, however, and when public broadcasting began in the early 1920s, Secretary of Commerce Herbert Hoover attempted to regulate the stations. Court decisions in 1923 and 1926, however, struck down the government's power to regulate licenses, to fail to renew them, or even to decide on which wavelengths the stations should operate.[2] At about the same time, the courts were working out the concept of "homestead" private property rights in the airwaves, notably in the case of *Tribune Co.* v. *Oak Leaves Broadcasting Station* (Circuit Court, Cook County, Illinois, 1926). In this case the court held that the operator of an existing station had a property right, acquired by prior use, sufficient to enjoin a new station from using a radio frequency in any way so as to cause interference with the signals of the prior station.[3] And so order was being brought out of the chaos by means of the assignment of property rights. But it was precisely this development that the government rushed in to forestall.

The 1926 Zenith decision striking down the government's power to regulate or to fail to renew licenses, and forcing the Department of Commerce to issue licenses to any station that applied, produced a great boom in the broadcasting industry. Over two hundred new stations were created in the nine months after the decision. As a result, Congress rushed through a stopgap measure in July 1926 to *prevent* any property rights in radio frequencies, and resolved that all licenses should be limited to ninety days. By February 1927 the Congress passed the law establishing the Federal Radio Commission, which nationalized the airwaves and established powers similar to those of the

[2] In the decisions *Hoover* v. *Intercity Radio Co.*, 286 Fed. 1003 (Appeals D.C., 1923); and *United States* v. *Zenith Radio Corp.*, 12 F. 2d 614 (N.D. Ill., 1926). See the excellent article by Ronald H. Coase, "The Federal Communications Commission," *Journal of Law and Economics* (October 1959), pp. 4–5.

[3] Coase, *ibid.*, p. 31n.

current FCC. That the aim of the knowledgeable politicians was *not* to prevent chaos but to prevent private property in the airwaves as the solution to chaos is demonstrated by the legal historian H. P. Warner. Warner states that "grave fears were expressed by legislators, and those generally charged with the administration of communications . . . that government regulation of an effective sort might be permanently prevented through the accrual of property rights in licenses or means of access, and that thus franchises of the value of millions of dollars might be established for all time." [4] The net result, however, was to establish equally valuable franchises anyway, but in a monopolistic fashion through the largesse of the Federal Radio Commission and later FCC rather than through competitive homesteading.

Among the numerous direct invasions of freedom of speech exercised by the licensing power of the FRC and FCC, two cases will suffice. One was in 1931, when the FRC denied renewal of license to a Mr. Baker, who operated a radio station in Iowa. In denying renewal, the Commission said:

This Commission holds no brief for the Medical Associations and other parties whom Mr. Baker does not like. Their alleged sins may be at times of public importance, to be called to the attention of the public over the air in the right way. But this record discloses that Mr. Baker does not do so in any high-minded way. It shows that he continually and erratically over the air rides a personal hobby, his cancer cure ideas and his likes and dislikes of certain persons and things. Surely his infliction of all this on the listeners is not the proper use of a broadcasting license. Many of his utterances are vulgar, if not indeed indecent. Assuredly they are not uplifting or entertaining.[5]

Can we imagine the outcry if the federal government were to put a newspaper or a book publisher out of business on similar grounds?

[4] Harry P. Warner, *Radio and Television Law* (1958), p. 540. Quoted in Coase, *op. cit.*, p. 32.
[5] Decisions of the FRC, Docket No. 967, June 5, 1931. Quoted in Coase, *op. cit.*, p. 9.

A recent act of the FCC was to threaten nonrenewal of license of radio station KTRG in Honolulu, a major radio station in Hawaii. KTRG had been broadcasting libertarian programs for several hours a day for approximately two years. Finally, in late 1970, the FCC decided to open lengthy hearings moving toward nonrenewal of license, the threatened cost of which forced the owners to shut down the station permanently.[6]

Pornography

To the libertarian, the arguments between conservatives and liberals over laws prohibiting pornography are distressingly beside the point. The conservative position tends to hold that pornography is debasing and immoral and therefore should be outlawed. Liberals tend to counter that sex is good and healthy and that therefore pornography will only have good effects, and that depictions of violence—say on television, in movies, or in comic books—should be outlawed instead. Neither side deals with the crucial point: that the good, bad, or indifferent consequences of pornography, while perhaps an interesting problem in its own right, is completely irrelevant to the question of whether or not it should be outlawed. The libertarian holds that it is not the business of the law—the use of retaliatory violence —to enforce anyone's conception of morality. It is not the business of the law—even if this were practically possible, which is, of course, most unlikely—to make anyone good or reverent or moral or clean or upright. This is for each individual to decide for himself. It is only the business of legal violence to defend

---

[6] The best and most fully elaborated portrayal of how private property rights could be assigned in radio and television is in A. DeVany *et al,* "A Property System for Market Allocation of the Electromagnetic Spectrum: A Legal-Economic-Engineering Study," *Stanford Law Review* (June 1969). See also William H. Meckling, "National Communications Policy: Discussion," *American Economic Review, Papers and Proceedings* (May 1970), pp. 222–23. Since the DeVany article, the growth of community and cable television has further diminished the scarcity of frequencies and expanded the range of potential competition.

people against the use of violence, to defend them from violent invasions of their person or property. But if the government presumes to outlaw pornography, it *itself* becomes the genuine outlaw—for it is invading the property rights of people to produce, sell, buy, or possess pornographic material.

We do not pass laws to make people upright; we do not pass laws to force people to be kind to their neighbors or not to yell at the bus driver; we do not pass laws to force people to be honest with their loved ones. We do not pass laws to force them to eat X amount of vitamins per day. Neither is it the business of government, nor of any legal agency, to pass laws against the voluntary production or sale of pornography. Whether pornography is good, bad, or indifferent should be of no interest to the legal authorities.

The same holds true for the liberal bugbear of "the pornography of violence." Whether or not watching violence on television helps lead to actual crimes should not come under the purview of the state. To outlaw violent films because they *might* someday induce someone to commit a crime is a denial of man's free will, and a total denial, of course, of the right of those who will *not* commit crimes to see the film. But more important, it is no more justifiable—in fact, less so—to outlaw violent films for this reason than it would be, as we have noted, to lock up all teen-age Negro males because they have a greater tendency to commit crime than the rest of the population.

It should be clear, too, that prohibition of pornography is an invasion of property right, of the right to produce, sell, buy, and own. Conservatives who call for the outlawing of pornography do not seem to realize that they are thereby violating the very concept of property rights they profess to champion. It is also a violation of freedom of the press, which, as we have seen, is really a subset of the general right of private property.

Sometimes it seems that the *beau ideal* of many conservatives, as well as of many liberals, is to put everyone into a cage and coerce him into doing what the conservatives or liberals believe to be the moral thing. They would of course be differently styled cages, but they would be cages just the same. The conservative would ban illicit sex, drugs, gambling, and impiety, and coerce everyone to act according to his version of moral and religious behavior. The liberal would ban films of violence, unesthetic advertising, football, and racial discrimination, and, at the extreme, place everyone in a "Skinner box" to be run by a supposedly benevolent liberal dictator. But the effect would be the same: to reduce everyone to a subhuman level and to deprive everyone of the most precious part of his or her humanity—the freedom to choose.

The irony, of course, is that by forcing men to be "moral"—i.e., to *act* morally—the conservative or liberal jail-keepers would in reality deprive men of the very *possibility* of being moral. The concept of "morality" makes no sense unless the moral act is freely chosen. Suppose, for example, that someone is a devout Muslim who is anxious to have as many people as possible bow to Mecca three times a day; to him let us suppose this is the highest moral act. But if he wields coercion to *force* everyone to bow to Mecca, he is thereby depriving everyone of the opportunity to be moral—to *choose freely* to bow to Mecca. Coercion deprives a man of the freedom to choose and, therefore, of the possibility of choosing morally.

The libertarian, in contrast to so many conservatives and liberals, does not want to place man in any cage. What he wants for everyone is freedom, the freedom to act morally or immorally, as each man shall decide.

Sex Laws

In recent years, liberals have fortunately been coming to the conclusion that "any act between two (or more) consenting adults" should be legal. It is unfortunate that the liberals have not yet widened this criterion from sex to trade and exchange, for if they ever would, they would be close to becoming full-scale libertarians. For the libertarian is precisely interested in legalizing all interrelations whatever between "consenting adults." Liberals have also begun to call for the abolition of "victimless crimes," which would be splendid if "victims" were defined with greater precision as victims of aggressive violence.

Since sex is a uniquely private aspect of life, it is particularly intolerable that governments should presume to regulate and legislate sexual behavior, yet of course this has been one of the State's favorite pastimes. Violent acts such as rape, of course, are to be classed as crimes in the same way as any other act of violence against persons.

If labor and persons in general are to be free, then so should there be freedom for *prostitution*. Prostitution is a voluntary sale of a labor service, and the government has no right to prohibit or restrict such sales. It should be noted that many of the grimmer aspects of the streetwalking trade have been brought about by the outlawing of brothels. As long-lasting houses of prostitution operated by madams anxious to cultivate goodwill among customers over a long time span, brothels used to compete to provide high-quality service and build up their "brand name." The outlawing of brothels has forced prostitution into a "black-market," fly-by-night existence, with all the dangers and general decline in quality this always entails. Recently, in New York City, there has been a tendency for the police to crack down on prostitution with the excuse that the trade is no longer "victimless," since many prostitutes commit crimes against their customers. To outlaw trades that may attract crime, however, would in the same way justify prohibition because many fights take place in bars. The answer is not to outlaw the voluntary and truly lawful activity, but for the police to see to it that the genuine crimes do not get committed. It should be clear that advocacy of freedom for prostitution does not, for the libertarian, in the least imply advocacy of prostitution itself. In short, if a particularly puritanical government were to outlaw all cosmetics, the libertarian would call for legalizing cosmetics without in any sense implying that he favors—or for that matter, opposes—the use of cosmetics themselves. On the contrary, depending upon his personal ethics or esthetics, he might well agitate against the use of cosmetics after they become legalized; his attempt is always to persuade rather than to compel.

If sex should be free, then *birth control* should, of course, be free as well. It is unfortunately characteristic of our society, however, that scarcely has birth control been made legal when people—in this case liberals—arise to agitate for birth control being made *compulsory*. It is true, of course, that if my neighbor has a baby this may well affect me for good or ill. But, then, almost everything that anyone does may affect one or more people. To the libertarian, this is scarcely justification for using force, which may *only* be used to combat or restrain force itself. There is no right more personal, no freedom more precious, than for any woman to decide to have, or not to have, a baby, and it is totalitarian in the extreme for any government to presume to den   that right. Besides, if any family has more children than   an support in comfort, the family itself will bear the main burden; hence, the almost universal result that the wish to preserve a treasured rise in living standards will induce a voluntary reduction of births by the families themselves.

This brings us to the more complex case of *abortion*. For the libertarian, the "Catholic" case against abortion, even if finally rejected as invalid, cannot be dismissed out of hand. For the essence of that case—not really "Catholic" at all in a theological sense—is that abortion destroys a human life and is therefore murder, and hence cannot be condoned. More than that, if abortion is truly murder, then the Catholic—or any other person who shares this view—cannot just shrug his shoulders and say that "Catholic" views should not be imposed upon non-Catholics. Murder is not an expression of religious preference; no sect, in the name of "freedom of religion," can or should get away with committing murder with the plea that its religion so commands. The vital question then becomes: should abortion be considered as murder?

Most discussion of the issue bogs down in *minutiae* about *when* human life begins, when or if the fetus can be considered to be alive, etc. All this is really irrelevant to the issue of the *legality* (again, not necessarily the *morality*) of abortion. The Catholic antiabortionist, for example, declares that all that he wants for the fetus is the rights of any human being—i.e., the right not to be murdered. But there is more involved here, and this is the crucial consideration. If we are to treat the fetus as having the same rights as humans, then let us ask: What *human* has the right to remain, unbidden, as an unwanted parasite within some other human being's body? This is the nub of the issue: the absolute right of every person, and hence every woman, to the ownership of her own body. What the mother is doing in an abortion is causing an unwanted entity within her body to be ejected from it: If the fetus dies, this does not rebut the point that no being has a right to live, unbidden, as a parasite within or upon some person's body.

The common retort that the mother either originally wanted or at least was responsible for placing the fetus within her body is, again, beside the point. Even in the stronger case where the mother originally wanted the child, the mother, as the property owner in her own body, has the right to change her mind and to eject it.

Wiretapping

Wiretapping is a contemptible invasion of privacy and of property right, and of course should be outlawed as an invasive act. Few, if any, people would condone private wiretapping. The controversy arises with those who maintain that the police should be able to tap the wires of persons they *suspect* as criminals. Otherwise, how would criminals be caught?

In the first place, from the pragmatic viewpoint, it is rare that wiretapping is effective in such "one-shot" crimes as bank robbery. Wiretapping is generally used in cases where the "business" is set up on a regularized and continuing basis—such as narcotics and gambling—and is therefore vulnerable to espionage and "bugging." Secondly, we remain with our contention that it is itself criminal to invade the property of anyone not yet convicted of a crime. It may well be true, for example, that if the government employed a ten-million man espionage force to spy upon and tap the wires of the entire population, the total amount of private crime would be reduced—just as it would if all ghetto residents or teen-age males were promptly incarcerated. But what would this be compared to the mass crime that would thus be committed, legally and without shame, by the government itself?

There is one concession we might make to the police argument, but it is doubtful the police would be happy with the concession. It is proper to invade the property of a thief, for example, who has himself invaded to a far greater extent the property of others. Suppose the police decide that John Jones is a jewel thief. They tap his wires, and use this evidence to convict Jones of the crime. We might say that this tapping is legitimate, and should go unpunished: *provided*, however, that if Jones should prove *not* to be a thief, the police and the judges who may have issued the court order for the tap are now to be adjudged *criminals themselves* and sent to jail for their crime of unjust wiretapping. This reform would have two happy consequences: no policeman or judge would participate in wiretapping unless he was dead certain the victim is indeed a criminal; and the police and judges would at last join everyone else as equally subject to the rule of the criminal law. Certainly equality of liberty requires that the law applies to everyone; therefore any invasion of the property of a noncriminal by *anyone* should be outlawed, regardless of who committed the deed. The policeman who guessed wrong and thereby aggressed against a noncriminal should therefore be considered just as guilty as any "private" wiretapper.

Gambling

There are few laws more absurd and iniquitous than the laws against gambling. In the first place, the law, in its broadest sense, is clearly unenforceable. If every time Jim and Jack made a quiet bet on a football game, or on an election, or on virtually anything else, this were illegal, an enormous multimillion-man gestapo would be required to enforce such a law and to spy on everyone and ferret out every bet. Another large super-espionage force would then be needed to spy on the spies to make sure that they have not been bought off. Conservatives like to retort to such arguments—used against laws outlawing sexual practices, pornography, drugs, etc.—that the prohibition against murder is not fully enforceable either, but this is no argument for repeal of *that* law. This argument, however, ignores a crucial point: the mass of the public, making an instinctive libertarian distinction, abhors and condemns murder and does not engage in it; hence, the prohibition becomes broadly enforceable. But the mass of the public is not as convinced of the criminality of gambling, hence continues to engage in it, and the law—properly—becomes unenforceable.

Since the laws against quiet betting are clearly unenforceable, the authorities decide to concentrate on certain highly *visible* forms of gambling, and confine their activities to them: roulette, bookies, "numbers" betting—in short, on those areas where gambling is a fairly regularized activity. But then we have a peculiar and surely totally unsupportable kind of ethical judgment: roulette, horse betting, etc., are somehow morally evil and must be cracked down upon by the massed might of the police, whereas quiet betting is morally legitimate and need not be bothered.

In New York State, a particular form of imbecility developed over the years: until recent months, all forms of horse betting were illegal *except* those made at the tracks themselves. Why horse betting at Aqueduct or Belmont race track should be perfectly moral and legitimate while betting on the same race with your friendly neighborhood bookie should be sinful and bring down the awful majesty of the law defies the imagination. Unless, of course, if we consider the point of the law to force betters to swell the coffers of the tracks. Recently, a new wrinkle has developed. The City of New York has *itself* gone into the horse-betting business, and betting at city-owned stores is perfectly fine and proper, while betting with competing private bookies continues to be sinful and outlawed. Clearly, the point of the system is first to confer a special privilege upon the race tracks, and then upon the city's own betting installation. Various states are also beginning to finance their ever-growing expenditures through lotteries, which thus become conferred with the cloak of morality and respectability.

A standard argument for outlawing gambling is that, if the poor workman is allowed to gamble, he will improvidently blow his weekly pay check and thereby render his family destitute. Aside from the fact that he can now spend his payroll on friendly betting, this paternalistic and dictatorial argument is a curious one. For it proves far too much: If we must outlaw gambling because the masses might spend too much of their substance, why should we not outlaw many other articles of mass consumption? After all, if a workman is determined to blow his pay check, he has many opportunities to do so: he can improvidently spend too much on a TV set, a hi-fi, liquor, baseball equipment, and countless other goodies. The logic of prohibiting a man from gambling for his own or his family's good leads straight to that totalitarian cage, the cage in which Pappa Government tells the man exactly what to do, how to spend his money, how many vitamins he must ingest, and forces him to obey the State's dictates.

Narcotics and Other Drugs

The case for outlawing any product or activity is essentially the same twofold argument we have seen used to justify the compulsory commitment of mental patients: it will harm the person involved, or it will lead that person to commit crimes against others. It is curious that the general—and justified—horror of drugs has led the mass of the public to an irrational enthusiasm for outlawing them. The case against outlawing narcotic and hallucinogenic drugs is far weaker than the case against Prohibition, an experiment which the grisly era of the 1920s has hopefully discredited for all time. For while narcotics are undoubtedly more harmful than is alcohol, the latter can also be harmful, and outlawing something because it may harm the user leads straight down the logical garden path to our totalitarian cage, where people are prohibited from eating candy and are forced to eat yogurt "for their own good." But in the far more imposing argument about harm to others, alcohol is much more likely to lead to crimes, auto accidents, etc. than narcotics, which render the user preternaturally peaceful and passive. There is, of course, a very strong connection between addiction and crime, but the connection is the *reverse* of any argument for prohibition. Crimes are committed by addicts driven to theft by the high price of drugs caused by the outlawry itself! If narcotics were legal, the supply would greatly increase, the high costs of black markets and police payoffs would disappear, and the price would be low enough to eliminate most addict-caused crime.

This is not to argue, of course, for prohibition of alcohol; once again, to outlaw something which *might* lead to crime is an illegitimate and invasive assault on the rights of person and property, an assault which, again, would far more justify the immediate incarceration of all teen-age males. Only the overt commission of a crime should be illegal, and the way to combat crimes committed under the influence of alcohol is to be more diligent about the crimes themselves, not to outlaw the alcohol. And this would have the further beneficial effect of reducing crimes *not* committed under the influence of alcohol.

Paternalism in this area comes not only from the right; it is curious that while liberals generally favor legalizing marijuana and sometimes of heroin, they seem to yearn to outlaw cigarettes, on the ground that cigarette smoking often causes cancer. Liberals have already managed to use federal control of television to outlaw cigarette advertising on that medium—and thereby to level a grave blow against the very freedom of speech liberals are supposed to cherish.

Once again: Every man has the right to choose. Propagandize against cigarettes as much as you want, but leave the individual free to run his own life. Otherwise, we may as well outlaw all sorts of possible carcinogenic agents—including tight shoes, improperly fitting false teeth, excessive exposure to the sun, as well as excessive intake of ice cream, eggs, and butter which might lead to heart disease. And, if such prohibitions prove unenforceable, again the logic is to place people in cages so that they will receive the proper amount of sun, the correct diet, properly fitting shoes, and so on.

Police Corruption

In the fall of 1971, the Knapp Commission focussed public attention on the problem of widespread police corruption in New York City. Midst the drama of individual cases, there is a danger of overlooking what is clearly the central problem, a problem of which the Knapp Commission itself was perfectly aware. In virtually every case of corruption, the policemen were involved in regularly functioning businesses which, by government fiat, had been declared illegal. And yet a vast number of people, by demanding these goods and services, have shown that they do not agree that such activities should be placed in the same category as murder, theft, or assault. Indeed, in practically no case did the "purchase" of the police involve these heinous crimes. In almost all cases, they consisted of the police looking the other way while legitimate, voluntary transactions took place.

The common law makes a vital distinction between a crime that is a *malum in se* and one that is merely a *malum prohibitum*. A *malum in se* is an act which the mass of the people instinctively feel is a reprehensible crime which should be punished. This coincides roughly with the libertarian's definition of a crime as an invasion of person or property: assault, theft, and murder. Other crimes are activities made into crimes by government edict: it is in this far more widely tolerated area that police corruption occurs.

In short, police corruption occurs in those areas where entrepreneurs supply voluntary services to consumers, but where the government has decreed that these services are illegal: narcotics, prostitution, and gambling. Where gambling, for example, is outlawed, the law places into the hands of the police assigned to the gambling detail the power to sell the privilege of engaging in the gambling business. In short, it is as if the police were empowered to issue special licenses to engage in these activities, and then proceeded to sell these unofficial but vital licenses at whatever price the traffic will bear. One policeman testified that, if the law were to be fully enforced, not a single construction site in New York City could continue functioning, so intricately did the government wrap construction sites in a web of trivial and impossible regulations. In short, whether consciously or not, the government proceeds as follows: first it outlaws a certain activity—drugs, gambling, construction, or whatever—then the governmental police sell to would-be entrepreneurs in the field the privilege of entering and continuing in business.

At best, the result of these actions is the imposition of higher cost, and more restricted output, of the activity than would have occurred in a free market. But the effects are still more pernicious. Often, what the policemen sell is not just permission to function, but what is in effect a privileged monopoly. In that case, a gambler pays off the police not just to continue in business but also to freeze out any competitors who might want to enter the industry. The consumers are then saddled with privileged monopolists, and are barred from enjoying the advantages of competition. It is no wonder, then, that when Prohibition was finally repealed in the early 1930s, the main opponents of repeal were, along with fundamentalist and Prohibitionist groups, the organized bootleggers, who had enjoyed special monopolistic privileges from their special arrangements with the police and other enforcement arms of government.

The way, then, to eliminate police corruption is simple but effective: abolish the laws against voluntary business activity and against all "victimless crimes." Not only would corruption be eliminated, but a large number of police would then be freed to operate against the *real* criminals, the aggressors against person and property. This, after all, is supposed to be the function of the police in the first place.

We should realize, then, that the problem of police corruption, as well as the broader question of government corruption in general, should be placed in a wider context. The point is that *given* the unfortunate and unjust laws prohibiting, regulating, and taxing certain activities, corruption is highly beneficial to society. In a number of countries, without corruption that nullified government prohibitions, taxes, and exactions, virtually no trade or industry would be carried on at all. Corruption greases the wheels of trade. The solution, then, is not to deplore corruption and redouble enforcement against it, but to abolish the crippling policies and laws of government that make corruption necessary.

Gun Laws

For most of the activities in this chapter, liberals tend to favor freedom of trade and activity while conservatives yearn for rigorous enforcement and maximum crackdowns against violators of the law. Yet, mysteriously, in the drive for gun laws the positions tend to be reversed. Every time a gun is used in a violent crime, liberals redouble their agitation for the severe restriction, if not prohibition of private ownership of guns, while conservatives oppose such restrictions on behalf of individual freedom.

If, as libertarians believe, every individual has the right to own his person and property, it then follows that he has the right to employ violence to defend himself against the violence of criminal aggressors. But for some odd reason, liberals have systematically tried to deprive innocent persons of the means for defending themselves against aggression. Despite the fact that the Second Amendment to the Constitution guarantees that "the right of the people to keep and bear arms shall not be infringed," the government has systematically eroded much of this right. Thus, in New York State, as in most other states, the Sullivan Law prohibits the carrying of "concealed weapons" without a license issued by the authorities. Not only has the carrying of guns been grievously restricted by this unconstitutional edict, but the government has extended this prohibition to almost any object that could possibly serve as a weapon— even those that could only be used for self-defense. As a result, potential victims of crime have been barred from carrying knives, tear-gas pens, or even hatpins, and people who have used such weapons in defending themselves against assault have themselves been prosecuted by the authorities. In the cities, this invasive prohibition against concealed weapons has in effect stripped victims of any possible self-defense against crime. (It is true that there is no official prohibition against carrying an *unconcealed* weapon, but a man in New York City who, several years ago, tested the law by walking the streets carrying a rifle was promptly arrested for "disturbing the peace.") Furthermore, victims are so hamstrung by provisions against "undue" force in self-defense that the criminal is automatically handed an enormous built-in advantage by the existing legal system.

It should be clear that no physical object is *in itself* aggressive; *any* object, whether it be a gun, a knife, or a stick, can be used for aggression, for defense, or for numerous other purposes unconnected with crime. It makes no more sense to outlaw or restrict the purchase and ownership of guns than it does to outlaw the possession of knives, clubs, hatpins, or stones. And how are all of these objects to be outlawed, and if outlawed, how is the prohibition to be enforced? Instead of pursuing innocent people carrying or possessing various objects, then, the law should be concerned with combatting and apprehending real criminals.

There is, moreover, another consideration which reinforces our conclusion. If guns are restricted or outlawed, there is no reason to expect that determined criminals are going to pay much attention to the law. The criminals, then, will always be able to purchase and carry guns; it will only be their innocent victims who will suffer from the solicitous liberalism that imposes laws against guns and other weapons. Just as drugs, gambling, and pornography should be made legal, so too should guns and any other objects that might serve as weapons of self-defense.

7

Education

Public and Compulsory Schooling

UNTIL THE LAST FEW YEARS there were few institutions in America that were held more sacred—especially by liberals—than the public school. Devotion to the public school had seized even those early Americans—such as Jeffersonians and Jacksonians—who were libertarian in most other respects. In recent years the public school was supposed to be a crucial ingredient of democracy, the fount of brotherhood, and the enemy of elitism and separateness in American life. The public school was the embodiment of the alleged right of every child to an education, and it was upheld as a crucible of understanding and harmony between men of all occupations and social classes who would rub elbows from an early age with all their neighbors.

Going hand in hand with the spread of public education have been *compulsory attendance laws*, which have forced all children up to a high—and continually increasing—minimum age, to attend either a public school or a private school certified as suitable by the state apparatus. In contrast to earlier decades, when a relatively small proportion of the population went to school in the higher grades, the entire mass of the population has thus been coerced by the government into spending a large portion of the most impressionable years of their lives in public institutions. We could easily have analyzed compulsory attendance laws in our chapter on involuntary servitude, for what institution is more evidently a vast system of incarceration? In recent years, Paul Goodman and other critics of education have trenchantly exposed the nation's public schools—and to a lesser extent their private appendages—as a vast prison system for the nation's youth, dragooning countless millions of unwilling and unadaptable children into the schooling structure. The New Left tactic of breaking into the high schools shouting "Jailbreak!" may have been absurd and ineffective, but it certainly expressed a great truth about the school system. For if we are to dragoon the entire youth population into vast prisons in the guise of "education," with teachers and administrators serving as surrogate wardens and guards, why should we not expect vast unhappiness, discontent, alienation, and rebellion on the part of the nation's youth? The only surprise should be that the rebellion was so long in coming. But now it is increasingly acknowledged that something is terribly wrong with America's proudest institution; that, especially in urban areas, the public schools have become cesspools of crime, petty theft, and drug addiction, and that little or no genuine education takes place amidst the warping of the minds and souls of the children.[1]

Part of the reason for this tyranny over the nation's youth is misplaced altruism on the part of the educated middle class. The workers, or the "lower classes," they felt, should have the opportunity to enjoy the schooling the middle classes value so highly. And if the parents or the children of the masses should be so benighted as to balk at this glorious opportunity set be-

[1] Thus, see Paul Goodman, *Compulsory Mis-education and the Community of Scholars* (New York: Vintage Press, 1964), and numerous works by Goodman, John Holt, Jonathan Kozol, Herbert Kohl, Ivan Illich, and many others.

fore them, well, then, a little coercion must be applied—"for their own good," of course.

A crucial fallacy of the middle-class school worshippers is confusion between formal schooling and *education* in general. Education is a lifelong process of learning, and learning takes place not only in school, but in all areas of life. When the child plays, or listens to parents or friends, or reads a newspaper, or works at a job, he or she is becoming *educated*. Formal schooling is only a small part of the educational process, and is really only suitable for formal subjects of instruction, particularly in the more advanced and systematic subjects. The elementary subjects, reading, writing, arithmetic and their corollaries, can easily be learned at home and outside the school.

Furthermore, one of the great glories of mankind is its diversity, the fact that each individual is unique, with unique abilities, interests, and aptitudes. To coerce into formal schooling children who have neither the ability nor the interest in this area is a criminal warping of the soul and mind of the child. Paul Goodman has raised the cry that most children would be far better off if they were allowed to work at an early age, learn a trade, and begin to do that which they are most suited for. America was built by citizens and leaders, many of whom received little or no formal schooling, and the idea that one must have a high-school diploma—or nowadays, an A.B. degree—before he can begin to work and to live in the world is an absurdity of the current age. Abolish compulsory attendance laws and give children their head, and we will return to a nation of people far more productive, interested, creative, and happy. Many thoughtful opponents of the New Left and the youth rebellion have pointed out that much of the discontent of youth and their divorce from reality is due to the ever-longer period in which youth must remain at school, wrapped in a cocoon of dependence and irresponsibility. Well and good, but what is the main reason for this ever-lengthening cocoon? Clearly the whole system, and in particular the compulsory attendance laws, which preach that everyone must go perpetually to school—first to high school, now to college, and soon perhaps for a Ph.D. degree. It is the compulsion toward mass schooling that creates both the discontent and the ever-continuing shelter from the "real world." In no other nation and in no other age has this mania for mass schooling so taken hold.

It is remarkable that the old libertarian right and the New Left, from very different perspectives and using very different rhetoric, came to a similar perception of the despotic nature of mass schooling. Thus, Albert Jay Nock, the great individualist theorist of the 1920s and '30s, denounced the educational system for forcing the "ineducable" masses into the schools out of a vain egalitarian belief in the equal educability of every child. Instead of allowing those children with the needed aptitude and ability to go to school, all children are being coerced into schools for their own supposed good, and the result is a distortion of the lives of those not suited for school and the wrecking of proper schooling for the truly educable. Nock also perceptively criticized the conservatives who attacked "progressive education" for diluting educational standards by giving courses in automobile driving, basket weaving, or choosing a dentist. Nock pointed out that if you force a whole host of children who cannot absorb classical education into school, then you *have* to shift education in the direction of vocational training, suitable for the lowest common denominator. The fatal flaw is not progressive education, but the drive toward universal schooling to which progressivism was a makeshift response.[2]

Such New Left critics as John McDermott and Paul Goodman charge, for their part, that the middle class has been forcing working class children, many of them with completely different values and aptitudes, into a public school system designed to force these children into a middle-class mould. It

---

[2] Thus, see Albert Jay Nock, *The Theory of Education in the United States* (Chicago: Henry Regnery, 1949); and Nock, *Memoirs of a Superfluous Man* (New York: Harper & Bros., 1943).

should be clear that whether one favors one class or the other, one ideal of schooling or another, the substance of the criticism is very much the same: that a whole mass of children are being dragooned into an institution for which they have little interest or aptitude.

Indeed, if we look into the history of the drive for public schooling and compulsory attendance in this and other countries, we find at the root not so much misguided altruism as a conscious scheme to coerce the mass of the population into a mould desired by the Establishment. Recalcitrant minorities were to be forced into a majority mould; all citizens were to be inculcated in the civic virtues, notably and always including obedience to the State apparatus. Indeed, if the mass of the populace is to be educated in government schools, how could these schools *not* become a mighty instrument for the inculcation of obedience to the State authorities? Martin Luther, a leader in the first modern drive for compulsory State education, phrased the plea typically in his famous letter of 1524 to the rulers of Germany:

Dear rulers. . . . I maintain that the civil authorities are under obligation to compel the people to send their children to school. . . . If the government can compel such citizens as are fit for military service to bear spear and rifle, to mount ramparts, and perform other martial duties in time of war, how much more has it a right to the people to send their children to school, because in this case we are warring with the devil, whose object it is secretly to exhaust our cities and principalities. . . .[3]

Thus, for Luther, the State schools were to be an indispensable part of the "war with the devil," i.e., with Catholics, Jews, infidels, and competing Protestant sects. A modern admirer of Luther and of compulsory education was to remark that "the permanent and positive value of Luther's pronouncement of 1524 lies . . . in the hallowed associations which it established

[3] See John William Perrin, *The History of Compulsory Education in New England*, 1896.

for Protestant Germany between the national religion and the educational duties of the individual and the state. Thus, doubtless, was created that healthy public opinion which rendered the principle of compulsory school attendance easy of acceptance in Prussia at a much earlier date than in England." [4]

The other great Protestant founder, John Calvin, was no less zealous in promoting mass public schooling, and for similar reasons. It is therefore not surprising that the earliest compulsory schooling in America was established by the Calvinist Puritans in Massachusetts Bay, those men who were so eager to plant an absolutist Calvinist theocracy in the New World. In June 1642, only a year after the Massachusetts Bay colony enacted its first set of laws, the colony established the first system of compulsory education in the English-speaking world. The law declared:

For as much as the good education of children is of singular behoof and benefit to any commonwealth, and whereas many parents and masters are too indulgent and negligent of their duty of that kind, it is ordered that the selectmen of every town . . . shall have a vigilant eye over their neighbors, to see first that none of them shall suffer so much barbarism in any of their families, as not to endeavor to teach, by themselves or others, their children and apprentices. . . . [5]

Five years later, Massachusetts Bay followed up this law with the establishment of public schools.

Thus, from the beginning of American history, the desire to mould, instruct, and render obedient the mass of the population was the major impetus behind the drive toward public schooling. In colonial days, public schooling was used as a device to suppress religious dissent, as well as to imbue unruly servants with the virtues of obedience to the State. It is typical, for example, that in the course of their suppression of the Quakers, Massachusetts and Connecticut forbade that despised

---

[4] A. E. Twentyman, "Education; Germany," *Encyclopaedia Britannica*, 14th Ed. (1929), VII, pp. 999–1000.

[5] See Perrin, *op. cit.*

sect from establishing their own schools. And Connecticut, in a vain attempt to suppress the "New Light" movement, in 1742 forbade that sect from establishing any of their own schools. Otherwise, the Connecticut authorities reasoned, the New Lights "may tend to train youth in ill principles and practices, and introduce such disorders as may be of fatal consequences to the public peace and weal of this colony." [6] It is hardly a coincidence that the only truly free colony in New England—Rhode Island—was also the one colony in the area devoid of public schooling.

The motivation for public and compulsory schooling after Independence scarcely differed in essentials. Thus, Archibald D. Murphey, the father of the public school system in North Carolina, called for such schools as follows:

. . . all the children will be taught in them. . . . In these schools the precepts of morality and religion should be inculcated, and habits of subordination and obedience be formed. . . . Their parents know not how to instruct them. . . . The state, in the warmth of her affection and solicitude for their welfare, must take charge of those children, and place them in school where their minds can be enlightened and their hearts can be trained to virtue.[7]

One of the most common uses of compulsory public schooling has been to oppress and cripple national ethnic and linguistic minorities or colonized peoples—to force them to abandon their own language and culture on behalf of the language and culture of the ruling groups. The English in Ireland and Quebec, and nations throughout Central and Eastern Europe and in Asia—all dragooned their national minorities into the public schools run by their masters. One of the most potent stimuli for discontent and rebellion by these oppressed peoples was the desire to rescue their language and heritage from the

[6] See Merle Curti, *The Social Ideas of American Educators* (New York: Charles Scribner's Sons, 1935).

[7] *The Papers of Archibald D. Murphey* (Raleigh, N.C.: University of North Carolina Press, 1914), II, 53–54.

weapon of public schools wielded by their oppressors. Thus, the laissez-faire liberal Ludwig von Mises has written that, in linguistically mixed countries,

. . . continued adherence to a policy of compulsory education is utterly incompatible with efforts to establish lasting peace. . . .

The question of which language is to be made the basis of instruction assumes crucial importance. A decision one way or the other can, over the years, determine the nationality of a whole area. The school can alienate children from the nationality to which their parents belong and can be used as a means of oppressing whole nationalities. Whoever controls the schools has the power to injure other nationalities and to benefit his own.

Furthermore, Mises points out, the coercion inherent in rule by one nationality makes it impossible to solve the problem by formally allowing each parent to send his child to a school using a language of his own nationality:

It is often not possible for an individual—out of regard for his means of livelihood—to declare himself openly for one or another nationality. Under a system of interventionism, it could cost him the patronage of customers belonging to other nationalities or a job with an entrepreneur of a different nationality. . . . If one leaves to the parents the choice of the school to which they wish to send their children, then one exposes them to every conceivable form of political coercion. In all areas of mixed nationality, the school is a political prize of the highest importance. It cannot be deprived of its political character so long as it remains a public and compulsory institution. There is, in fact, only *one* solution: the state, the government, the laws must not in any way concern themselves with schooling or education. Public funds must not be used for such purposes. The rearing and instruction of youth must be left entirely to parents and to private associations and institutions.[8]

In fact, one of the major motivations of the legion of mid-nineteenth century American "educational reformers" who es-

---

[8] Ludwig von Mises, *The Free and Prosperous Commonwealth* (Princeton, N.J.: D. Van Nostrand Co., 1962), pp. 114–15.

tablished the modern public school system was precisely to use
it to cripple the cultural and linguistic life of the waves of immigrants into America, and to mould them, as educational re-
former Samuel Lewis stated, into "one people." It was the desire
of the Anglo-Saxon majority to tame, channel, and restructure
the immigrants, and in particular to smash the parochial school
system of the Catholics, that formed the major impetus for educational "reform." The New Left critics who perceive the role
of the public schools of today in crippling and moulding the
minds of ghetto children are only grasping the current embodiment of a long-cherished goal held by the public school Establishment—by the Horace Manns and the Henry Barnards
and the Calvin Stowes. It was Mann and Barnard, for example,
who urged the use of the schools for indoctrination against the
"mobocracy" of the Jacksonian movement. And it was Stowe,
author of an admiring tract on the Prussian compulsory school
system originally inspired by Martin Luther, who wrote of the
schools in unmistakably Lutheran and military terms:

If a regard to the public safety makes it right for a government to
compel the citizens to do military duty when the country is invaded,
the same reason authorizes the government to compel them to provide for the education of their children. . . . A man has no more
right to endanger the state by throwing upon it a family of ignorant
and vicious children, than he has to give admission to the spies of
an invading army.[9]

Forty years later, Newton Bateman, a leading educator, spoke
of the State's "right of eminent domain" over the "minds and
souls and bodies" of the nation's children: Education, he asserted, "cannot be left to the caprices and contingencies of individuals. . . ."[10]

[9] Calvin E. Stowe, *The Prussian System of Public Instruction and its
Applicability to the United States* (Cincinnati, 1830), pp. 61ff. On the
elitist motivations of the educational reformers, see Michael B. Katz, *The
Irony of Early School Reform* (Boston: Beacon Press, 1970).
[10] Quoted in Edward C. Kirkland, *Dream and Thought in the Business
Community, 1860–1900* (Chicago: Quadrangle Books, 1964), p. 54.

The most ambitious attempt by the public school partisans to maximize their control over the nation's children came in Oregon during the early 1920s. The state of Oregon, unhappy even with allowing private schools certified by the state, passed a law on November 7, 1922, outlawing private schools and compelling all children to attend public school. Here was the culmination of the educationists' dream. At last, all children were to be forced into the "democratizing" mould of uniform education by the state authorities. The law, happily, was declared unconstitutional by the Supreme Court of the United States in 1925 (*Pierce* v. *Society of Sisters,* June 1, 1925). The Supreme Court declared that "the child is not the mere creature of the State," and asserted that the Oregon law clashed with the "fundamental theory of liberty upon which all governments in this Union repose." The public school fanatics never tried to go that far again. But it is instructive to realize what the forces were that attempted to outlaw all competing private education in the state of Oregon. For the spearheads of the law were *not,* as we might expect, liberal or progressive educators or intellectuals; the spearhead was the Ku Klux Klan, then strong in the northern states, which was eager to crush the Catholic parochial school system, and to force all Catholic and immigrant children into the neo-Protestantizing and "Americanizing" force of the public school. The Klan, it is interesting to note, opined that such a law was necessary for the "preservation of free institutions." It is well to ponder that the much-vaunted "progressive" and "democratic" public school system had its most ardent supporters in the most bigoted by-ways of American life, among people anxious to stamp out diversity and variety in America.[11]

Uniformity or Diversity?

While current educationists do not go as far as the Ku Klux Klan, it is important to realize that the very *nature* of the pub-

[11] See Lloyd P. Jorgenson, "The Oregon School Law of 1922: Passage and Sequel," *Catholic Historical Review* (October 1968), pp. 455–460.

lic school *requires* the imposition of uniformity and the stamping out of diversity and individuality in education.

For it is in the nature of any governmental bureaucracy to live by a set of rules, and to impose those rules in a uniform and heavy-handed manner. If it did not do so, and the bureaucrat were to decide individual cases ad hoc, he would then be accused, and properly so, of not treating each taxpayer and citizen in an equal and uniform manner. He would be accused of discrimination and of fostering special privilege. Furthermore, it is administratively more convenient for the bureaucrat to establish uniform rules throughout his jurisdiction. In contrast to the private, profit-making business, the government bureaucrat is neither interested in efficiency nor in serving his customers to the best of his ability. Having no need to make profits and sheltered from the possibility of suffering losses, the bureaucrat can and does disregard the desires and demands of his consumer-customers. His major interest is in "not making waves," and this he accomplishes by even-handedly applying a uniform set of rules, regardless of how inapplicable they may be in any given case.

The public school bureaucrat, for his part, is faced with a host of crucial and controversial decisions in deciding on the pattern of formal schooling in his area. He must decide: should schooling be—traditional or progressive? free enterprise or socialistic? competitive or egalitarian? liberal arts or vocational? segregated or integrated? sex education or not? religious or secular? or various shades between these poles. The point is that *whatever* he decides, and even if he decides according to the wishes of the majority of the public, there will always be a substantial number of parents and children who will be totally deprived of the kind of education they desire. If the decision is for traditional discipline in the schools, then the more progressive-minded parents lose out, and vice versa; and the same is true for all the other critical decisions. The more that education becomes public, the more will parents and children be deprived of the education they feel they need. The more that education becomes public, the more will heavy-handed uniformity stamp out the needs and desires of individuals and minorities.

Consequently, the greater the sphere of public as opposed to private education, the greater the scope and intensity of conflict in social life. For if one agency is going to make the decision: sex education or no, traditional or progressive, integrated or segregated, etc., then it becomes particularly important to gain control of the government and to prevent one's adversaries from taking power themselves. Hence, in education as well as in all other activities, the more that government decisions replace private decision-making, the more various groups will be at each others' throats in a desperate race to see to it that the one and only decision in each vital area goes its own way.

Contrast the deprivation and intense social conflict inherent in government decision-making with the state of affairs on the free market. If education were strictly private, then each and every group of parents could and would patronize its own kind of school. A host of diverse schools would spring up to meet the varied structure of educational demands by parents and children. Some schools would be traditional, others progressive. Schools would range through the full traditional-progressive scale; some schools would experiment with egalitarian and grade-less education, others would stress the rigorous learning of subjects and competitive grading; some schools would be secular, others would emphasize various religious creeds; some schools would be libertarian and stress the virtues of free enterprise, others would preach various kinds of socialism.

Let us consider, for example, the structure of the magazine or book publishing industry today, remembering too that magazines and books are themselves an extremely important form of education. The magazine market, being roughly free, contains all manner of magazines to suit a wide variety of tastes and demands by consumers: there are nationwide, all-purpose magazines; there are liberal, conservative, and all manner of ideological journals; there are specialized scholarly publications; and there are a myriad of magazines devoted to special interests and hobbies like bridge, chess, hi-fi, etc. A similar structure appears in the free book market: there are wide-circulation books, books appealing to specialized markets, books of all ideological persuasions. Abolish public schools and the free, varied, and diverse magazine and book markets would be parallelled by a similar kind of "school market." In contrast, if there were only one magazine for each city or state, think of the battles and conflicts that would rage: should the magazine be conservative, liberal, or socialist; how much space should it devote to fiction or bridge, etc.? The pressures and conflicts would be intense, and no resolution would be satisfactory, for *any* decision would deprive countless numbers of people of what they want and require. What the libertarian is calling for, then, is not as *outré* as it might at first appear; what he is calling for is a school system as free and varied as most other educational media are today.

To focus again on other educational media, what then would we think of a proposal for the government, federal or state, to use the taxpayers' money to set up a nationwide chain of public magazines or newspapers, and then to compel all people, or all children, to read them? Further, what would we think of the government outlawing all other newspapers and magazines, or at the very least outlawing all newspapers or magazines that do not come up to certain "standards" of what a government commission thinks children ought to read? Such a proposal would surely be regarded with horror throughout the country, yet this is precisely the sort of regime that government has established in the schools. A compulsory public press would rightly be considered an invasion of the basic freedom of the press; is not scholastic freedom at least as important as press freedom? Aren't both vital media for public information and education, for free inquiry and search for the truth? In fact, the suppression of free schooling should be regarded with even greater horror than the suppression of a free press, since here the tender and unformed minds of children are more directly involved.

It is intriguing that at least some public school advocates

have recognized the analogy between schooling and the press and have pursued their logic to the latter area. Thus, prominent in Boston politics in the 1780s and 1790s was the arch-Federalist "Essex Junto," a group of leading merchants and lawyers originally hailing from Essex County, Massachusetts. The Essexmen were particularly anxious for an extensive public school system in order to have the youth "taught the proper subordination." Essexman Stephen Higginson frankly declared that "the people must be taught to confide in and revere their rulers." And seeing with firm consistency that newspapers were as important a form of education as formal schooling, another leading Essex merchant and theoretician, Jonathan Jackson, denounced the free press for being necessarily subservient to its readership, and advocated a state-owned newspaper that could be independent of its readers and therefore inculcate the proper virtues into the citizenry.[12]

Professor E. G. West has also offered an instructive analogy between the provision of schooling and of food, surely an industry of at least an equal importance for children as well as adults. West writes:

Protection of a child against starvation or malnutrition is presumably just as important as protection against ignorance. It is difficult to envisage, however, that any government, in its anxiety to see that children have minimum standards of food and clothing, would pass laws for compulsory and universal eating, or that it should entertain measures which lead to increased taxes or rates in order to provide children's food, "free" at local authority kitchens or shops. It is still more difficult to imagine that most people would unquestioningly accept this system, especially where it had developed to the stage that for "administrative reasons" parents were allocated to those shops which happened to be nearest their homes. . . . Yet strange as such hypothetical measures may appear when applied to

[12] See David Hackett Fischer, "The Myth of the Essex Junto," *William and Mary Quarterly* (April 1964), pp. 191–235. Also see Murray N. Rothbard, "Economic Thought: Comment," in D. T. Gilchrist, ed., *The Growth of the Seaport Cities, 1790–1825* (Charlottesville, Va.: University Press of Virginia, 1967), pp. 178–79.

the provision of food and clothing they are nevertheless typical of . . . state education. . . .[13]

Several libertarian thinkers, from "left" and "right"-wing ends of the libertarian spectrum, have delivered trenchant critiques of the totalitarian nature of compulsory public schooling. Thus, left-libertarian British critic Herbert Read:

Mankind is naturally differentiated into many types, and to press all these types into the same mold must inevitably lead to distortions and repressions. Schools should be of many kinds, following different methods and catering for different dispositions. It might be argued that even a totalitarian state must recognize this principle but the truth is that differentiation is an organic process, the spontaneous and roving associations of individuals for particular purposes. . . . The whole structure of education as the natural process we have envisaged, falls to pieces if we attempt to make that structure . . . artificial.[14]

And the great late-nineteenth-century individualist English philosopher Herbert Spencer asked:

For what is meant by saying that a government ought to educate the people? Why should they be educated? What is the education for? Clearly to fit the people for social life—to make them good citizens? And who is to say what are good citizens? The government: there is no other judge. And who is to say how these good citizens may be made? The government: there is no other judge. Hence the proposition is convertible into this—a government ought to mold children into good citizens. . . . It must first form for itself a definite conception of a pattern citizen; and having done this, must elaborate such system of discipline as seems best calculated to produce citizens after that pattern. This system of discipline it is bound to enforce to the uttermost. For if it does otherwise, it allows men to become different from what in its

---

[13] E. G. West, *Education and the State* (London: Institute of Economic Affairs, 1965), pp. 13–14.

[14] Herbert Read, *The Education of Free Men* (London: Freedom Press, 1944), pp. 27–28.

judgment they should become, and therefore fails in that duty it is charged to fulfill.[15]

And the twentieth-century American individualist writer Isabel Paterson declared:

Educational texts are necessarily selective, in subject matter, language, and point of view. Where teaching is conducted by private schools, there will be a considerable variation in different schools; the parents must judge what they want their children taught, by the curriculum offered. . . . Nowhere will there be any inducement to teach the "supremacy of the state as a compulsory philosophy." But every politically controlled educational system will inculcate the doctrine of state supremacy sooner or later, whether as the divine right of kings, or the "will of the people" in "democracy." Once that doctrine has been accepted, it becomes an almost superhuman task to break the stranglehold of the political power over the life of the citizen. It has had his body, property, and mind in its clutches from infancy. An octopus would sooner release its prey.

A tax-supported, compulsory educational system is the complete model of the totalitarian state.[16]

As E. G. West indicated, bureaucratic convenience has invariably led the states to prescribe geographical public school districts, to place one school in each district, and then to force each public school child to attend school in the district closest to his residence. While in a free private school market most children would undoubtedly attend schools near their homes, the present system compels a monopoly of one school per district, and thereby coerces uniformity throughout each area. Children who, for whatever reason, would prefer to attend a school in another district are prohibited from doing so. The result is enforced geographic homogeneity, and it also means that the character of each school is completely dependent on its residential neighborhood. It is then inevitable that public

[15] Herbert Spencer, *Social Statics* (London: John Chapman, 1851), pp. 332–33.
[16] Isabel Paterson, *The God of the Machine* (New York: G. P. Putnam, 1943), pp. 257–58.

schools, instead of being totally uniform, will be uniform *within* each district, and the composition of pupils, the financing of each school, and the quality of education will come to depend upon the values, the wealth, and the tax base, of each geographical area. The fact that wealthy school districts will have costlier and higher-quality teaching, higher teaching salaries, and better working conditions than the poorer districts, then becomes inevitable. Teachers will regard the better schools as the superior teaching posts, and the better teachers will gravitate to the better school districts, while the poorer ones must remain in the lower-income areas. Hence, the operation of district public schools inevitably results in the negation of the very egalitarian goal which is supposed to be a major aim of the public school system in the first place.

Moreover, if the residential areas are racially segregated, as they often tend to be, the result of a compulsory geographical monopoly is the compulsory racial segregation of the public schools. Those parents who prefer integrated schooling have to come up against the geographical monopoly system. Furthermore, just as some wag has said that nowadays "Whatever isn't prohibited is compulsory," the recent tendency of the public school bureaucrats has not been to institute voluntary bussing of children to widen parental discretion, but to swing in the opposite direction and institute compulsory bussing and compulsory racial integration of the schools—often resulting in a grotesque transfer of children far from their homes. Once again, the typical government pattern: either compulsory segregation or compulsory integration. The voluntary way—leaving the decisions up to the individual parents involved—cuts across the grain of any State bureaucracy.

It is curious that recent movements for local parental control of public education have sometimes been called "extreme right-wing" and at other times "extreme left-wing," when the libertarian motivation has been precisely the same in either case. Thus, when parents have opposed the compulsory bussing of their children to distant schools, the educational Establishment has condemned these movements as "bigoted" and "right-wing." But when, similarly, Negro parents—as in the case of Ocean Hill-Brownsville in New York City—have demanded local parental control of the school system, this drive in its turn has been condemned as "extreme left-wing" and "nihilistic." The most curious part of the affair is that the parents in both cases have failed to recognize their common desire for local parental control, and have themselves condemned the "bigots" or "militants" in the other group. Tragically, neither the local white nor black groups have recognized their common cause against the educational Establishment: against dictatorial control of their children's education by an educational bureaucracy which is trying to ram down their throats a form of schooling which *it* believes must be imposed upon the recalcitrant masses. One crucial task of libertarians is to highlight the common cause of all groups of parents against the State's educational tyranny. Of course, it must also be pointed out that parents can *never* get the State off their educational backs until the public school system is totally abolished and schooling becomes free once more.

The geographical nature of the public school system has also led to a coerced pattern of residential segregation, in income and consequently in race, throughout the country and particularly in the suburbs. As everyone knows, the United States since World War II has seen an expansion of population, not in the inner central cities, but in the surrounding suburban areas. As new and younger families have moved to the suburbs, by far the largest and growing burden of local budgets has been to pay for the public schools, which have to accommodate a young population with a relatively high proportion of children per capita. These schools invariably have been financed from growing property taxation, which largely falls on the suburban residences. This means that the wealthier the suburban family, and the more expensive its home, the greater will be its tax contribution for the local school. Hence, as the burden of school taxes increases steadily, the suburbanites try desperately to encourage an inflow of wealthy residents and expensive homes, and to *discourage* an inflow of poorer citizens. There is, in short, a break-even point of the price of a house beyond which a new family in a new house will more than pay for its children's education in its property taxes. Families in homes below that cost level will not pay enough in property taxes to finance their children's education and hence will throw a greater tax burden on the existing population of the suburb. Realizing this, suburbs have generally adopted rigorous zoning laws which prohibit the erection of housing below a minimum cost level—and thereby freeze out any inflow of poorer citizens. Since the proportion of Negro poor is far greater than white poor, this effectively also bars Negroes from joining the move to the suburbs. And since in recent years there has been an increasing shift of jobs and industry from the central city to the suburbs as well, the result is an increasing pressure of unemployment on the Negroes— a pressure which is bound to intensify as the job shift accelerates. The abolition of the public schools, and therefore of the school burden-property tax linkage, would go a long way toward removing zoning restrictions and ending the suburb as an upper middle-class-white preserve.

Burdens and Subsidies

The very existence of the public school system, furthermore, involves a complex network of coerced levies and subsidies, all of which are difficult to justify on any ethical grounds whatever. In the first place, public schools force those parents who wish to send their children to private schools to shoulder a double burden: they are coerced into subsidizing public school children, and they also have to pay for their own children's education. Only the evident breakdown of public education in the large cities has maintained a flourishing private school system there; in higher education, where the breakdown has not been as stark, private colleges are rapidly being put out of business by the competition from tax-subsidized free tuition and tax-financed higher salaries. Similarly, since public schools must constitutionally be secular, this means that religious parents must be forced to subsidize the secular public schools. While "separation of church and State" is a noble principle—and a subset of the libertarian principle of separating *everything* from the State —it is surely going too far in the other direction to force the religious to subsidize the nonreligious through State coercion.

The existence of the public school also means that unmarried and childless couples are coerced into subsidizing families with children. What is the ethical principle here? And now that population growth is no longer fashionable, consider the anomaly of liberal antipopulationists advocating a public school system that not only subsidizes families with children, but subsidizes them in *proportion to the number of children* they have. We need not subscribe to the full dimensions of the current antipopulation hysteria to question the wisdom of deliberately subsidizing the number of children per family by government action. This means, too, that poor single people and poor childless couples are forced to subsidize wealthy families with children. Does this make any ethical sense at all?

In recent years, the public school forces have promulgated the doctrine that "Every child has a right to an education," and therefore that the taxpayers should be coerced into granting that right. But this concept totally misconstrues the concept of "right." A "right," philosophically, must be something embedded in the nature of man and reality, something that can be preserved and maintained at any time and in any age. The "right" of self-ownership, of defending one's life and property, is clearly that sort of right: it can apply to Neanderthal cavemen, in modern Calcutta, or in the contemporary United States. Such a right is independent of time or place. But a "right to a job" or to "three meals a day" or to "twelve years of schooling" cannot be so guaranteed. Suppose that such things *cannot* exist, as was true in Neanderthal days or in modern Calcutta? To speak of a "right" as something which can only be fulfilled in modern industrial conditions is not to speak of a human, natural right at all. Furthermore, the libertarian "right" of self-ownership does not require the coercion of one set of people to provide such a "right" for another set. *Every* man can enjoy the right of self-ownership, without special coercion upon anyone. But in the case of a "right" to schooling, this can only be provided if other people are coerced into fulfilling it. The "right" to schooling, to a job, three meals, etc., is then not embedded in the nature of man, but requires for its fulfillment the existence of a group of exploited people who are coerced into providing such a "right."

Furthermore, the entire concept of a "right to education" should always be placed in the context that formal schooling is only a small fraction of any person's education in life. If every child really has a "right" to education, then why not a "right" to reading newspapers and magazines, and then why should not the government tax everyone to provide free public magazines for everyone who wishes to obtain them?

Professor Milton Friedman, an economist at the University of Chicago, has performed an important service in separating out money sums from various aspects of government subsidy, in education as well as in other areas. While Friedman unfortunately accepts the view that every child should have his schooling provided by the taxpayers, he points out the *non sequitur* in using this as an argument for public schools: It is quite feasible for the taxpayer to subsidize every child's education without having any public schools whatsoever! [17] In Friedman's now famous "voucher plan," the government would give to every parent a voucher entitling him to pay a certain amount of tuition for each child, in *any school* of the parent's choice. The voucher plan would continue the tax-financed provision of education for every child, yet enable the abolition of the vast monopolistic, inefficient, dictatorial public school bureaucracy. The parent could then send his child to any sort of private

[17] Milton Friedman, *Capitalism and Freedom* (Chicago: University of Chicago Press, 1962), pp. 85–107.

school that he wished, and the range of choice for every parent and child would then be maximized. The child could then go to any type of school—progressive or traditional, religious or secular, free-enterprise or socialistic—the parent desired. The monetary subsidy would then be totally separated from the government's actual provision of schooling through a public school system.

While the Friedman plan would be a great improvement over the present system in permitting a wider range of parental choice and enabling the abolition of the public school system, the libertarian finds many grave problems yet remaining. In the first place, the immorality of coerced subsidy for schooling would still continue in force. Secondly, it is inevitable that the power to subsidize brings with it the power to regulate and control: The government is not about to hand out vouchers for *any* kind of schooling whatever. Clearly, then, the government would only pay vouchers for private schools *certified* as fitting and proper by the State, which means detailed control of the private schools by the government—control over their curriculum, methods, form of financing, etc. The power of the State over private schools, through its power to certify or not to certify for vouchers, will be even greater than it is now.[18]

Since the Oregon case, the public school advocates have never gone so far as to abolish private schools, but these schools remain regulated and confined in numerous ways. Each state, for example, provides that every child must be educated in schools it certifies, which again coerces the schools into a curricular mould desired by the government. In order to "qualify" as certified private schools, all sorts of pointless and costly regulations have to be fulfilled, by the school as well as by the teacher, who must often take a host of meaningless "education" courses in order to be deemed qualified to teach. Many fine private schools are now operating technically "illegally," be-

---

[18] For a libertarian critique of the voucher scheme, see George Pearson, *Another Look at Education Vouchers* (Wichita, Kan.: Center for Independent Education).

cause they refuse to conform to the often stultifying government requirements. Perhaps the gravest injustice is that, in
most states, parents are prohibited from teaching their children
themselves, since the state will not agree that they constitute a
proper "school." There are a vast number of parents who are
more than qualified to teach their children themselves, particularly the elementary grades. Furthermore, they are more qualified than any outside party to judge the abilities and the required pacing of each child, and to gear education to the individual needs and abilities of each child. No formal school, confined to uniform classrooms, can perform that sort of service.

"Free" schools, whether current public schools or future
vouchered schools, are of course not *really* free; someone, that
is, the taxpayers, must pay for the educational services involved.
But with service severed from payment, there tends to be an
oversupply of children into the schools (apart from the compulsory attendance laws which have the same effect), and a
lack of interest by the child in the educational service for which
his family does not have to pay. As a result, a large number of
children unsuitable for or uninterested in school who would be
better off either at home or working, are dragooned into going
to school and into staying there far longer than they should.
The resulting mania for mass schooling has led to a mass of
discontented and imprisoned children, along with the general
view that everyone *has* to finish high school (or even college) to
be worthy of being employed. Adding to this pressure has been
the hysterical growth of "antidropout" propaganda in the mass
media. Part of this development is the fault of business, for
employers are quite happy to have their labor force trained, not
by the employers or on the job, but at the expense of the hapless taxpayer. How much of the burgeoning of mass public
schooling is a means by which employers foist the cost of training their workers upon the taxpayers at large?

One would expect that this training, being without cost to
employers, will be highly expensive, inefficient, and far too
lengthy. There is in fact increasing evidence that a vast amount

of current schooling is not needed for productive employment. As Arthur Stinchcombe asks:

Is there anything that a high school can teach which employers of manual labor would be willing to pay for, if it were learned well? In general, the answer is no. Neither physical abilities nor reliability, the two main variables of interest in employers of manual labor, are much influenced by schooling. Employers concerned with securing reliable workers may require high school diplomas as evidence of good discipline. Otherwise they can train workers better and cheaper than a high school can, on the job.[19]

And, as Professor Banfield points out, most job skills are learned on the job anyway.[20]

The relative uselessness of the public school system for training manual labor is demonstrated by the fascinating work of MIND, a private educational service now operated by the Corn Products Refining Company of Greenwich, Conn. MIND deliberately chose high-school dropouts who were unskilled for manual jobs, and in a few short weeks, using intensive training and teaching machines, was able to teach these dropouts basic skills and typing, and place them in corporate jobs. Ten years of public schooling had taught these youngsters less than a few weeks of private, job-oriented training! Allowing youngsters to drop out from enforced dependency into becoming independent and self-supporting could only have immeasurable benefits for the youngsters themselves and for the rest of society.

There is considerable evidence linking compulsory attendance laws with the growing problem of juvenile delinquency, particularly in frustrated older children. Thus, Stinchcombe found that rebellious and delinquent behavior is "largely a reaction to the school itself"; and the British Crowther Committee found that when in 1947 the minimum school-leaving age was raised

19 Arthur L. Stinchcombe, *Rebellion in a High School* (Chicago: Quadrangle Books, 1964), p. 180. Quoted in Edward C. Banfield, *The Unheavenly City* (Boston: Little, Brown & Co., 1970), p. 136.
20 Banfield, *ibid.*, p. 292.

by the government from 14 to 15, there was an immediate and sharp increase in the delinquencies committed by the newly incarcerated fourteen-year-olds.[21]

Part of the blame for compulsory attendance and mass public schooling must also be laid at the door of the labor unions which, in order to reduce competition from young, adolescent workers, try to force the youth out of the labor market and into educational institutions for as long a time as possible. Thus, both labor unions and employers exert powerful pressure for compulsory schooling and therefore for the nonemployment of most of the nation's youth.

Higher Education

With the exception of the effects of compulsory attendance laws, the same strictures we have levelled against public schools can also be directed against public higher education, with one noteworthy addition. There is increasing evidence that, certainly in the case of public higher education, the coerced subsidy is largely in the direction of forcing poorer citizens to subsidize the education of the wealthier! There are three basic reasons: the tax structure for schools is not particularly "progressive," i.e., does not tax the wealthier in greater proportion; the kids going to college generally have wealthier parents than the kids who do not; and the kids going to college will, as a result, acquire a higher lifetime working income than those who do not go. Hence a net redistribution of income from the poorer to the richer via the public college! Where is the ethical justification here?

Professors Weisbrod and Hansen have already demonstrated this redistribution effect in their studies of public higher education in Wisconsin and California. They found, for example, that the average family income of Wisconsinites without children in Wisconsin state universities was $6,500 in 1964–65,

---

[21] See Banfield, *op. cit.*, pp. 149ff.

while the average family income of families *with* children at the University of Wisconsin was $9,700. In California the respective figures were $7,900 and $12,000, and the subsidy disparity was even greater because the tax structure was much less "progressive" in the latter state. Douglas Windham found a similar redistribution effect from poorer to wealthier in the state of Florida. Hansen and Weisbrod concluded, from their California study:

> . . . on the whole, the effect of these subsidies is to promote greater rather than less inequality among people of various social and economic backgrounds by making available substantial subsidies that lower income families are either not eligible for or cannot make use of because of other conditions and constraints associated with their income position.

> What we have found true in California—an exceedingly unequal distribution of subsidies provided through public higher education —quite probably is even more true for other states. No state has such an extensive system of local Junior Colleges as does California, and for this reason, no state has such a large percentage of its high school graduates going on to public higher education. As a result we can be rather confident that California has a smaller percentage of its young people receiving a zero subsidy than do other states.[22]

Furthermore, the states, in addition to putting private colleges into financial jeopardy by their unfair, tax-subsidized competition, enforce strict controls on private higher education through various regulations. Thus, in New York State, no one can establish any institution called a "college" or "university" unless he posts a $500,000 bond with the state of New York.

---

[22] W. Lee Hansen and Burton A. Weisbrod, *Benefits, Costs, and Finance of Public Higher Education* (Chicago: Markham Pub. Co., 1969), p. 78. On Wisconsin and its comparison with California, see W. Lee Hansen, "Income Distribution Effects of Higher Education," *American Economic Review, Papers and Proceedings* (May 1969), pp. 335–40. On the general problem of redistribution from poorer to richer in the modern "welfare state," see Leonard Ross, "The Myth that Things are Getting Better," *New York Review of Books* (Aug. 12, 1971), pp. 7–9.

Clearly, this severely discriminates against small, poorer educational institutions, and effectively keeps them out of higher education. Also, the regional associations of colleges, through their power of "accreditation," can effectively put any college that does not conform to Establishment canons of curriculum or financing out of business. For example, these associations strictly refuse to accredit *any* college, no matter how excellent its instruction, that is proprietary or profit-making, rather than trustee-governed. Since proprietary colleges, having a far greater incentive to be efficient and to serve the consumer, will tend to be more successful financially, this discrimination places another heavy economic burden on private higher education. In recent years, two successful proprietary private colleges, Marjorie Webster Junior College in Washington, D.C., and Royalston College in Vermont, have been almost put out of business by the refusal to accredit such colleges. While one might say that the regional associations are private and not public, they work hand in hand with the federal government, which, for example, refuses to provide the usual scholarships or GI benefits to unaccredited colleges.[23]

Governmental discrimination against proprietary colleges (and other institutions, as well) does not stop at accreditation and scholarships. The entire income tax structure discriminates against them even more severely. By exempting trustee-run organizations from income taxes and by levying heavy taxes on profit-making institutions, the federal and state governments cripple and repress what could be the most efficient and solvent form of private education. The libertarian solution to this inequity, of course, is *not* to place equal burdens on the trustee colleges, but to remove the tax burdens on the proprietary schools. The libertarian ethic is not to impose equal slavery on everyone, but to arrive at equal freedom.

Trustee governance is, in general, a poor way to run any

[23] On the Marjorie Webster Junior College case, see James D. Koerner, "The Case of Marjorie Webster," *The Public Interest* (Summer, 1970), pp. 40–64.

institution. In the first place, in contrast to profit-making firms, partnerships, or corporations, the trustee-run firm is not fully owned by *anyone*. The trustees *cannot* make profits from successful operation of the organization, so there is no incentive to be efficient, or to serve the firm's customers properly. As long as the college or other organization does not suffer excessive deficits it can peg along at a low level of performance. Since the trustees cannot make profits by bettering their service to customers, they tend to be lax in their operations. Furthermore, they are hobbled in financial efficiency by the terms of their charters; for example, the trustees of a college are forbidden from saving their institution by converting part of the campus into a commercial enterprise—say a profit-making parking lot.

The short-changing of the customers is aggravated in the case of current trustee-colleges, where the students pay only a small fraction of the cost of their education, the major part being financed by subsidy or endowment. The usual market situation, where the producers sell the product and the consumers pay the full amount, is gone, and the disjunction between service and payment leads to an unsatisfactory state of affairs for everyone. The consumers, for example, feel that the managers are calling the tune. In contrast, as one libertarian remarked at the height of the student riots of the late 1960s, "nobody sits in at Berlitz." Furthermore, the fact that the "consumers" are really the governments, foundations, or alumni who pay the largest share of the bill, means that higher education inevitably gets skewed in the direction of their demands rather than toward the education of students. As Professors Buchanan and Devletoglou state:

The interposition of the government between the universities and their student-consumers has created a situation in which universities cannot meet demand and tap directly resources for satisfying student-consumer preferences. In order to get resources, universities have to compete with other tax-financed activities (armed forces, lower schools, welfare programs, and so forth). In the process, student-consumer demand is neglected, and the resulting student unrest provides the ingredients for the chaos we observe. . . . The mounting dependence on governmental financial support, as this has been translated into the institution of free tuition, may itself be one significant source of current unrest.[24]

The libertarian prescription for our educational mess can, then, be summed up simply: Get the government out of the educational process. The government has attempted to indoctrinate and mould the nation's youth through the public school system, and to mould the future leaders through state operation and control of higher education. Abolition of compulsory attendance laws would end the schools' role as prison custodians of the nation's youth, and would free all those better off outside the schools for independence and for productive work. The abolition of the public schools would end the crippling property tax burden and provide a vast range of education to satisfy all the freely exercised needs and demands of our diverse and varied population. The abolition of government schooling would end the unjust coerced subsidy granted to large families, and, often, toward the upper classes and against the poor. The miasma of government, of moulding the youth of America in the direction desired by the State, would be replaced by freely chosen and voluntary actions—in short, by a genuine and truly free education, both in and out of formal schools.

[24] James M. Buchanan and Nicos E. Devletoglou, *Academia in Anarchy: An Economic Diagnosis* (New York: Basic Books, 1970), pp. 32–33.

8

Welfare and the
Welfare State

Why the Welfare Crisis?

ALMOST EVERYONE, regardless of ideology, agrees that there is something terribly wrong with the accelerating, runaway welfare system in the United States, a system in which an ever-increasing proportion of the population lives as idle, compulsory claimants on the production of the rest of society. A few figures and comparisons will sketch in some of the dimensions of this galloping problem. In 1934, in the middle of the greatest depression in American history, at a nadir of our economic life, total direct welfare expenditures were $900 million. In the fiscal year 1966–67, after nearly a quarter century of the greatest boom in American history, when we had reached the status of having the highest standard of living in the history of the world with a low level of unemployment, total direct welfare expenditures were $8.3 billion. Now some of this enormous 800% increase can be accounted for by inflation, which diluted the value and purchasing power of the dollar. If we correct both figures for inflation by putting them both in terms of "constant 1958 dollars" (i.e., where each dollar has roughly the same purchasing power that the dollar could command in 1958), the 1934 welfare figure becomes $2.1 billion and the 1966–67 figure is $7.2 billion—still a 250% increase, from a time of deepest depression to a time of affluence. If we adjust the figures still further to correct for population growth (American total population was 126 million in 1934, 198 million in 1966–67), we still get a doubling of welfare expenditures (in constant dollars) per person: $17 in 1934, $36 in 1966–67. And the totals are undoubtedly much larger now, as a result of the accelerating expansion of the welfare system. A few more comparisons: from 1952 to 1970—during years of great prosperity—the total number of people on welfare quintupled, from 2 to 10 million. The population of children 18 years and younger during these same years increased by 42%; the number on welfare, however, increased by 400%. Coupled with a static total population, the number of welfare recipients in New York City jumped from 330,000 in 1960 to 1.2 million in 1971. Clearly, a welfare crisis is upon us.

The crisis is shown to be far greater if we include in "welfare payments" all social welfare aids to the poor. Thus, federal "aid to the poor" nearly tripled from 1960 to 1969, leaping from $9.5 billion to $27.7 billion. State and local social welfare expenditures zoomed from $3.3 billion in 1935 to $46 billion, a 1300% increase! Total social welfare expenditures for 1969, federal, state, and local, amounted to a staggering $73.7 billion.[1]

Most people think of being on welfare as a process external to the welfare clients themselves, as almost a natural disaster (like a tidal wave or volcanic eruption) that occurs beyond and despite the will of the people on welfare. The usual dictum is that "poverty" is the cause of individuals or families being on welfare. But on whatever criterion one wants to define poverty, on the basis of any chosen income level, it is undeniable that the number of people or families below that "poverty line" has

[1] See Henry Hazlitt, *Man vs. the Welfare State* (New Rochelle, N. Y.: Arlington House, 1969), pp. 59–60.

been steadily *decreasing* since the 1930s, not *vice versa*. Thus, the extent of poverty can scarcely account for the spectacular growth in the welfare clientele.

The solution to the puzzle becomes clear once one realizes that the number of welfare recipients has what is called in economics a "positive supply function"; in other words, that when the *incentives* to go on welfare rise, the welfare rolls will lengthen, and that a similar result will occur if the *disincentives* to go on welfare become weaker. Oddly enough, nobody challenges this finding in any *other* area of the economy. Suppose, for example, that someone (whether the government or a dotty billionaire is not important here) offers an extra $10,000 to everyone who will work in a shoe factory. Clearly, the supply of eager workers in the shoe business will multiply. The same will happen when *dis*incentives are reduced, e.g., if the government promises to relieve every shoe worker from paying income taxes. If we begin to apply the same analysis to welfare clientele as to all other areas of economic life, the answer to the welfare puzzle becomes crystal-clear.

What, then, are the important incentives/disincentives for going on welfare, and how have they been changing? Clearly, an extremely important factor is the relation between the income to be gained on welfare, *as compared with* the income to be earned from productive work. Suppose, to put it simply, that the "average," or going wage (very roughly, the wage open to an "average" worker), in a certain area is $7,000 a year. Suppose, also, that the income to be obtained from welfare is $3,000 a year. This means that the average net gain to be made from working (before taxes) is $4,000 a year. Suppose now that the welfare payments go up to $5,000 (or, alternatively, that the average wage is reduced to $5,000.) The differential—the *net* gain to be made from working—has now been cut in half, reduced from $4,000 to $2,000 a year. It stands to reason that the result will be an enormous increase in the welfare rolls (which will increase still more when we consider that the $7,000 workers will have to pay higher taxes in order to support a swollen and virtually nontaxpaying welfare clientele). We would then expect that if—as, of course, has been the case—welfare payment levels have been rising faster than average wages, an increasing number of people will flock to the welfare rolls. This effect will be still greater if we consider that, of course, not everyone earns the "average"; it will be the "marginal" workers, the ones earning below the average, who will flock to the welfare rolls. In our example, if the welfare payment rises to $5,000 a year, what can we expect to happen to the workers making $4,000? $5,000? or even $6,000? The $5,000-a-year man who previously earned a net of $2,000 higher than the welfare client now finds that his differential has been reduced to zero, that he is making no more—even *less* after taxes!—than the welfare client kept in idleness by the state. Is it any wonder that he will begin to flock to the welfare bonanza?

Specifically, during the period between 1952 and 1970, when the welfare rolls quintupled from 2 to 10 million, the average monthly benefit of a welfare family more than doubled, from $82 to $187, an increase of almost 130% at a time when consumer prices were rising by only 50%. Furthermore, in 1968, the Citizens Budget Commission of New York City compared the ten states in the Union having the fastest rise in welfare rolls with the ten states enjoying the lowest rate of growth. The Commission found that the average monthly welfare benefit in the ten fastest-growing states was twice as high as in the ten slowest states. (Monthly welfare payments per person averaged $177 in the former group of states, and only $88 in the latter.)[2]

Another example of the impact of high welfare payments and of their relation to wages available from working was cited by

[2] See Roger A. Freeman, "The Wayward Welfare State," *Modern Age* (Fall, 1971), pp. 401–02. In a detailed state-by-state study, Professors Brehm and Saving estimated that over 60% of the number of welfare clients in each state in 1951 could be accounted for by the level of welfare payments in that state; by the end of the '50s, the percentage had increased to over 80%. C. T. Brehm and T. R. Saving, "The Demand for General Assistance Payments," *American Economic Review* (December 1964), pp. 1002–1018.

the McCone Commission investigating the Watts riot of 1965. The Commission found that a job at the minimum wage paid about $220 a month, out of which had to come such work-related expenses as clothing and transportation. In contrast, the average welfare family in the area received from $177 to $238 a month, out of which no work-related expenses had to be deducted.[3]

Another powerful factor in swelling the welfare rolls is the increasing disappearance of the various sturdy disincentives for going on welfare. The leading disincentive has always been the stigma that every person on the welfare dole used to feel, the stigma of being parasitic and living off production instead of contributing to production. This stigma has been socially removed by the permeating values of modern liberalism; furthermore, the government agencies and social workers themselves have increasingly rolled out the red carpet to welcome and even urge people to get on welfare as quickly as possible. The "classical" view of the social worker was to help people to help themselves, to aid people in achieving and maintaining their independence and to stand on their own feet. For welfare clients, the aim of social workers used to be to help them get *off* the welfare rolls as quickly as possible. But now social workers have the opposite aim: to try to get as many people *on* welfare as possible, to advertise and proclaim their "rights." The result has been a continuing easing of eligibility requirements, a reduction in red tape, and the withering away of the enforcing of residency, work, or even income requirements for being on the dole. Anyone who suggests, however faintly, that welfare recipients should be required to accept employment and get off the dole is considered a reactionary moral leper. And with the old stigma increasingly removed, people now tend more and more to move rapidly toward welfare instead of shrinking from it. Irving

[3] Governor's Commission on the Los Angeles Riots, *Violence in the City—An End or a Beginning?* December 2, 1965, p. 72; quoted in Edward C. Banfield, *The Unheavenly City* (Boston: Little, Brown & Co., 1970), p. 288.

Kristol has trenchantly written of the "welfare explosion" of the 1960s:

This "explosion" was created—in part intentionally, in larger part unwittingly by public officials and public employees who were executing public policies as part of a "War on Poverty." And these policies had been advocated and enacted by many of the same people who were subsequently so bewildered by the "welfare explosion." Not surprisingly it took them a while to realize that the problem they were trying to solve was the problem they were creating.

Here . . . are the reasons behind the "welfare explosion" of the 1960s:

1. The number of poor people who are eligible for welfare will increase as one elevates the official definitions of "poverty" and "need." The War on Poverty elevated these official definitions; therefore, an increase in the number of "eligibles" automatically followed.

2. The number of eligible poor who actually apply for welfare will increase as welfare benefits go up—as they did throughout the 1960s. When welfare payments (and associated benefits, such as Medicaid and food stamps) compete with low wages, many poor people will rationally prefer welfare. In New York City today, as in many other large cities, welfare benefits not only compete with low wages; they outstrip them.

3. The reluctance of people actually eligible for welfare to apply for it—a reluctance based on pride or ignorance or fear—will diminish if any organized campaign is instituted to "sign them up." Such a campaign was successfully launched in the 1960s by (a) various community organizations sponsored and financed by the Office of Economic Opportunity, (b) the Welfare Rights Movement, and (c) the social work profession, which was now populated by college graduates who thought it their moral duty to help people get on welfare—instead of, as used to be the case, helping them get off welfare. In addition, the courts cooperated by striking down various legal obstacles (for example, residence requirements). . . .

Somehow, the fact that more poor people are on welfare, receiving more generous payments, does not seem to have made this country a nice place to live—not even for the poor on welfare, whose condition seems not noticeably better than when they were poor and off welfare. Something appears to have gone wrong; a liberal and compassionate social policy has bred all sorts of unanticipated and perverse consequences.[4]

The spirit that used to animate the social work profession was a far different—and a libertarian—one. There were two basic principles: (a) that all relief and welfare payments should be voluntary, by private agencies, rather than by the coercive levy of government; and (b) that the object of giving should be to help the recipient become independent and productive as soon as possible. Of course, in ultimate logic, (b) follows from (a), since no private agency is able to tap the virtually unlimited funds that can be mulcted from the long-suffering taxpayer. Since private aid funds are strictly limited, there is therefore no room for the idea of welfare "rights" as an unlimited and permanent claim on the production of others. As a further corollary of the limitation on funds, the social workers also realized that there was no room for aid to malingerers, those who refused to work, or who used the aid as a racket; hence came the concept of the "deserving" as against the "undeserving" poor. Thus, the nineteenth-century laissez-faire English agency, the Charity Organisation Society, included among the undeserving poor ineligible for aid those who did not need relief, impostors, and the man whose "condition is due to improvidence or thriftlessness, and there is no hope of being able to make him independent of charitable . . . assistance in the future." [5]

English laissez-faire liberalism, even though it generally ac-

---

[4] Irving Kristol, "Welfare: The best of intentions, the worst of results," *Atlantic Monthly* (August 1971), p. 47.

[5] Charity Organisation Society, *15th Annual Report*, 1883, p. 54; quoted in Charles Loch Mowat, *The Charity Organisation Society, 1869–1913* (London: Methuen & Co., 1961), p. 35.

cepted "Poor Law" governmental welfare, insisted that there be a strong disincentive effect: not only strict eligibility rules for assistance, but also making the workhouse conditions unpleasant enough to insure that workhouse relief would be a strong deterrent rather than an attractive opportunity. For the "undeserving poor," those responsible for their own fate, abuse of the relief system could only be curbed by "making it as distasteful as possible to the applicants; that is, by insisting (as a general rule) on a labour test or residence in a workhouse." [6]

While a strict deterrent is far better than an open welcome and a preachment about the recipients' "rights," the libertarian position calls for the complete abolition of governmental welfare and reliance on private charitable aid, based as it necessarily will be on helping the "deserving poor" on the road to independence as rapidly as possible. There was, after all, little or no governmental welfare in the United States until the Depression of the 1930s, and yet—in an era of a far lower general standard of living—there was no mass starvation in the streets. A highly successful private welfare program in the present-day is the one conducted by the three-million-member Mormon Church. This remarkable people, hounded by poverty and persecution, emigrated to Utah and nearby states in the nineteenth century, and by thrift and hard work raised themselves to a general level of prosperity and affluence. Very few Mormons are on welfare; Mormons are taught to be independent, self-reliant, and to shun the public dole. Mormons are devout believers and have therefore successfully internalized these admirable values. Furthermore, the Mormon Church operates an extensive private welfare plan for its members—based, again, on the principle of helping their members toward independence as rapidly as possible.

Note, for example, the following principles from the "Welfare Plan" of the Mormon Church. "Ever since its organization

[6] Charity Organisation Society, *2nd Annual Report*, 1870, p. 5; quoted in Mowat, *ibid.*, p. 36.

in 1830, the Church has encouraged its members to establish and maintain their economic independence; it has encouraged thrift and fostered the establishment of employment-creating industries; it has stood ready at all times to help needy faithful members." In 1936, the Mormon Church developed a "Church Welfare Plan, . . . a system under which the curse of idleness would be done away with, the evils of a dole abolished, and independence, industry, thrift and self-respect be once more established amongst our people. The aim of the Church is to help the people to help themselves. Work is to be enthroned as the ruling principle of the lives of our Church membership." [7] Mormon social workers in the program are instructed to act accordingly: "Faithful to this principle, welfare workers will earnestly teach and urge Church members to be self-sustaining to the full extent of their powers. No true Latter-Day Saint will, while physically able, voluntarily shift from himself the burden of his own support. So long as he can, under the inspiration of the Almighty and with his own labors, he will supply himself with the necessities of life." [8] The immediate objectives of the welfare program are to: "1. Place in gainful employment those who are able to work. 2. Provide employment within the Welfare Program, in so far as possible, for those who cannot be placed in gainful employment. 3. Acquire the means with which to supply the needy, for whom the Church assumes responsibility, with the necessities of life." [9] Insofar as possible, this program is carried on in small, decentralized, grass-roots groups: "Families, neighbors, quorums and wards and other Church organizational units may find it wise and desirable to form small groups for extending mutual help one to the other. Such groups may plant and harvest crops, process foods, store food, clothing and fuel, and carry out other projects for their mutual benefit." [10]

[7] *Welfare Plan of the Church of Jesus Christ of Latter-Day Saints* (The General Church Welfare Committee, 1960), p. 1.

[8] *Ibid.*, p. 4.

[9] *Ibid.*, p. 4.

[10] *Ibid.*, p. 5.

Specifically, the Mormon bishops and priesthood quorums are enjoined to aid their brethren to self-help: "In his temporal administrations the bishop looks at every able-bodied needy person as a purely temporary problem, caring for him until he can help himself. The priesthood quorum must look at its needy member as a continuing problem until not alone his temporal needs are met but his spiritual ones also. As a concrete example—a bishop extends help while the artisan or craftsman is out of work and in want; a priesthood quorum assists in establishing him in work and tries to see that he becomes fully self-supporting and active in his priesthood duties." Concrete rehabilitation activities for needy members enjoined upon the priesthood quorums include: "1. Placing quorum members and members of their families in permanent jobs. In some instances through trade school training, apprenticeships, and in other ways, quorums have assisted their quorum members to qualify themselves for better jobs. 2. Assisting quorum members and their families to get established in businesses of their own. . . ." [11]

The prime objective of the Mormon Church is to find jobs for their needy. To this end, "The finding of suitable jobs, under the Welfare Program, is a major responsibility of priesthood quorum members. They and members of the Relief Society should be constantly on the alert for employment opportunities. If every member of the ward welfare committee does well his or her work in this respect, most of the unemployed will be placed in gainful employment at the group or ward level." [12] Other members are rehabilitated as self-employed, the church may aid with a small loan, and the member's priesthood quorum may guarantee repayment from its funds. Those Mormons who cannot be placed in jobs or rehabilitated as self-employed "are to be given, in so far as possible, work at productive labor on Church properties. . . ." The Church is insistent on work by the recipient as far as possible: "It is imperative that people

[11] *Ibid.*, p. 19.
[12] *Ibid.*, p. 22.

being sustained through the bishops storehouse program work to the extent of their ability, thus earning what they receive. . . . Work of an individual on welfare projects should be considered as temporary rather than permanent employment. It should nevertheless continue so long as assistance is rendered to the individual through the bishops storehouse program. In this way the spiritual welfare of people will be served as their temporal needs are supplied. Feelings of diffidence will be removed. . . ." [13] Failing other work, the bishop may assign welfare recipients to aid individual members who are in need of help, the aided members reimbursing the Church at prevailing wage rates. In general, in return for their assistance, the welfare recipients are expected to make whatever contributions they can to the Church welfare program, either in funds, produce, or by their labor.[14]

Complementary to this comprehensive system of private aid on the principle of fostering independence, the Mormon Church sternly discourages its members from going on public welfare. "It is requested that local Church officers stress the importance of each individual, each family and each Church community becoming self-sustaining and independent of public relief." And: "To seek and accept direct public relief all too often invites the curse of idleness and fosters the other evils of dole. It destroys one's independence, industry, thrift and self-respect." [15]

There is no finer model than the Mormon Church for a private, voluntary, rational, individualistic welfare program. Let government welfare be abolished, and one would expect that numerous such programs for rational mutual aid would spring up throughout the country.

The inspiring example of the Mormon Church is a demonstration that the major determinant of who or how many people go on public welfare is their cultural and moral values rather

13 *Ibid.*, p. 25.
14 *Ibid.*, pp. 25, 46.
15 *Ibid.*, pp. 46, 48.

than their level of income. Another example is the group of Albanian-Americans in New York City.

Albanian-Americans are an extremely poor group, and in New York they are almost invariably poor slum dwellers. Statistics are scanty, but their average income is undoubtedly lower than that of the more highly publicized blacks and Puerto Ricans. Yet there is not a single Albanian-American on welfare. Why? Because of their pride and independence. As one of their leaders stated: "Albanians do not beg, and to Albanians, taking welfare is like begging in the street." [16]

A similar case is the decaying, poor, largely Polish-American and almost totally Catholic community of Northside, in Brooklyn, New York. Despite the low incomes, blight, and old and deteriorating housing in the area, there are virtually no welfare recipients in this community of 15,000. Why? Rudolph J. Stobierski, president of the Northside Community Development Council, supplied the answer: "They consider welfare an insult." [17]

In addition to the impact of religion and ethnic differences on values, Professor Banfield, in his brilliant book, *The Unheavenly City*, has demonstrated the importance of what he calls "upper-class" or "lower-class" culture in influencing the values of their members. The definitions of "class" in Banfield are not strictly income or status levels, but they tend to overlap strongly with these more common definitions. His definitions of class center on the different attitudes toward the present and the future: upper- and middle-class members tend to be future-oriented, purposeful, rational, and self-disciplined. Lower-class people, on the other hand, tend to have a strong present-orientation, are capricious, hedonistic, purposeless, and therefore unwilling to pursue a job or a career with any consistency. People with the former values therefore *tend* to have higher incomes and better jobs, and lower-class people *tend* to be poor,

[16] *The New York Times*, April 13, 1970.
[17] Nadine Brozan, in *The New York Times*, Feb. 14, 1972.

jobless, or on welfare. In short, the economic fortunes of people tend over the long run to be their own internal responsibility, rather than to be determined—as liberals always insist—by external factors. Thus, Banfield quotes Daniel Rosenblatt's findings on the lack of interest in medical care due to the "general lack of future orientation" among the urban poor:

For example, regular checkups of automobiles to detect incipient defects are not in the general value system of the urban poor. In similar fashion, household objects are often worn out and discarded rather than repaired at an early stage of disintegration. Installment buying is easily accepted without an awareness of the length of payments.

The body can be seen as simply another class of objects to be worn out but not repaired. Thus, teeth are left without dental care; later there is often small interest in dentures, whether free or not. In any event, false teeth may be little used. Corrective eye examinations, even for those people who wear glasses, are often neglected—regardless of clinic facilities. It is as though the middle class thinks of the body as a machine to be preserved and kept in perfect running order whether through prosthetic devices, rehabilitation, cosmetic surgery, or perpetual treatment, whereas the poor think of the body as having a limited span of utility: to be enjoyed in youth and then, with age and decrepitude, to be suffered and endured stoically.[18]

Banfield points out, furthermore, that lower-class death rates are, and have been for generations, far higher than for upper-class persons. Much of the differential is caused not by poverty or low incomes per se, as much as by the values or culture of the lower-class citizens. Thus, prominent and particularly lower-class causes of death are alcoholism, narcotics addiction, homicide, and venereal disease. Infant mortality has also been far higher among the lower classes, ranging up to two and three

---

[18] Daniel Rosenblatt, "Barriers to Medical Care for the Urban Poor," in A. Shostak and W. Gomberg, eds., *New Perspectives on Poverty* (Englewood Cliffs, N.J.: Prentice-Hall, 1965), pp. 72–73; quoted in Banfield, *The Unheavenly City*, pp. 286–87.

times that of the upper groups. That this is due to cultural values rather than to income level may be seen in Banfield's comparison of turn-of-the century Irish immigrants with Russian Jewish immigrants in New York City. The Irish immigrants were, in those days, generally present-minded and "lower-class" in attitudes, while the Russian Jews, though living in overcrowded tenements and on an income level probably lower than the Irish, were unusually future-minded, purposive, and "upper-class" in their values and attitudes. At the turn of the century, the life expectancy at the age of 10 of an Irish immigrant was only 38 years, whereas for the Russian Jewish immigrant it was more than 50 years. Furthermore, whereas in 1911–16, in a study of seven cities, the infant mortality rate was over three times as high for the lowest as compared to the highest income groups, the Jewish infant mortality rate was extremely low.[19]

As in illness or mortality, so in unemployment—which obviously has a close relation to both poverty and welfare. Banfield cites the findings of Professor Michael J. Piore on the essential "unemployability" of many or most of the persistently low-income unemployed. Piore discovered that their difficulty was not so much in finding or learning the skills for steady, well-paying jobs as in the lack of personal fibre in sticking to such jobs. These people are inclined to high absenteeism, leaving

---

[19] See Banfield, *op. cit.*, pp. 210–16, 303. Infant mortality comparisons can be found in O. W. Anderson, "Infant Mortality and Social and Cultural Factors: Historical Trends and Current Patterns," in E. G. Jaco, ed., *Patients, Physicians, and Illness* (New York: The Free Press, 1958), pp. 10–22; the seven cities study is in R. M. Woodbury, *Causal Factors in Infant Mortality: A Statistical Study Based on Investigation in Eight Cities*, U. S. Children's Bureau Publication #142 (Washington, D.C.: U. S. Govt. Printing Office, 1925), 1925), p. 157. On Irish and Jewish life expectancy see James J. Walsh, "Irish Mortality in New York and Pennsylvania," *Studies: An Irish Quarterly Review* (December 1921), p. 632. On the necessity for changing values and life styles in order to reduce infant mortality, see C. V. Willie and W. B. Rothney, "Racial, Ethnic and Income Factors in the Epidemiology of Neonatal Mortality," *American Sociological Review* (August 1962), p. 526.

their jobs without notice, being insubordinate, and sometimes stealing from the employer.[20] Furthermore, Peter Doeringer's study of the Boston "ghetto" labor market in 1968 found that about 70 percent of job applicants referred by neighborhood employment centers received job offers—but that over half of these offers were rejected, and of those accepted only about 40 percent of the new workers kept their jobs for as long as one month. Doeringer concluded: "Much of the ghetto unemployment appears to be a result of work instability rather than job scarcity." [21]

It is highly instructive to compare the descriptions of this common refusal of the lower-class unemployed to engage in steady work by the frostily disapproving Professor Banfield and by the highly approving leftist sociologist Alvin Gouldner. Banfield: "Men accustomed to a street-corner style of life, to living off women on welfare, and to 'hustling' are seldom willing to accept the dull routines of the 'good' job." [22] Pondering the lack of success of welfare workers in luring these men "away from a life of irresponsibility, sensuality, and freewheeling aggression," Gouldner proclaims that they judge the proferred bargain to be unattractive: "Give up promiscuous sex, give up freely expressed aggression, and wild spontaneity . . . and you, or your children, may be admitted to the world of three square meals a day, to a high school or perhaps even a college education, to the world of charge accounts, of secure jobs and respectability." [23] The interesting point is that from both ends

[20] Michael J. Piore, "Public and Private Responsibilities in On-the-Job Training of Disadvantaged Workers," M.I.T. Dept. of Economics Working Paper #23, June 1968. Cited in Banfield, *op. cit.*, pp. 105, 285.

[21] Peter B. Doeringer, *Ghetto Labor Markets—Problems and Programs*, Harvard Institute of Economic Research, Discussion Paper #33, June 1968, p. 9; quoted in Banfield, *op. cit.*, pp. 112, 285–86.

[22] Banfield, *op. cit.*, p. 105. Also *Ibid.*, p. 112.

[23] Alvin W. Gouldner, "The Secrets of Organizations," in *The Social Welfare Forum*, Proceedings of the National Conference on Social Welfare (New York: Columbia University Press, 1963), p. 175; quoted in Banfield, *op. cit.*, pp. 221–22, 305.

of the ideological spectrum both Banfield and Gouldner agree on the essential nature of this process, despite their contrasting value judgments on it: that much of persistent lower-class unemployment, and hence poverty, is voluntary on the part of the unemployed themselves.

Gouldner's attitude is typical of liberals and leftists in the present day: that it is shameful to try to foist, even noncoercively, "bourgeois" or "middle-class values" on the gloriously spontaneous and "natural" lower-class culture. Fair enough, perhaps; but then don't expect—or call upon—those same hard-working bourgeoisie to be coerced into supporting and subsidizing those very parasitic values of idleness and irresponsibility which they abhor—and which are clearly dysfunctional for the survival of any society. If people wish to be "spontaneous," let them do so on their own time and with their own resources, and let them then take the consequences of this decision, and not use State coercion to force the hard-working and "unspontaneous" to bear those consequences instead. In short, abolish the welfare system.

If the major problem with the lower-class poor is irresponsible present-mindedness, and if it takes the inculcation of "bourgeois" future-minded values to get people off welfare and dependency (*pace* the Mormons), then at the very least these values should be encouraged and not discouraged in society. The left-liberal attitudes of social workers discourage the poor directly by fostering the idea of welfare as a "right" and as a moral claim upon production. Furthermore, the easy availability of the welfare check obviously promotes present-mindedness, unwillingness to work, and irresponsibility among the recipients —thus perpetuating the vicious cycle of poverty-welfare. As Banfield puts it, "there is perhaps no better way to make converts to present-mindedness than to give a generous welfare check to everyone." [24]

Generally, in their attacks on the welfare system conserva-

---

[24] Banfield, *op. cit.*, p. 221.

tives have focussed on the ethical and moral evils of coercively mulcting the taxpayers to support the idle, while the leftist critics have concentrated on the demoralization of the welfare "clients" through their dependency on the largesse of the State and its bureaucracy. Actually, both sets of criticisms are right; there is no contradiction between them. We have seen that voluntary programs such as those of the Mormon Church are keenly alive to this problem. And in fact, earlier laissez-faire critics of the dole were just as concerned with the demoralization as with the coercion over those forced to pay for welfare.

Thus, the nineteenth-century English laissez-faire advocate Thomas Mackay declared that welfare reform "consists in a re-creation and development of the arts of independence." He called "not for more philanthropy, but rather for more respect for the dignity of human life, and more faith in its ability to work out its own salvation." And Mackay poured his scorn on the advocates of greater welfare, on "the vicarious philanthropist who, in a reckless race after a cheap popularity, uses the rate [tax] extorted from his neighbors to multiply the occasions of stumbling set before the . . . crowd who are only too ready to fall into dependence. . . ." [25] Mackay added that the "legal endowment of destitution" implied by the welfare system "introduces a most dangerous and at times demoralising influence into our social arrangements. Its real necessity is by no means proved. Its apparent necessity arises mainly from the fact that the system has created its own dependent population." [26] Elaborating on the theme of dependence, Mackay observed that "the bitterest element in the distress of the poor arises, not from mere poverty, but from the feeling of dependence which must of necessity be an ingredient in every measure of public relief. This feeling cannot be removed, but is rather intensified by liberal measures of public relief." [27]

Mackay concluded that "the only way in which the legislator

[25] Thomas Mackay, *Methods of Social Reform* (London: John Murray, 1896), p. 13.
[26] *Ibid.*, pp. 38–39.
[27] *Ibid.*, pp. 259–60.

or the administrator can promote the reduction of pauperism is by abolishing or restricting the legal endowments provided for pauperism. The country can have, there is no doubt of it, exactly as many paupers as it chooses to pay for. Abolish or restrict that endowment . . . and new agencies are called into activity, man's natural capacity for independence, the natural ties of relationship and friendship, and under this head I would include private as distinguished from public charity. . . ." [28]

The Charity Organisation Society, England's leading private charity agency in the late nineteenth century, operated precisely on this principle of aid to foster self-help. As Mowat, the historian of the Society notes: "The C.O.S. embodied an idea of charity which claimed to reconcile the divisions in society, to remove poverty and to produce a happy, self-reliant community. It believed that the most serious aspect of poverty was the degradation of the character of the poor man or woman. Indiscriminate charity only made things worse; it demoralised. True charity demanded friendship, thought, the sort of help that would restore a man's self-respect and his ability to support himself and his family." [29]

Perhaps one of the grimmest consequences of welfare is that it actively discourages self-help by crippling the financial incentive for rehabilitation. It has been estimated that, on the average, every dollar invested by handicapped persons in their own rehabilitation brings them from $10 to $17 in the present value of increased future earnings. But this incentive is crippled by the fact that, by becoming rehabilitated, they will lose their welfare relief, social security disability payments, and workmen's compensation. As a result, most of the disabled decide not to invest in their own rehabilitation. [30] Many people, moreover, are by now familiar with the crippling disincentive

[28] *Ibid.*, pp. 268–69.

[29] Mowat, *op. cit.*, pp. 1–2.

[30] Estelle James, "Review of *The Economics of Vocational Rehabilitation*," *American Economic Review* (June 1966), p. 642; also see Yale Brozen, "Welfare Without the Welfare State," *The Freeman* (December 1966), pp. 50–51.

effects of the social security system, which—in glaring contrast to all private insurance funds—cuts off payments if the recipient should be brazen enough to work and earn an income after age 62.

In these days, when most people look askance at population growth, few antipopulationists have focussed on another unfortunate effect of the welfare system: Since welfare families are paid proportionately to the number of their children, the system provides an important subsidy for the production of more children. Furthermore, the people being induced to have more children are precisely those who can afford it least; the result can only be to perpetuate their dependence on welfare, and, in fact, to develop generations who are permanently dependent on the welfare dole.

Burdens and Subsidies of the Welfare State

Does the modern welfare state really help the poor? The commonly held notion, the idea that has propelled the welfare state and maintained it in being, is that the welfare state redistributes income and wealth from the rich to the poor: the progressive tax system takes money from the rich while numerous welfare and other services distribute the money to the poor. But even liberals, the great advocates and abettors of the welfare state, are beginning to realize that every part and aspect of this idea is merely a cherished myth. Government contracts, notably of the military, funnel tax funds into the pockets of favored corporations and well-paid industrial workers. Minimum wage laws tragically generate unemployment, especially so among the poorest and least-skilled or educated workers— in the South, among teen-age Negroes in the ghettoes, and among the vocationally handicapped. Because a minimum wage, of course, does not guarantee any worker's employment; it only prohibits, by force of law, anyone from being employed at the wage which would pay his employer to hire him. It therefore compels unemployment. Economists have demonstrated that raises in the federal minimum wage have created the well-known Negro-white teen-age employment gap, and have driven the rate of male Negro teen-age unemployment from an early postwar rate of about 8 percent to what is now well over 35 percent—an unemployment rate among teen-age Negroes that is far more catastrophic than the massive general unemployment rate of the 1930s (20–25 percent.)[31]

We have already seen how state higher education redistributes income from poorer to wealthier citizens. A host of government licensing restrictions, permeating occupation after occupation, exclude poorer and less skilled workers from these jobs. It is becoming recognized that urban renewal programs, supposedly designed to aid the slum housing of the poor, in fact demolish their housing and force the poor into more crowded and less available housing, all for the benefit of wealthier subsidized tenants, construction unions, favored real estate developers, and downtown business interests. Unions, once the pampered favorites of liberals, are now generally seen to use their governmental privileges to exclude poorer and minority-group workers. Farm price supports, jacked ever higher by the federal government, mulct the taxpayers in order to push food prices higher and higher, thereby injuring particularly the poor consumers and helping—*not* poor farmers, but the wealthy farmers commanding a large amount of acreage. (Since farmers are paid per pound or per bushel of product, the support program largely benefits the wealthy farmers; in fact, since farmers are often paid *not* to produce, the resulting taking of acreage out of production causes severe unemployment among the poorest segment of the farm population—the farm tenants and farm workers.) Zoning laws in the burgeoning suburbs of the United States serve to keep out the poorer citizens by legal coercion, very often Negroes who are attempting to move out of the inner cities to follow increasing job opportunities in the suburbs. The

[31] Among numerous studies, see Yale Brozen and Milton Friedman, *The Minimum Wage: Who Pays?* (Washington, D.C.: Free Society Association, April 1966); and John M. Peterson and Charles T. Stewart, Jr., *Employment Effects of Minimum Wage Rates* (Washington, D.C.: American Enterprise Institute, August 1969).

U.S. Postal Service charges high monopoly rates on the first-class mail used by the general public in order to subsidize the distribution of newspapers and magazines. The FHA subsidizes the mortgages of well-to-do homeowners. The Federal Bureau of Reclamation subsidizes irrigation water to well-to-do farmers in the West, thereby depriving the urban poor of water and forcing them to pay higher water charges. The Rural Electrification Administration and the Tennessee Valley Authority subsidize electric service to well-to-do farmers, suburbanites, and corporations. As Professor Brozen sardonically observes: "Electricity for poverty-stricken corporations such as the Aluminum Corporation of America and the DuPont Company is subsidized by the tax-free status of the Tennessee Valley Authority (27 percent of the price of electricity goes to pay the taxes imposed on privately operated utilities)." [32] And the government regulation monopolizes and cartelizes much of industry, thereby driving up prices to consumers and restricting production, competitive alternatives, or improvements in products (e.g., railroad regulation, public utility regulation, airline regulation, oil proration laws). Thus, the Civil Aeronautics Board allocates airline routes to favored companies and keeps out and even drives out of business smaller competitors. State and federal oil proration laws provide for absolute maximum limits on crude oil production, thereby driving up oil prices, prices that are further kept up by import restrictions. And government throughout the country grants an absolute monopoly in each area to gas, electric, and telephone companies, thus protecting them from competition, and sets their rates in order to guarantee them a fixed profit. Everywhere and in every area the story is the same: a systematic mulcting of the mass of the population by the "welfare state." [33]

---

[32] Brozen, "Welfare Without the Welfare State," pp. 48–49.

[33] In addition to Brozen, *op. cit.*, see Yale Brozen, "The Untruth of the Obvious," *The Freeman* (June 1968), pp. 328–40. See also Yale Brozen, "The Revival of Traditional Liberalism," *New Individualist Review* (Spring, 1965), pp. 3–12; Sam Peltzman, "CAB: Freedom from Competition," *New Individualist Review* (Spring, 1963), pp. 16–23; Martin Ander-

Most people believe that the American tax system basically taxes the rich far more than it taxes the poor and is therefore a method of redistributing income from higher to lower income classes. (There are, of course, many *other* kinds of redistribution, e.g., from the taxpayers to Lockheed or General Dynamics.) But even the federal income tax, which everybody assumes to be "progressive" (taxing the rich far more than the poor, with the middle classes in between), does not really work that way when we take into account other aspects of this tax. For example, the social security tax is blatantly and starkly "regressive," since it is a soak-the-poor-and-middle-class tax: a person making the base income ($8,000) pays fully as much social security tax—and the amount is rising every year—as someone making $1,000,000 a year. Capital gains, mostly accruing to wealthy stockholders and owners of real estate, pay far less than income taxes; private trusts and foundations are tax exempt, and interest earned on state and municipal government bonds are also exempt from the federal income tax. We wind up with the following estimate of what percentage of income is paid, overall, by each "income class" in federal taxes:

1965

Income Classes	Percent of Income Paid in Federal Tax
Under $2,000	19
$2,000–$4,000	16
$4,000–$6,000	17
$6,000–$8,000	17
$8,000–$10,000	18
$10,000–$15,000	19
Over $15,000	32
AVERAGE	22

If federal taxes are scarcely "progressive," the impact of state and local taxes is almost fiercely regressive. Property taxes are

---

son, *The Federal Bulldozer* (Cambridge: MIT Press, 1964). An introduction to the oil price story is Hendrik S. Houthakker, "No Use for Controls," *Barrons* (Nov. 8, 1971), pp. 7–8.

(a) proportional, (b) hit only owners of real estate, and (c) depend on the political vagaries of local assessors. Sales and excise taxes hit the poor more than anyone else. The following is the estimate of the percentage of income extracted, overall, by state and local taxes:

1965

Income Classes	Percent of Income Paid in State and Local Taxes
Under $2,000	25
$2,000–$4,000	11
$4,000–$6,000	10
$6,000–$8,000	9
$8,000–$10,000	9
$10,000–$15,000	9
Over $15,000	7
AVERAGE	9

Following are the combined estimates for the total impact of taxation—federal, state, and local—on income classes:

1965

Income Classes	Percent of Income Paid in All Taxes [34]
Under $2,000	44
$2,000–$4,000	27
$4,000–$6,000	27
$6,000–$8,000	26
$8,000–$10,000	27
$10,000–$15,000	27
Over $15,000	38
AVERAGE	31

Still more recent (1968) estimates of the total impact of taxes on all levels of government amply confirm the above, while also showing a far greater relative rise in the three years of the tax burden on the lowest income groups:

[34] For the estimates, see Joseph A. Pechman, "The Rich, the Poor, and the Taxes they Pay," *Public Interest* (Fall, 1969), p. 33.

1968

Income Classes	Percent of Income Paid in All Taxes [35]
Under $2,000	50
$2,000–$4,000	35
$4,000–$6,000	31
$6,000–$8,000	30
$8,0000–$10,000	29
$10,000–$15,000	30
$15,000–$25,000	30
$25,000–$50,000	33
$50,000 and over	45

Many economists try to mitigate the impact of these telltale figures by saying that the people in the "Under $2,000" category, for example, receive more in welfare and other "transfer" payments than they pay out in taxes; but of course this ignores the vital fact that the *same* people in each category are *not* the welfare receivers *and* the taxpayers. The latter group is socked heavily in order to subsidize the former. In short, the poor (and the middle class) are taxed in order to pay for the subsidized public housing of *other* poor—*and* middle-income groups. And it is the working poor who are socked a staggering amount to pay for the subsidies of the welfare poor.

There is plenty of income redistribution in this country: to Lockheed, to welfare recipients, and so on and on . . . , but the "rich" are not being taxed to pay for the "poor." The redistribution is *within* income categories; some poor are forced to pay for other poor.

Other tax estimates confirm this chilling picture. The Tax Foundation, for example, estimates that federal, state, and local taxes extract 34 percent of the overall income of those who make less than $3,000 a year.[86]

[35] R. A. Herriott and H. P. Miller, "The Taxes We Pay," *The Conference Board Record* (May 1971), p. 40.

[86] See William Chapman, "Study Shows Taxes Hit Poor," *New York Post* (February 10, 1971), p. 46; *U.S. News* (December 9, 1968); Rod Manis, *Poverty: A Libertarian View* (Los Angeles: Rampart College, n.d.); Yale Brozen, "Welfare Without the Welfare State," *op. cit.*

The object of this discussion is not, of course, to advocate a "really" progressive income tax structure, a real soaking of the rich, but to point out that the modern welfare state, highly touted as soaking the rich to subsidize the poor, does no such thing. In fact, soaking the rich would have disastrous effects, not just for the rich but for the poor and middle classes themselves. For it is the rich who provide a proportionately greater amount of saving, investment capital, entrepreneurial foresight, and financing of technological innovation that has brought the United States to by far the highest standard of living—for the mass of the people—of any country in history. Soaking the rich would not only be profoundly immoral, it would drastically penalize the very virtues: thrift, business foresight, and investment, that have brought about our remarkable standard of living. It would truly be killing the goose that lays the golden eggs.

What Can Government Do?

What, then, *can* the government do to help the poor? The only correct answer is also the libertarian answer: Get out of the way. Let the government get out of the way of the productive energies of all groups in the population, rich, middle class, and poor alike, and the result will be an enormous increase in the welfare and the standard of living of everyone, and most particularly of the poor who are the ones supposedly helped by the miscalled "welfare state."

There are four major ways in which the government can get out of the way of the American people. First, it can abolish— or at the very least drastically reduce—the level of all taxation, taxation which cripples productive energies, savings, investment, and technological advance. In fact, the creation of jobs and increase of wage rates resulting from abolishing these taxes would benefit the lower-income groups *more* than anyone else. As Professor Brozen points out: "With less attempt to use state power to compress the inequality in the distribution of income, inequality would diminish more rapidly. Low wage rates would rise more rapidly with a higher rate of saving and capital formation, and inequality would diminish with the rise in income of wage earners." [37] The best way to help the poor is to slash taxes and allow savings, investment, and creation of jobs to proceed unhampered. As Dr. F. A. Harper pointed out years ago, productive investment is the "greatest economic charity." Wrote Harper:

According to one view, sharing a crust of bread is advocated as the method of charity. The other advocates savings and tools for the production of additional loaves of bread, which is the greatest economic charity.

The two views are in conflict because the two methods are mutually exclusive in absorbing one's time and means in all the choices he makes day by day. . . .

The reason for the difference in view really stems from different concepts about the nature of the economic world. The former view stems from the belief that the total of economic goods is a constant. The latter view is built on the belief that expansion in production is possible without any necessary limit.

The difference between the two views is like the difference between a two- and three-dimensional perspective of production. The two-dimensional size is fixed at any instant of time, but the third dimension and therefore the size of the total is expandable without limit by savings and tools. . . .

All the history of mankind denies that there is a fixed total of economic goods. History further reveals that savings and expansion of tools constitute the only way to any appreciable increase." [38]

The libertarian writer Isabel Paterson put the case eloquently:

As between the private philanthropist and the private capitalist acting as such, take the case of the truly needy man, who is not in-

[37] Brozen, "Welfare Without the Welfare State," p. 47.
[38] F. A. Harper, "The Greatest Economic Charity," in M. Sennholz, ed., *On Freedom and Free Enterprise* (Princeton, N. J.: D. Van Nostrand, 1956), p. 106.

capacitated, and suppose that the philanthropist gives him food and clothes and shelter—when he has used them, he is just where he was before, except that he may have acquired the habit of dependence. But suppose someone with no benevolent motive whatever, simply wanting work done for his own reasons, should hire the needy man for a wage. The employer has not done a good deed. Yet the condition of the employed man has actually been changed. What is the vital difference between the two actions?

It is that the unphilanthropic employer has brought the man he employed *back into the production line*, on the great circuit of energy; whereas the philanthropist can only divert energy in such manner that there can be no return into production, and therefore less likelihood of the object of his benefaction finding employment. . . .

If the full roll of *sincere* philanthropists were called, from the beginning of time, it would be found that all of them together by their strictly philanthropic activities have never conferred upon humanity one-tenth of the benefit derived from the normally self-interested efforts of Thomas Alva Edison, to say nothing of the greater minds who worked out the scientific principles which Edison applied. Innumerable speculative thinkers, inventors, and organizers, have contributed to the comfort, health, and happiness of their fellow men—because that was not their objective.[39]

Secondly, and as a corollary to a drastic reduction or abolition of taxation would come an equivalent reduction in government expenditures. No longer would scarce economic resources be siphoned off into wasteful and unproductive expenditures: into the multibillion dollar space program, public works, the military-industrial complex, or whatever. Instead, these resources would be available to produce goods and services desired by the mass of the consuming population. The outpouring of goods and services would provide new and better goods to the consumers at far lower prices. No longer would we suffer the inefficiencies and the injury to productivity of government sub-

[39] Isabel Paterson, *The God of the Machine* (New York: G. P. Putnam's Sons, 1943), pp. 248–50.

sidies and contracts. Furthermore, the diversion of most of the nation's scientists and engineers to wasteful military and other governmental research and expenditure would be released for peaceful and productive activities and inventions benefitting the nation's consumers.[40]

Thirdly, if the government also cut out the numerous ways in which it taxes the poorer to subsidize the wealthier, such as we have named above (higher education, farm subsidies, irrigation, Lockheed, etc.), this in itself would stop the government's deliberate exactions upon the poor. By ceasing to tax the poorer in order to subsidize the richer, the government would aid the poor by removing its burdens from their productive activity.

Finally, one of the most significant ways in which the government could aid the poor is by removing its own direct roadblocks from their productive energies. Thus, minimum wage laws disemploy the poorest and least productive members of the population. Government privileges to trade unions enable them to keep the poorer and minority-group workers from productive and high-wage employment. And licensing laws, the outlawing of gambling, and other government restrictions prevent the poor from starting small businesses and creating jobs on their own. Thus, the government has everywhere clamped onerous restrictions on peddling, ranging from outright prohibition to heavy license fees. Peddling was the classic path by which immigrants, poor and lacking capital, were able to become entrepreneurs and eventually to become big businessmen. But now this route has been cut off—largely to confer monopoly privileges on each city's retail stores, who fear that they would lose profits if faced with the highly mobile competition of street peddlers.

Typical of how government has frustrated the productive

---

[40] On the massive diversion of scientists and engineers to government in recent years, see H. L. Nieburg, *In the Name of Science* (Chicago: Quadrangle, 1966); on the inefficiencies and misallocations of the military-industrial complex, see Seymour Melman, ed., *The War Economy of the United States* (New York: St. Martin's Press, 1971).

activities of the poor is the case of the neurosurgeon Dr.
Thomas Matthew, founder of the black self-help organization
NEGRO, which floats bonds to finance its operations. In the
mid-1960s, Dr. Matthew, over the opposition of the New York
City government, established a successful interracial hospital in
the black section of Jamaica, Queens. He soon found, however,
that public transportation in Jamaica was so abysmal that
transportation service was totally inadequate for the hospital's
patients and staff. Finding bus service inadequate, Dr. Matthew
purchased a few busses and established a regular bus service in
Jamaica, service that was regular, efficient, and successful. The
problem was that Dr. Matthew did not have a city license to
operate a bus line—that privilege is reserved to inefficient but
protected monopolies. The ingenious Dr. Matthew, discovering
that the city did not allow any unlicensed busses to charge fares,
made his bus service free, except that any riders who wished
could buy a 25¢ company bond instead whenever they rode
the busses.

So successful was the Matthew bus service that he proceeded
to establish another bus line in Harlem; but it was at this point,
in early 1968, that the New York City government took fright
and cracked down. The government went to court and put both
lines out of business for operating without licenses.

A few years later, Dr. Matthew and his colleagues seized an
unused building in Harlem owned by the city government.
(The New York City government is the city's biggest "slum-
lord," owning as it does a vast amount of useful buildings abandoned because of nonpayment of high property taxes and rot-
ting away, rendered useless and uninhabitable.) In this building, Dr. Matthew established a low-cost hospital—at a time of
soaring hospital costs and scarcity of hospital space. The city
has tried its best to put this hospital, too, out of business, claiming "fire violations." Again and again, in area after area, the
role of government has been to thwart the economic activities
of the poor. It is no wonder that when Dr. Matthew was asked
by a white official of the New York City government how it

could best aid Negro self-help projects, Matthew replied: "Get out of our way, and let us try something."

Another example of how government functions occurred a few years ago, when the federal and New York City governments loudly proclaimed that they would rehabilitate a group of thirty-seven buildings in Harlem. But instead of following the usual practice of private industry and awarding rehabilitation contracts on each house individually, the government instead awarded one contract on the entire thirty-seven building package. By doing so, the government made sure that small, black-owned construction firms would not be able to bid, and so the prize contract naturally went to a large white-owned company. Still another example: In 1966, the federal Small Business Administration proudly proclaimed a program for encouraging new black-owned small business. But the government put certain key restrictions on its loans. First, it decided that any borrower must be "at the poverty level." Now since the very poor are not apt to be setting up their own businesses, this restriction ruled out many small businesses by owners with moderately low incomes—just the ones likely to be small entrepreneurs. To top this, the New York SBA added a further restriction: All blacks seeking such loans must "prove a real need in their community" for filling a recognizable "economic void"—the need and the void to be proved to the satisfaction of remote bureaucrats far from the actual economic scene.[41]

A fascinating gauge of whether or to what extent government is helping or hurting the poor in the "welfare state" is provided by a recent unpublished study by the Institute for Policy Studies of Washington, D.C. An inquiry was made on the estimated flow of government money (federal and district) *into* the low-income Negro ghetto of Shaw-Cardozo in Washington, D.C., as compared to the *outflow* that the area pays in taxes to the government. In fiscal 1967, the Shaw-

---

[41] On the Matthew and Small Business Administration cases, see Jane Jacobs, *The Economy of Cities* (New York: Random House, 1969), pp. 225–28.

Cardozo area had a population of 84,000 (of whom 79,000 were black) with a median family income of $5,600 per year. Total earned personal income for the residents of the area for that year amounted to $126.5 million. The value of total government benefits flowing into the district (ranging from welfare payments to the estimated expenditure on public schools) during fiscal 1967 was estimated at $45.7 million. A generous subsidy, amounting to almost 40 percent of total Shaw-Cardozo income? Perhaps, but against this we have to offset the total outflow of taxes from Shaw-Cardozo, best estimated at $50.0 million—a net *outflow* from this low-income ghetto of $4.3 million! Can it still be maintained that abolition of the entire massive, unproductive welfare state structure would hurt the poor? [42]

Government could then best help the poor—and the rest of society—by getting out of the way: by removing its vast and crippling network of taxes, subsidies, inefficiencies, and monopoly privileges. As Professor Brozen summed up his analysis of the "welfare state":

The state has typically been a device for producing affluence for a few at the expense of many. The market has produced affluence for many with little cost even to a few. The state has not changed its ways since Roman days of bread and circuses for the masses, even though it now pretends to provide education and medicine as well as free milk and performing arts. It still is the source of monopoly privilege and power for the few behind its facade of providing welfare for the many—welfare which would be more abundant if politicians would not expropriate the means they use to provide the illusion that they care about their constituents. [43]

---

[42] Data adapted from an unpublished study by Earl F. Mellor, "Public Goods and Services: Costs and Benefits, A Study of the Shaw-Cardozo Area of Washington, D.C." (presented to the Institute for Policy Studies, Washington, D.C., October 31, 1969).

[43] Brozen, "Welfare Without the Welfare State," p. 52.

The Negative Income Tax

Unfortunately, the recent trend—embraced by a wide spectrum of advocates (with unimportant modifications) from President Nixon to Milton Friedman on the right to a large number on the left—is to abolish the current welfare system *not* in the direction of freedom but toward its very opposite. This new trend is the "guaranteed annual income" or "negative income tax," or President Nixon's "Family Assistance Plan." Citing the inefficiencies, inequities, and red tape of the present system, the guaranteed annual income would make the dole easy, "efficient," and automatic: The income tax authorities will pay money each year to families earning below a certain base income—this automatic dole to be financed, of course, by taxing working families making *more* than the base amount. Estimated costs of this seemingly neat and simple scheme are supposed to be only a few billion dollars per year.

But there is an extremely important catch: the costs are estimated *on the assumption* that everyone—the people on the universal dole as well as those financing it—will continue to work to the same extent as before. But this assumption begs the question. For the chief problem is the enormously crippling disincentive effect the guaranteed annual income will have on taxpayer and recipient alike.

The one element that saves the present welfare system from being an utter disaster is precisely the red tape and the stigma involved in going on welfare. The welfare recipient still bears a psychic stigma, even though weakened in recent years, and he still has to face a typically inefficient, impersonal, and tangled bureaucracy. But the guaranteed annual income, *precisely* by making the dole efficient, easy, and automatic, will remove the major obstacles, the major disincentives, to the "supply function" for welfare, and will lead to a massive flocking to the guaranteed dole. Moreover, everyone will now consider the new dole as an automatic "right" rather than as a privilege or gift, and all stigma will be removed.

Suppose, for example, that $4,000 per year is declared the "poverty line," and that everyone earning income below that line receives the difference from Uncle Sam automatically as a result of filling out his income tax return. Those making zero income will receive $4,000 from the government, those making $3,000 will get $1,000, and so on. It seems clear that there will be no real reason for *anyone* making less than $4,000 a year to keep on working. Why should he, when his nonworking neighbor will wind up with the same income as himself? In short, the net income from working will then be zero, and the entire working population below the magic $4,000 line will quit work and flock to its "rightful" dole.

But this is not all; what of the people making either $4,000, or slightly or even moderately above that line? The man making $4,500 a year will soon find that the lazy slob next door who refuses to work will be getting his $4,000 a year from the federal government; his own *net* income from 40 hours a week of hard work will be only $500 a year. So he will quit work and go on the negative-tax dole. The same will undoubtedly hold true for those making $5,000 a year, etc.

The baleful process is not over. As all the people making below $4,000 and even considerably above $4,000 leave work and go on the dole, the total dole payments will skyrocket enormously, and they can only be financed by taxing *more* heavily the higher income folk who will continue to work. But then *their* net, after-tax incomes will fall sharply, until many of *them* will quit work and go on the dole too. Let us contemplate the man making $6,000 a year. He is, at the outset, faced with a net income from working of only $2,000, and if he has to pay, let us say, $500 a year to finance the dole of the nonworkers, his net after-tax income will be only $1,500 a year. If he then has to pay *another* $1,000 to finance the rapid expansion of others on the dole, his net income will fall to $500 and he will go on the dole Thus, the logical conclusion of the guaranteed annual income will be a vicious spiral into disaster, heading toward the logical and impossible goal of virtually no one working, and everyone on the dole.

In addition to all this, there are some important extra considerations. In practice, of course, the dole, once set at $4,000, will not remain there; irresistible pressure by welfare clients and other pressure groups will inexorably raise the base level every year, thereby bringing the vicious spiral and economic disaster that much closer. In practice, too, the guaranteed annual income will *not*, as in the hopes of its conservative advocates, *replace* the existing patchwork welfare system; it will simply be added *on top of* the existing programs. This, for example, is precisely what happened to the states' old-age relief programs. The major talking point of the New Deal's federal social security program was that it would efficiently *replace* the then existing patchwork old-age relief programs of the states. In practice, of course, it did no such thing, and old-age relief is far higher now than it was in the 1930s. An ever-rising social security structure was simply placed on top of existing programs. In practice, finally, President Nixon's sop to conservatives that able-bodied recipients of the new dole would be forced to work is a patent phony. They would, for one thing, only have to find "suitable" work, and it is the universal experience of state unemployment relief agencies that almost no "suitable" jobs are ever found.[44]

The various schemes for a guaranteed annual income are no genuine replacement for the universally acknowledged evils of the welfare system; they would only plunge us still more deeply into those evils. The only workable solution is the libertarian one: the abolition of the welfare dole in favor of freedom and voluntary action for all persons, rich and poor alike.

[44] For a brilliant critique of the guaranteed annual income, negative income tax, and Nixon schemes, see Hazlitt, *Man vs. the Welfare State*, pp. 62–100. Also see Hazlitt, "The Coming Crisis in Welfare," *National Review* (April, 18, 1967), pp. 416–18.

9

The Public Sector,
I: Government
in Business

PEOPLE TEND TO FALL into habits and into unquestioned ruts, especially in the field of government. On the market, in society in general, we expect and accommodate rapidly to change, to the unending marvels and improvements of our civilization. New products, new life styles, new ideas are often embraced eagerly. But in the area of government we follow blindly in the path of centuries, content to believe that whatever has been must be right. In particular, government, in the United States and elsewhere, for centuries and seemingly from time immemorial has been supplying us with certain essential and necessary services, services which nearly everyone concedes are important: defense (including army, police, judicial, and legal), firefighting, streets and roads, water, sewage and garbage disposal, postal service, etc. So identified has the State become in the public mind with the provision of these services that an attack on State financing *appears* to many people as an attack on the service itself. Thus if one maintains that the State should not supply court services, and that private enterprise on the market could supply such service more efficiently as well as more morally, people tend to think of this as denying the importance of courts themselves.

The libertarian who wants to replace government by private enterprises in the above areas is thus treated in the same way as he would be if the government had, for various reasons, been supplying shoes as a tax-financed monopoly from time immemorial. If the government and only the government had had a monopoly of the shoe manufacturing and retailing business, how would most of the public treat the libertarian who now came along to advocate that the government get out of the shoe business and throw it open to private enterprise? He would undoubtedly be treated as follows: people would cry, "How could you? You are opposed to the public, and to poor people, wearing shoes! And *who* would supply shoes to the public if the government got out of the business? Tell us that! Be constructive! It's easy to be negative and smart-alecky about government; but tell us *who* would supply shoes? Which people? How many shoe stores would be available in each city and town? How would the shoe firms be capitalized? How many brands would there be? What material would they use? What lasts? What would be the pricing arrangements for shoes? Wouldn't regulation of the shoe industry be needed to see to it that the product is sound? And who would supply the poor with shoes? Suppose a poor person didn't have the money to buy a pair?"

These questions, ridiculous as they seem to be and are with regard to the shoe business, are just as absurd when applied to the libertarian who advocates a free market in fire, police, postal service, or any other government operation. The point is that the advocate of a free market in *anything* cannot provide a "constructive" blueprint of such a market in advance. The essence and the glory of the free market is that individual firms and businesses, competing on the market, provide an ever-changing orchestration of efficient and progressive goods and services: continually improving products and markets, advancing technology, cutting costs, and meeting changing consumer demands as swiftly and as efficiently as possible. The libertarian economist can try to offer a few guidelines on how markets *might* develop where they are now prevented or restricted from developing; but he can do little more than point the way toward freedom, to call for government to get out of the way of the productive and ever-inventive energies of the public as expressed in voluntary market activity. No one can predict the number of firms, the size of each firm, the pricing policies, etc., of any future market in any service or commodity. We just know—by economic theory and by historical insight—that such a free market will do the job infinitely better than the compulsory monopoly of bureaucratic government.

How will the poor pay for defense, fire protection, postal service, etc., can basically be answered by the counter-question: how do the poor pay for *anything* they now obtain on the market? The difference is that we know that the free private market will supply these goods and services far more cheaply, in greater abundance, and of far higher quality than monopoly government does today. Everyone in society would benefit, and *especially* the poor. And we also know that the mammoth tax burden to finance these and other activities would be lifted from the shoulders of everyone in society, including the poor.

We have seen above that the universally acknowledged pressing problems of our society are all wrapped up in government operations. We have also seen that the enormous social conflicts entwined in the public school system would all disappear when each group of parents was allowed to finance and support whichever education it preferred for their children. The grave inefficiencies and the intense conflicts are all inherent in government operation. If the government, for example, provides monopoly services (e.g., in education or in water supply), then whichever decisions the government makes are coercively imposed on the hapless minority—whether it is a question of educational policies for the schools (integration or segregation, progressive or traditional, religious or secular, etc.), or even for the kind of water to be sold (e.g., fluoridated or unfluoridated).

It should be clear that no such fierce arguments occur where each group of consumers can purchase the goods or services they demand. There are no battles between consumers, for example, over what kind of newspapers should be printed, churches established, books printed, records marketed, or automobiles manufactured. Whatever is produced on the market reflects the diversity as well as the strength of consumer demand.

On the free market, in short, the consumer is king, and any business firm that wants to make profits and avoid losses tries its best to serve the consumer as efficiently and at as low a cost as possible. In a government operation, in contrast, everything changes. *Inherent in all government operation is a grave and fatal split between service and payment*, between the providing of a service and the payment for receiving it. The government bureau does not get its income as does the private firm, from serving the consumer well or from consumer purchases of its products exceeding its costs of operation. No, the government bureau acquires its income from mulcting the long-suffering taxpayer. Its operations therefore become inefficient, and costs zoom, since government bureaus need not worry about losses or bankruptcy; they can make up their losses by additional extractions from the public till. Furthermore, the consumer, instead of being courted and wooed for his favor, becomes a mere annoyance to the government, someone who is "wasting" the *government's* scarce resources. In government operations, the consumer is treated like an unwelcome intruder, an interference in the quiet enjoyment by the bureaucrat of his steady income.

Thus, if consumer demand should increase for the goods or services of any private business, the private firm is delighted; it woos and welcomes the new business and expands its operations eagerly to fill the new orders. Government, in contrast, generally meets this situation by sourly urging or even ordering consumers to "buy" less, and allows shortages to develop, along with deterioration in the quality of its service. Thus, the increased consumer use of government streets in the cities is met by aggravated traffic congestion and by continuing denunciations and threats against people who drive their own cars. The New York City administration, for example, is continually threatening to outlaw the use of private cars in Manhattan, where congestion has been most troublesome. It is only government, of course, that would ever think of bludgeoning consumers in this way; it is only government that has the audacity to "solve" traffic congestion by forcing private cars (or trucks or taxis or whatever) off the road. According to this principle, of course, the "ideal" solution to traffic congestion is simply to outlaw all vehicles!

But this sort of attitude toward the consumer is not confined to traffic on the streets. New York City, for example, has suffered periodically from a water "shortage." Here is a situation where, for many years, the city government has had a compulsory monopoly of the supply of water to its citizens. Failing to supply enough water, and failing to price that water in such a way as to clear the market, to equate supply and demand (which private enterprise does automatically), New York's response to water shortages has always been to blame *not* itself, but the consumer, whose sin has been to use "too much" water. The city administration could only react by outlawing the sprinkling of lawns, restricting use of water, and demanding that people drink less water. In this way, government transfers its own failings to the scapegoat user, who is threatened and bludgeoned instead of being served well and efficiently.

There has been similar response by government to the ever-accelerating crime problem in New York City. Instead of providing efficient police protection, the city's reaction has been to force the innocent citizen to stay out of crime-prone areas. Thus, after Central Park in Manhattan became a notorious center for muggings and other crime in the night hours, New York City's "solution" to the problem was to impose a curfew, banning use of the park in those hours. In short, if an innocent citizen wants to stay in Central Park at night, it is he who is arrested for disobeying the curfew; it is, of course, easier to arrest him than to rid the park of crime.

In short, while the long-held motto of private enterprise is that "the customer is always right," the implicit maxim of government operation is that the customer is always to be blamed.

Of course, the political bureaucrats have a standard response to the mounting complaints of poor and inefficient service: "The taxpayers must give us more money!" It is not enough that the "public sector," and its corollary in taxation, has been growing far more rapidly in this century than the national income. It is not enough that the flaws and headaches of government operation have multiplied along with the increased burden of the government budget. We are supposed to pour still more money down the governmental rathole!

The proper counter-argument to the political demand for more tax money is the question: "How is it that private enterprise doesn't have these problems?" How is it that hi-fi manufacturers or photocopy companies or computer firms or whatever do not have trouble finding capital to expand their output? Why don't *they* issue manifestoes denouncing the investing public for not providing *them* with more money to serve consumer needs? The answer is that consumers pay for the hi-fi sets or the photocopy machines or the computers, and that investors, as a result, know that they can make money by investing in those businesses. On the private market, firms that successfully serve the public find it easy to obtain capital for expansion; inefficient, unsuccessful firms do not, and eventually have to go out of business. But there is no profit-and-loss mechanism in *government* to induce investment in efficient operations and to penalize and drive the inefficient or obsolete ones out of business. There are no profits or losses in government operations inducing either expansion or contraction of operations. In government, then, no one truly "invests," and no one can insure that successful operations will expand and unsuccessful ones disappear. In contrast, government must raise its "capital" by literally conscripting it through the coercive mechanism of taxation.

Many people, including some government officials, think that these problems could be solved if only "government were run like a business." The government then sets up a pseudocorporate monopoly, run by government, which is supposed to set affairs on a "business basis." This has been done, for example, in the case of the Post Office—now the U.S. "Postal Service"— and in the case of the ever-crumbling and decaying New York City Transit Authority. The "corporations" are enjoined to end their chronic deficits and are allowed to float bonds on the bond market. It is true that direct users then would be taking some of the burden off the mass of taxpayers, which include users and nonusers alike. But there are fatal flaws inherent in any government operation which cannot be avoided by this pseudobusiness device. In the first place, government service is always a monopoly or semimonopoly. Often, as in the case of the Postal Service or the Transit Authority, it is a compulsory monopoly—all or nearly all private competition is outlawed. The monopoly means that government service will be far more costly, higher priced, and poorer in quality than would be the case in the free market. Private enterprise gains a profit by cutting costs as much as it can. Government, which cannot go bankrupt or suffer losses in any case, need not cut costs; protected from competition as well as losses, it need only cut its service or simply raise prices. A second fatal flaw is that, try as it may, a government corporation can *never* be run as a business because its *capital* continues to be conscripted from the taxpayer. There is no way of avoiding that; the fact that the government corporation may raise bonds on the market still rests on the ultimate power of taxation to redeem these bonds.

Finally, there is another critical problem inherent in any government operation of a business. One of the reasons that private firms are models of efficiency is because the free market establishes prices which permit them to *calculate*, to figure out what their costs are and therefore what they must do to make profits and avoid losses. It is through this price system, as well as through the motivation to increase profits and avoid losses, that goods and services are properly allocated in the market among all the intricate branches and areas of production that make up the modern industrial "capitalist" economy. It is economic calculation that makes this marvel possible; in contrast, central planning, such as is attempted under socialism, is deprived of accurate pricing, and therefore *cannot* calculate costs and prices. This is the major reason that central socialist planning has increasingly proved to be a failure as the communist countries have become industrialized. It is because central planning cannot determine prices and costs with any accuracy that the communist countries of Eastern Europe have been moving rapidly away from socialist planning and toward a free-market economy.

If central planning, then, thrusts the economy into hopeless calculational chaos, and into irrational allocations and production operations, the advance of government activities inexorably introduces ever greater *islands* of such chaos into the economy, and makes calculation of costs and rational allocation of production resources more and more difficult. As government operations expand and the market economy withers, the calculational chaos becomes more and more disruptive and the economy increasingly unworkable.

The ultimate libertarian program may be summed up in one phrase: the *abolition* of the public sector, the conversion of all operations and services performed by the government into activities performed voluntarily by the private-enterprise economy. Let us now turn from general considerations of government as contrasted with private activity to some of the major areas of government operation and how they could be performed by the free-market economy.

10

The Public Sector, II: Streets and Roads

Protecting the Streets

ABOLITION OF THE PUBLIC SECTOR means, of course, that *all* pieces of land, all land areas, including streets and roads, would be owned privately, by individuals, corporations, cooperatives, or any other voluntary groupings of individuals and capital. The fact that all streets and land areas would be private would by itself solve many of the seemingly insoluble problems of private operation. What we need to do is to reorient our thinking to consider a world in which all land areas are privately owned.

Let us take, for example, police protection. How would police protection be furnished in a totally private economy? *Part* of the answer becomes evident if we consider a world of totally private land and street ownership. Consider the Times Square area of New York City, a notoriously crime-ridden area where there is little police protection furnished by the city authorities. Every New Yorker knows, in fact, that he lives and walks the streets, and not only Times Square, virtually in a state of "anarchy," dependent solely on the normal peacefulness and good will of his fellow citizens. Police protection in New York is minimal, a fact dramatically revealed in a recent week-long police strike when, lo and behold!, crime in no way increased from its normal state when the police are supposedly alert and on the job. At any rate, suppose that the Times Square area, including the streets, was privately owned, say by the "Times Square Merchants Association." The merchants would know full well, of course, that if crime was rampant in their area, if muggings and holdups abounded, then their customers would fade away and would patronize competing areas and neighborhoods. Hence, it would be to the economic interest of the merchants' association to supply efficient and plentiful police protection, so that customers would be attracted to, rather than repelled from, their neighborhood. Private business, after all, is always trying to attract and keep its customers. But what good would be served by attractive store displays and packaging, pleasant lighting and courteous service, if the customers may be robbed or assaulted if they walk through the area?

The merchants' association, furthermore, would be induced, by their drive for profits and for avoiding losses, to supply not only sufficient police protection but also courteous and pleasant protection. Governmental police have not only no incentive to be efficient or worry about their "customers'" needs; they also live with the ever-present temptation to wield their power of force in a brutal and coercive manner. "Police brutality" is a well-known feature of the police system, and it is held in check only by remote complaints of the harassed citizenry. But if the private merchants' police should yield to the temptation of brutalizing the merchants' customers, those customers will quickly disappear and go elsewhere. Hence, the merchants' association will see to it that its police are courteous as well as plentiful.

Such efficient and high-quality police protection would prevail throughout the land, throughout all the private streets and land areas. Factories would guard their street areas, merchants their streets, and road companies would provide safe and efficient police protection for their toll roads and other privately owned roads. The same would be true for residential neighborhoods. We can envision two possible types of private street ownership in such neighborhoods. In one type, all the land owners in a certain block might become the joint *owners* of that block, let us say as the "85th St. Block Company." This company would then provide police protection, the costs being paid either by the homeowners directly or out of tenants' rent if the street includes rental apartments. Again, homeowners will of course have a direct interest in seeing that their block is safe, while landlords will try to attract tenants by supplying safe streets in addition to the more usual services such as heat, water, and janitorial service. To ask *why* landlords should provide safe streets in the libertarian, fully private society is just as silly as asking *now* why they should provide their tenants with heat or hot water. The force of competition and of consumer demand would make them supply such services. Furthermore, whether we are considering homeowners or rental housing, in *either case* the capital value of the land and the house will be a function of the safety of the street as well as of the other well-known characteristics of the house and the neighborhood. Safe and well-patrolled streets will raise the value of the landowners' land and houses in the same way as well-tended houses do; crime-ridden streets will lower the value of the land and houses as surely as dilapidated housing itself does. Since landowners always prefer higher to lower market values for their property, there is a built-in incentive to provide efficient, well-paved, and safe streets.

Another type of private street-ownership in residential areas might be private street companies, which would own only the streets, not the houses or buildings on them. The street companies would then charge landowners for the service of maintaining, improving, and policing their streets. Once again, safe, well-lit, and well-paved streets will induce landowners and tenants to flock to those streets; unsafe, badly lit and badly maintained streets will drive those owners and users away. A happy and flourishing use of the streets by landlords and automobiles will raise the profits and stock values of the street companies; an unhappy and decaying regard for streets by their owners will drive the users away and lower the profits and the stock values of the private street companies. Hence, the street-owning companies will do their best to provide efficient street service, including police protection, to secure happy users; they will be driven to do this by their desire to make profits and to increase the value of their capital, and by their equally active desire not to suffer losses and erosion of their capital. It is infinitely better to rely on the pursuit of economic interest by landowners or street companies than to depend on the dubious "altruism" of bureaucrats and government officials.

At this point in the discussion, someone is bound to raise the question: If streets are owned by street companies, and granting that they generally would aim to please their customers with maximum efficiency, what if some kooky or tyrannical street owner should suddenly decide to block access to his street to an adjoining home owner? How could the latter get in or out? Could he be blocked permanently, or be charged an enormous amount to be allowed entrance or exit? The answer to this question is the same as to a similar problem about land-ownership: Suppose that everyone owning homes surrounding someone's property would suddenly not allow him to go in or out? The answer is that everyone, in purchasing homes or street service in a libertarian society, would make sure that the purchase or lease contract provides full access for whatever term of years is specified. With this sort of "easement" provided in advance by contract, no such sudden blockade would be allowed, since it would be an invasion of the property right of the landowner.

There is of course nothing new or startling in the *principle* of this envisioned libertarian society. We are already familiar with the energizing effects of inter-location and inter-transportation competition. For example, when the private railroads were being built throughout the nation in the nineteenth century, the railroads and their competition provided a remarkable

energizing force for developing their respective areas. Each railroad tried its best to induce immigration and economic development in its area in order to increase its profits, land values,
and value of its capital; and each hastened to do so, lest people
and markets leave their area and move to the ports, cities, and
lands served by competing railroads. The same principle would
be at work if all streets and roads were private as well. Similarly, we are already familiar with police protection provided
by private merchants and organizations. *Within* their property, stores provide guards and watchmen; banks provide guards;
factories employ watchmen; shopping centers retain guards, etc.
The libertarian society would simply extend this healthy and
functioning system to the *streets* as well. It is scarcely accidental
that there are far more assaults and muggings on the *streets*
outside stores than in the stores themselves; this is because the
stores are supplied with watchful private guards while on the
streets we must all rely on the "anarchy" of government police
protection. Indeed, in various blocks of New York City there
has already arisen in recent years, in response to the galloping
crime problem, the hiring of private guards to patrol the blocks
by voluntary contributions of the landlords and homeowners on
that block. Crime on these blocks has already been substan-
tially reduced. The problem is that these efforts have been
halting and inefficient because those streets are not *owned* by
the residents, and hence there is no effective mechanism for
gathering the capital to provide efficient protection on a permanent basis. Furthermore, the patrolling street guards cannot
legally be armed because they are not on their owners' property, and they cannot, as store or other property owners can,
challenge anyone acting in a suspicious but not yet criminal
manner. They cannot, in short, do the things, financially or administratively, that *owners* can do with their property.

Furthermore, police paid for by the landowners and residents
of a block or neighborhood would not only end police brutality
against customers; this system would end the current spectacle
of police being considered by many communities as alien "im-

perial" colonizers, there not to serve but to oppress the community. In America today, for example, we have the general rule in our cities of black areas patrolled by police hired by central urban governments, governments that are perceived to be alien to the black communities. Police supplied, controlled, and paid for by the residents and landowners of the communities themselves would be a completely different story; they would be supplying, and perceived to be supplying, services to their customers rather than coercing them on behalf of an alien authority.

A dramatic contrast of the merits of public vs. private protection is provided by one block in Harlem. On West 135th Street between Seventh and Eighth Avenues is the station house of the 82nd Precinct of the New York City Police Department. Yet the august presence of the station house did not prevent a rash of night robberies of various stores on the block. Finally, in the winter of 1966, fifteen merchants on the block banded together to hire a guard to walk the block all night; the guard was hired from the Leroy V. George protection company to provide the police protection not forthcoming from their property taxes.[1]

The most successful and best organized private police forces in American history have been the railway police, maintained by many railroads to prevent injury or theft to passengers or freight. The modern railway police were founded at the end of World War I by the Protective Section of the American Railway Association. So well did they function that by 1929 freight claim payments for robberies had declined by 93 percent. Arrests by the railway police, who at the time of the major study of their activities in the early 1930s totalled 10,000 men, resulted in a far higher percentage of convictions than earned by police departments, ranging from 83 percent to 97 percent. Railway police were armed, could make normal arrests, and

---

[1] See William C. Wooldridge, *Uncle Sam the Monopoly Man* (New Rochelle, N.Y.: Arlington House, 1970), pp. 111ff.

were portrayed by an unsympathetic criminologist as having a widespread reputation for good character and ability.[2]

Street Rules

One of the undoubted consequences of all land areas in the country being owned by private individuals and companies would be a greater richness and diversity of American neighborhoods. The character of the police protection and the rules applied by the private police would depend on the wishes of the landowners or street owners, the owners of the given area. Thus, suspicious residential neighborhoods would insist that any people or cars entering the area have a prior appointment with a resident, or else be approved by a resident with a phone call from the gate. In short, the same rules for street property would be applied as are now often applied in private apartment buildings or family estates. In other, more raffish areas, everyone would be permitted to enter at will, and there might be varying degrees of surveillance in between. Most probably commercial areas, anxious not to rebuff customers, would be open to all. All this would give full scope to the desires and values of the residents and owners of all the numerous areas in the country.

It might be charged that all this will allow freedom "to discriminate" in housing or use of the streets. There is no question about that. Fundamental to the libertarian creed is every man's right to choose who shall enter or use his own property, provided of course that the other person is willing.

"Discrimination," in the sense of choosing favorably or unfavorably in accordance with whatever criteria a person may

---

[2] See Wooldridge, *op. cit.*, pp. 115–17. The criminological study was made by Jeremiah P. Shalloo, *Private Police* (Philadelphia: Annals of the American Academy of Political and Social Science, 1933). Wooldridge comments that Shalloo's reference to the good reputation of the railway police "contrasts with the present status of many big-city public forces; sanctions against misconduct are so ineffective or roundabout that they may as well not exist, however rhetorically comforting the forces' status as servants of the people may be." Wooldridge, *op. cit.*, p. 117.

employ, is an integral part of freedom of choice, and hence of a free society. But of course in the free market any such discrimination is costly, and will have to be paid for by the property owner concerned.

Suppose, for example, that someone in a free society is a landlord of a house or a block of houses. He *could* simply charge the free market rent and let it go at that. But then there are risks; he may choose to discriminate against renting to couples with young children, figuring that there is substantial risk of defacing his property. On the other hand, he may well choose to charge extra rent to compensate for the higher risk, so that the free-market rent for such families will tend to be higher than otherwise. This, in fact, will happen in most cases on the free market. But what of personal, rather than strictly economic, "discrimination" by the landlord? Suppose, for example, that the landlord is a great admirer of six-foot Swedish-Americans, and decides to rent his apartments only to families of such a group. In the free society it would be fully in his right to do so, but he would clearly suffer a large monetary loss as a result. For this means that he would have to turn away tenant after tenant in an endless quest for very tall Swedish-Americans. While this may be considered an extreme example, the effect is exactly the same, though differing in degree, for any sort of personal discrimination in the marketplace. If, for example, the landlord dislikes redheads and determines not to rent his apartments to them, he will suffer losses, although not as severely as in the first example.

In any case, anytime anyone practices such "discrimination" in the free market, he must bear the costs, either of losing profits or of losing services as a consumer. If a consumer decides to boycott goods sold by people he does not like, whether the dislike is justified or not, he then will go without goods or services which he otherwise would have purchased.

All property owners, then, in a free society, would set down the rules for use of, or admission to, their property. The more rigorous the rules the fewer the people who will engage in such use, and the property owner will then have to balance rigor of admission as against loss of income. A landlord might "discriminate," for example, by insisting, as George Pullman did in his "company town" in Illinois in the late nineteenth century, that all his tenants appear at all times dressed in jacket and tie; he might do so, but it is doubtful that many tenants would elect to move into or remain in such a building or development and the landlord would suffer severe losses.

The principle that property is administered by its owners also provides the rebuttal to a standard argument for government intervention in the economy. The argument holds that "after all, the government sets down traffic rules—red and green lights, driving on the right-hand side, maximum speed limits, etc. Surely everyone must admit that traffic would degenerate into chaos if not for such rules. Therefore, why should government not intervene in the rest of the economy as well?" The fallacy here is not that traffic should be regulated; of course such rules are necessary. But the crucial point is that such rules will always be laid down by whoever owns and therefore administers the roads. Government has been laying down traffic rules because it is the government that has always owned and therefore run the streets and roads; in a libertarian society of private ownership the *private* owners would lay down the rules for the use of their roads.

However, might not the traffic rules be "chaotic" in a purely free society? Wouldn't some owners designate red for "stop," others green or blue, etc.? Wouldn't some roads be used on the right-hand side and others on the left? Such questions are absurd. Obviously, it would be to the interest of all road owners to have uniform rules in these matters, so that road traffic could mesh smoothly and without difficulty. Any maverick road owner who insisted on a left-hand drive or green for "stop" instead of "go" would soon find himself with numerous accidents, and the disappearance of customers and users. The private railroads in nineteenth-century America faced similar problems and solved them harmoniously and without difficulty. Railroads allowed each other's cars on their tracks; they interconnected with each other for mutual benefit; the gauges of the different railroads were adjusted to be uniform; and uniform regional freight classifications were worked out for 6,000 items. Furthermore, it was the railroads and not government that took the initiative to consolidate the unruly and chaotic patchwork of time zones that had existed previously. In order to have accurate scheduling and timetables, the railroads *had* to consolidate; and in 1883 they agreed to consolidate the existing fifty-four time zones across the country into the four which we have today. The New York financial paper, the *Commercial and Financial Chronicle*, exclaimed that "the laws of trade and the instinct for self-preservation effect reforms and improvements that all the legislative bodies combined could not accomplish." [3]

Pricing Streets and Roads

If, in contrast, we examine the performance of governmental streets and highways in America, it is difficult to see how private ownership could pile up a more inefficient or irrational record. It is now widely recognized, for example, that federal and state governments, spurred by the lobbying of automobile companies, oil companies, tire companies, and construction contractors and unions, have indulged in a vast over-expansion of highways. The highways grant gross subsidies to the users and have played the major role in killing railroads as a viable enterprise. Thus, trucks can operate on a right-of-way constructed and maintained by the taxpayer, while railroads had to build and maintain their own trackage. Furthermore, the subsidized highway and road programs led to an over-expansion of automobile-using suburbs, the coerced bulldozing of countless homes and businesses, and an artificial burdening of the central cities. The cost to the taxpayer and to the economy has been enormous.

[3] See Edward C. Kirkland, *Industry Comes of Age: Business, Labor, and Public Policy, 1860–1897* (New York: Holt, Rinehart, and Winston, 1961), pp. 48–50.

Particularly subsidized has been the urban auto-using commuter, and it is precisely in the cities where traffic congestion
has burgeoned along with this subsidy to over-accumulation of
their traffic. Professor William Vickrey of Columbia University
has estimated that urban expressways have been built at a cost
of from 6¢ to 27¢ per vehicle mile, while users pay in gasoline
and other auto taxes only about 1¢ per vehicle-mile. The general taxpayer rather than the motorist pays for maintenance of
urban streets. Furthermore, the gasoline tax is paid *per mile*
regardless of the particular street or highway being used, and regardless of the time of day of the ride. Hence, when highways
are financed from the general gasoline tax fund, the users of
the low-cost rural highways are being taxed in order to subsidize the users of the far higher-cost urban expressways. Rural
highways typically cost only 2¢ per vehicle-mile to build and
maintain.[4]

In addition, the gasoline tax is scarcely a rational pricing system for the use of the roads, and no private firms would ever
price the use of roads in that way. Private business prices its
goods and services to "clear the market," so that supply equals
demand, and there are neither shortages nor goods going unsold.
The fact that gasoline taxes are paid per mile regardless of the
road means that the more highly demanded urban streets and
highways are facing a situation where the *price* charged is far
below the free-market price. The result is enormous and aggravated traffic congestion on the heavily traveled streets and
roads, especially in rush hours, and a virtually unused network
of roads in rural areas. A rational pricing system would at the
same time maximize profits for road owners and always provide clear streets free of congestion. In the current system, the
government holds the price to users of congested roads extremely low and far below the free-market price; the result is a
chronic shortage of road space reflected in traffic congestion.
The government has invariably tried to meet this growing

---

[4] From an unpublished study by William Vickrey, "Transit Fare Increases a Costly Revenue."

problem not by rational pricing but by building still more roads, socking the taxpayer for yet greater subsidies to drivers, and thereby making the shortage still worse. Frantically increasing the supply while holding the price of use far below the market simply leads to chronic and aggravated congestion. It is like a dog chasing a mechanical rabbit. Thus, the *Washington Post* has traced the impact of the federal highway program in the nation's capital:

Washington's Capital Beltway was one of the first major links in the system to be completed. When the last section was opened in the summer of 1964, it was hailed as one of the finest highways ever built.

It was expected to (a) relieve traffic congestion in downtown Washington by providing a bypass for north-south traffic and (b) knit together the suburban counties and cities ringing the capital.

What the Beltway actually became was (a) a commuter highway and local traffic circulator and (b) the cause of an enormous building boom that accelerated the flight of the white and the affluent from the central city.

Instead of relieving traffic congestion, the Beltway has increased it. Along with I-95, 70-S, and I-66, it has made it possible for commuters to move farther and farther from their downtown jobs.

It has also led to relocation of government agencies and retail and service firms from downtown to the suburbs, putting the jobs they create out of reach of many inner city dwellers.[5]

[5] Hank Burchard, "U.S. Highway System: Where to Now?," *Washington Post* (November 29, 1971). Or, as John Dyckman puts it: "in motoring facilities . . . additional accommodation creates additional traffic. The opening of a freeway designed to meet existing demand may eventually increase that demand until congestion on the freeway increases the travel time to what it was before the freeway existed." John W. Dyckman, "Transportation in Cities," in A. Schreiber, P. Gatons, and R. Clemmer, eds., *Economics of Urban Problems; Selected Readings* (Boston: Houghton Mifflin, 1971), p. 143. For an excellent analysis of how increased supply cannot end congestion when pricing is set far below market price, see Charles O. Meiburg, "An Economic Analysis of Highway Services," *Quarterly Journal of Economics* (November 1963), pp. 648–56.

What would a rational pricing system, a system instituted by private road owners, look like? In the first place, highways would charge tolls, especially at such convenient entrances to cities as bridges and tunnels, but not as is charged now. For example, toll charges would be much higher at rush-hour and other peak-hour traffic (e.g., Sundays in the summer) than in off-hours. In a free market, the greater demand at peak hours would lead to higher toll charges, until congestion would be eliminated and the flow of traffic steady. But people *have* to go to work, the reader will ask? Surely, but they don't *have* to go in their own cars. Some commuters will give up altogether and move back to the city; others will go in car pools; still others will ride in express busses or trains. In this way, use of the roads at peak hours would be restricted to those most willing to pay the market-clearing price for their use. Others, too, will endeavor to shift their times of work so as to come in and leave at staggered hours. Weekenders would also drive less or stagger their hours. Finally, the higher profits to be earned from, say, bridges and tunnels, will lead private firms to build more of them. Road building will be governed not by the clamor of pressure groups and users for subsidies, but by the efficient demand and cost calculations of the market-place.

While many people can envision the working of private *highways*, they boggle at the thought of private urban streets. How would *they* be priced? Would there be toll gates at every block? Obviously not, for such a system would be clearly uneconomic, prohibitively costly to the owner and driver alike. In the first place, the street owners will price *parking* far more rationally than at present. They will price parking on congested downtown streets very heavily, in response to the enormous demand. And contrary to common practice nowadays, they will charge proportionately far *more* rather than less for longer, all-day parking. In short, the street owners will try to induce rapid turnover in the congested areas. All right for parking; again, this is readily understandable. But what about *driving* on congested urban streets? How could this be priced? There are numerous possible ways. In the first place the downtown street owners might require anyone driving on their streets to buy a license, which could be displayed on the car as licenses and stickers are now. But, furthermore, they might require anyone driving at peak hours to buy and display an extra, very costly license. There are other ways. Modern technology may make feasible the requirement that all cars equip themselves with a meter, a meter which will not only click away per mile, but may speed up in a predetermined manner on congested streets and roads at peak hours. Then the car owner could receive a bill at the end of the month. A similar plan was set forth a decade ago by Professor A. A. Walters:

The particular administrative instruments which might be used include . . . special mileometers (similar to those used by taxis). . . . The special mileometers would record mileage when the "flag" is up and a charge would be levied on this mileage. This would be suitable for large urban areas such as New York, London, Chicago, etc. "Flag-up" streets could be specified for certain hours of the day. Vehicles might be allowed to travel on those streets without a special mileometer provided that they bought and displayed a daily "sticker." The occasional traffic on "sticker" authority would have been charged more than the maximum amount paid by those on mileometer authority. The supervision of the scheme would be fairly simple. Cameras could be set up to record those cars without sticker or flag, and a suitable fine could be levied for contravention.[6]

---

[6] Professor Walters adds that with a suitably large application of the mileometer method, the cost of each mileometer could probably be reduced to about $10. A. A. Walters, "The Theory and Measurement of Private and Social Cost of Highway Congestion," *Econometrica* (October 1961), p. 684. Also see Meiburg, *op. cit.*, p. 652; Vickrey, *op. cit.*, Dyckman, "Transportation in Cities," *op. cit.*, pp. 135–51; John F. Kain, "A Re-appraisal of Metropolitan Transport Planning," in Schreiber, Gatons, and Clemmer, *op. cit.*, pp. 152–66; John R. Meyer, "Knocking Down the Straw Men," in B. Chinitz, ed., *City and Suburb* (Englewood Cliffs, N.J.: Prentice-Hall, 1964), pp. 85–93; and James C. Nelson, "The Pricing of Highway, Waterway, and Airway Facilities," *American Economic Review, Papers and Proceedings* (May 1962), pp. 426–32.

Professor Vickrey has also suggested that TV cameras at the intersections of the most congested streets could record the license numbers of all cars, with motorists sent a bill each month in proportion to all the times that they crossed the intersection. Alternatively, he proposed that each car could be equipped with the Oxford electronic metering device; each car would then emit its own unique signal which would be picked up by the device placed at the given intersection.[7]

In any case, the problem of rational pricing for streets and highways would be an easy one for private enterprise and modern technology to solve. Businessmen on the free market have readily solved far more difficult problems; all that is needed is to allow them the room to function.

If all transportation were set completely free, if the roads, airlines, railroads, and waterways were freed of their labyrinthine networks of subsidies, controls, and regulations in a purely private system, how would the consumers allocate their transportation dollars? Would we return to railroad travel, for example? The best estimates of cost and demand for transportation predict that railroads would become the main staple for long-haul freight, airlines for long-range passenger service, trucks for short-haul freight, and busses for public commuter travel. While railroads, in short, would stage a comeback for long-haul freight, they would not be revivified for much passenger service. In recent years, many liberals who have become disenchanted with the overbuilding of highways have been calling for massive discouragement of highway use, and the subsidizing and building of subways and commuter railways on a vast scale for urban traffic. But these grandiose schemes ignore the enormous expense and waste that would be involved. For even if many of these highways should not have been built, they are *there*, and it would be folly not to take advantage of them. In recent years, some intelligent transportation economists have

---

[7] Douglass C. North and Roger LeRoy Miller, *The Economics of Public Issues* (New York: Harper & Row, 1971), p. 72.

raised their voices against the massive waste involved in constructing new rapid transit railroads (such as in the San Francisco Bay area) and have called instead for making use of the existing highways through employing express busses for commuting.[8]

It is not difficult to envision a network of private, unsubsidized and unregulated railroads and airlines; but could there be a system of private roads? Could such a system be at all feasible? One answer is that private roads have worked admirably in the past. In England before the eighteenth century, for example, roads, invariably owned and operated by local governments, were badly constructed and even more badly maintained. These public roads could never have supported the mighty Industrial Revolution that England experienced in the eighteenth century, the "revolution" that ushered in the modern age. The vital task of improving the almost impassable English roads was performed by private turnpike companies, which, beginning in 1706, organized and established the great network of roads which made England the envy of the world. The owners of these private turnpike companies were generally landowners, merchants, and industrialists in the area being served by the road, and they recouped their costs by charging tolls at selected tollgates. Often the collection of tolls was leased out for a year or more to individuals selected by competitive bids at auction. It was these private roads that developed an internal market in England, and that greatly lowered the costs of transport of coal and other bulky material. And since it was mutually beneficial for them to do so, the turnpike companies linked up with each other to form an interconnected road network throughout the land—all a result of private enterprise in action.[9]

---

[8] See for example the works of Meyer and Kain cited above, as well as Meyer, Kain, and Wohl, *The Urban Transportation Problem* (Cambridge: Harvard University Press, 1965).

[9] See T. S. Ashton, *An Economic History of England: the 18th Century* (New York: Barnes and Noble, 1955), pp. 78–90. See the same source, pp. 72–90, for the mighty network of private canals built throughout England during the same period.

As in England, so in the United States a little later in time. Faced again with virtually impassable roads built by local governmental units, private companies built and financed a great turnpike network throughout the northeastern states, from approximately 1800 to 1830. Once again, private enterprise proved superior in road building and ownership to the backward operations of government. The roads were built and operated by private turnpike corporations, and tolls were charged to the users. Again, the turnpike companies were largely financed by merchants and property owners along the routes, and they voluntarily linked themselves into an interconnected network of roads. And these turnpikes constituted the first really good roads in the United States.[10]

[10] See George Rogers Taylor, *The Transportation Revolution, 1815–1860* (New York: Rinehart & Co., 1951), pp. 22–28. Also see W. C. Wooldridge, *Uncle Sam the Monopoly Man*, pp. 128–36.

11

The Public Sector, III: Police, Law, and the Courts

Police Protection

THE MARKET AND PRIVATE ENTERPRISE do exist, and so most people can readily envision a free market in most goods and services. Probably the most difficult single area to grasp, however, is the abolition of government operations in the service of protection: police, the courts, etc.—the area encompassing defense of person and property against attack or invasion. How could private enterprise and the free market possibly provide *such* service? How could police, legal systems, judicial services, law enforcement, prisons—how could these be provided in a free market? We have already seen how a great deal of police protection, at the least, could be supplied by the various owners of streets and land areas. But we now need to examine this entire area systematically.

In the first place, there is a common fallacy, held even by most advocates of laissez-faire, that the government must supply "police protection," as if police protection were a single, absolute entity, a fixed quantity of something which the government supplies to all. But in actual fact there is no absolute commodity called "police protection" any more than there is an absolute single commodity called "food" or "shelter." It is true that everyone pays taxes for a seemingly fixed quantity of protection, but this is a myth. In actual fact, there are almost infinite degrees of all sorts of protection. For any given person or business, the police can provide everything from a policeman on the beat who patrols once a night, to two policemen patrolling constantly on each block, to cruising patrol cars, to one or even several round-the-clock personal bodyguards. Furthermore, there are many other decisions the police must make, the complexity of which becomes evident as soon as we look beneath the veil of the myth of absolute "protection." How shall the police allocate their funds which are, of course, always limited as are the funds of all other individuals, organizations, and agencies? How much shall the police invest in electronic equipment? fingerprinting equipment? detectives as against uniformed police? patrol cars as against foot police, etc?

The point is that the government has no rational way to make these allocations. The government only knows that it has a limited budget. Its allocations of funds are then subject to the full play of politics, boondoggling, and bureaucratic inefficiency, with no indication at all as to whether the police department is serving the consumers in a way responsive to their desires or whether it is doing so efficiently. The situation would be different if police services were supplied on a free, competitive market. In that case, consumers would pay for whatever degree of protection they wish to purchase. The consumers who just want to see a policeman once in a while would pay less than those who want continuous patrolling, and far less than those who demand twenty-four-hour bodyguard service. On the free market, protection would be supplied in proportion and in whatever way that the consumers wish to pay for it. A drive for efficiency would be insured, as it always is on the market, by the compulsion to make profits and avoid losses, and thereby to keep costs low and to serve the highest demands of the consumers. Any police firm that suffers from gross inefficiency would soon go bankrupt and disappear.

One big problem a government police force must always face is: what laws *really* to enforce? Police departments are theoretically faced with the absolute injunction, "enforce all laws," but in practice a limited budget forces them to allocate their personnel and equipment to the most urgent crimes. But the absolute dictum pursues them and works against a rational allocation of resources. On the free market, what would be enforced is whatever the customers are willing to pay for. Suppose, for example, that Mr. Jones has a precious gem he believes might soon be stolen. He can ask, and pay for, round-the-clock police protection at whatever strength he may wish to work out with the police company. He might, on the other hand, also have a private road on his estate he doesn't want many people to travel on—but he might not *care* very much about trespassers on that road. In that case, he won't devote any police resources to protecting the road. As on the market in general, it is up to the consumer—and since all of us are consumers this means each person individually decides how much and what kind of protection he wants and is willing to buy.

All that we have said about landowners' police applies to private police in general. Free-market police would not only be efficient, they would have a strong incentive to be courteous and to refrain from brutality against either their clients or their clients' friends or customers. A private Central Park would be guarded efficiently in order to maximize park revenue, rather than have a prohibitive curfew imposed on innocent—and paying—customers. A free market in police would reward efficient and courteous police protection to customers and penalize any falling off from this standard. No longer would there be the current disjunction between service and payment inherent in all government operations, a disjunction which means that police, like all other government agencies, acquire their revenue, not voluntarily and competitively from consumers, but from the taxpayers coercively.

In fact, as government police have become increasingly inefficient, consumers have been turning more and more to private forms of protection. We have already mentioned block or neighborhood protection. There are also private guards, insurance companies, private detectives, and such increasingly sophisticated equipment as safes, locks, and closed-circuit TV and burglar alarms. The President's Commission on Law Enforcement and the Administration of Justice estimated in 1969 that government police cost the American public $2.8 billion a year, while it spends $1.35 billion on private protection service and another $200 million on equipment, so that private protection expenses amounted to over half the outlay on government police. These figures should give pause to those credulous folk who believe that police protection is somehow, by some mystic right or power, necessarily and forevermore an attribute of State sovereignty.[1]

Every reader of detective fiction knows that private insurance detectives are far more efficient than the police in recovering stolen property. Not only is the insurance company impelled by economics to serve the consumer—and thereby try to avoid paying benefits—but the major focus of the insurance company is very different from that of the police. The police, standing as they do for a mythical "society," are primarily interested in catching and punishing the criminal; restoring the stolen loot to the victim is strictly secondary. To the insurance company and its detectives, on the other hand, the prime concern is recovery of the loot, and apprehension and punishment of the criminal is secondary to the prime purpose of aiding the victim of crime. Here we see again the difference between a private firm impelled to serve the customer-victim of crime and the public police, which is under no such economic compulsion.

We cannot blueprint a market that exists only as an hypothesis, but it is reasonable to believe that police service in the libertarian society would be supplied by the landowners or by insurance companies. Since insurance companies would be paying benefits to victims of crime, it is highly likely that they would supply police service as a means of keeping down crime

[1] See Wooldridge, *op. cit.*, pp. 111ff.

and hence their payment of benefits. It is certainly likely in any case that police service would be paid for in regular monthly premiums, with the police agency—whether insurance company or not—called on whenever needed.

This supplies what should be the first simple answer to a typical nightmare question of people who first hear about the idea of a totally private police: "Why, that means that if you're attacked or robbed you have to rush over to a policeman and start dickering on how much it will cost to defend you." A moment's reflection should show that no service is supplied in this way on the free market. Obviously, the person who wants to be protected by Agency A or Insurance Company B will pay regular premiums rather than wait to be attacked before buying protection. "But suppose an emergency occurs and a Company A policeman sees someone being mugged; will he stop to ask if the victim has bought insurance from Company A?" In the first place, this sort of street crime will be taken care of, as we noted above, by the police hired by whoever owns the street in question. But what of the unlikely case that a neighborhood does not have street police, and a policeman of Company A happens to see someone being attacked? Will he rush to the victim's defense? That, of course, would be up to Company A, but it is scarcely conceivable that private police companies would not cultivate goodwill by making it a policy to give free aid to victims in emergency situations and perhaps ask the rescued victim for a voluntary donation afterward. In the case of a homeowner being robbed or attacked, then of course he will call on whichever police company he has been using. He will call Police Company A rather than "the police" he calls upon now.

Competition insures efficiency, low price, and high quality, and there is no reason to assume *a priori*, as many people do, that there is something divinely ordained about having only *one* police agency in a given geographical area. Economists have often claimed that the production of certain goods or services is a "natural monopoly," so that more than one private agency could not long survive in a given area. Perhaps, although only a totally free market could decide the matter once and for all. Only the market can decide what and how many firms, and of what size and quality, can survive in active competition. But there is no reason to suppose in advance that police protection is a "natural monopoly." After all, insurance companies are not; and if we can have Metropolitan, Equitable, Prudential, etc., insurance companies coexisting side by side, why not Metropolitan, Equitable, and Prudential police protection companies? Gustave de Molinari, the nineteenth-century French free-market economist, was the first person in history to contemplate and advocate a free market for police protection. Molinari estimated that there would eventually turn out to be several private police agencies side by side in the cities, and one private agency in each rural area. Perhaps—but we must realize that modern technology makes much more feasible branch offices of large urban firms in even the most remote rural areas. A person living in a small village in Wyoming, therefore, could employ the services of a local protection company, *or* he might use a nearby branch office of the Metropolitan Protection Company.

"But how could a poor person afford private protection he would have to pay for instead of getting free protection, as he does now?" There are several answers to this question, one of the most common criticisms of the idea of totally private police protection. One is: that this problem of course applies to *any* commodity or service in the libertarian society, not just the police. But isn't protection necessary? Perhaps, but then so is food of many different kinds, clothing, shelter, etc. Surely these are at least as vital if not more so than police protection, and yet almost nobody says that *therefore* the government must nationalize food, clothing, shelter, etc., and supply these free as a compulsory monopoly. Very poor people would be supplied, in general, by private charity, as we saw in our chapter on welfare. Furthermore, in the specific case of police there would undoubtedly be ways of voluntarily supplying free police protection to the indigent—either by the police companies themselves for goodwill (as hospitals and doctors do now) or by special "police aid" societies that would do work similar to "legal aid" societies today. (Legal aid societies voluntarily supply free legal counsel to the indigent in trouble with the authorities.)

There are important supplementary considerations. As we have seen, police service is *not* "free"; it is paid for by the taxpayer, and the taxpayer is very often the poor person himself. He may very well be paying more in taxes for police now than he would in fees to private, and far more efficient, police companies. Furthermore, the police companies would be tapping a mass market; with the economies of such a large-scale market, police protection would undoubtedly be much cheaper. No police company would wish to price itself out of a large chunk of its market, and the cost of protection would be no more prohibitively expensive than, say, the cost of insurance today. (In fact, it would tend to be much cheaper than current insurance, because the insurance industry today is heavily regulated by government to keep out low-cost competition.)

There is a final nightmare which most people who have contemplated private protection agencies consider to be decisive in rejecting such a concept. Wouldn't the agencies always be clashing? Wouldn't "anarchy" break out, with perpetual conflicts between police forces as one person calls in "his" police while a rival calls in "his"?

There are several levels of answers to this crucial question. In the first place, since there would be no overall State, no central or even single local government, we would *at least* be spared the horror of inter-State wars, with their plethora of massive, superdestructive, and now nuclear, weapons. As we look back through history, isn't it painfully clear that the number of people killed in isolated neighborhood "rumbles" or conflicts is as nothing to the total mass devastation of inter-State wars? There are good reasons for this. To avoid emotionalism, let us take two hypothetical countries: "Ruritania" and "Walldavia." If both Ruritania and Walldavia were dissolved into a libertarian society, with no government and innumerable private individuals, firms, and police agencies, the only clashes that *could* break out would be local, and the weaponry would necessarily be strictly limited in scope and devastation. Suppose that in a Ruritanian city two police agencies clash and start shooting it out. At worst, they could *not* use mass bombing or nuclear destruction or germ warfare, since they themselves would be blown up in the holocaust. It is the slicing off of territorial areas into single, governmental monopolies that leads to mass destruction—for *then* if the single monopoly government of Walldavia confronts its ancient rival, the government of Ruritania, each can wield weapons of mass destruction and even nuclear warfare because it will be the "other guy" and the "other country" they will hurt. Furthermore, now that every person is a subject of a monopoly government, in the eyes of every other government he becomes irretrievably *identified* with "his" government. The citizen of France is identified with "his" government, and therefore if another government attacks France, it will attack the citizenry as well as the government of France. But if Company A battles with Company B, the *most* that can happen is that the respective customers of each company may be dragged into the battle—but *no one else.* It should be evident, then, that *even* if the worst happened, and a libertarian world would indeed become a world of "anarchy," we would *still* be much better off than we are now, at the mercy of rampant, "anarchic" nation-states, each possessing a fearsome monopoly of weapons of mass destruction. We must never forget that we are all living, and always have lived, in a world of "international anarchy," in a world of coercive nation-states unchecked by any overall world government, and there is no prospect of this situation changing.

A libertarian world, then, even if anarchic, would *still* not suffer the brutal wars, the mass devastation, the A-bombing, that our State-ridden world has suffered for centuries. Even if local police clash continually, there would be no more Dresdens, no more Hiroshimas.

But there is far more to be said. We should never concede that this local "anarchy" would be likely to occur. Let us separate the problem of police clashes into distinct and different parts: honest disagreements, and the attempt of one or more police forces to become "outlaws" and to extract funds or impose their rule by coercion. Let us assume for a moment that the police forces will be honest, and that they are only riven by honest clashes of opinion; we will set aside for a while the problem of outlaw police. Surely one of the very important aspects of protection service the police can offer their respective customers is quiet protection. Every consumer, every buyer of police protection, would wish above all for protection that is efficient and quiet, with no conflicts or disturbances. Every police agency would be fully aware of this vital fact. To assume that police would continually clash and battle with each other is absurd, for it ignores the devastating effect that this chaotic "anarchy" would have on the business of all the police companies. To put it bluntly, such wars and conflicts would be bad —very bad—for business. Therefore, on the free market, the police agencies would all see to it that there would be no clashes between them, and that all conflicts of opinion would be ironed out in private courts, decided by private judges or arbitrators.

To get more specific: in the first place, as we have said, clashes would be minimal because the street owner would have his guards, the storekeeper his, the landlord his, and the homeowner his own police company. Realistically, in the everyday world, there would be little room for direct clashes between police agencies. But suppose, as will sometimes occur, two neighboring home owners get into a fight, each accuses the other of initiating assault or violence, and each calls on his own police company, should they happen to subscribe to different companies. What then? Again, it would be pointless and economically as well as physically self-destructive for the two police companies to start shooting it out. Instead, every police company, to remain in business at all, would announce as a *vital part* of its service, the use of private courts or arbitrators to decide who is in the wrong.

The Courts

Suppose, then, that the judge or arbitrator decides Smith was in the wrong in a dispute, and that he aggressed against Jones. If Smith accepts the verdict then, whatever damages or punishment is levied, there is no problem for the theory of libertarian protection. But what if he does *not* accept it? Or suppose another example: Jones is robbed. He sets his police company to do detective work in trying to track down the criminal. The company decides that a certain Brown is the criminal. Then what? If Brown acknowledges his guilt, then again there is no problem and judicial punishment proceeds, centering on forcing the criminal to make restitution to the victim. But, again, what if Brown denies his guilt?

These cases take us out of the realm of police protection and into another vital area of protection: *judicial* service, i.e., the provision, in accordance with generally accepted procedures, of a method of trying as best as one can to determine *who* is the criminal, or *who* is the breaker of contracts, in any sort of crime or dispute. Many people, even those who acknowledge that there could be privately competitive police service supplied on a free market, balk at the idea of totally private courts. How in the world could *courts* be private? How would courts employ force in a world without government? Wouldn't eternal conflicts and "anarchy" *then* ensue?

In the first place, the monopoly courts of government are subject to the same grievous problems, inefficiencies, and contempt for the consumer as any other government operation. We all know that judges, for example, are *not* selected according to their wisdom, probity, or efficiency in serving the consumer, but are political hacks chosen by the political process. Furthermore, the courts are monopolies; if, for example, the courts in some town or city should become corrupt, venal, oppressive, or inefficient the citizen at present has no recourse. The aggrieved citizen of Deep Falls, Wyoming, must be governed by the local Wyoming court or not at all. In a libertarian society, there would be many courts, many judges to whom he could turn. Again, there is no reason to assume a "natural monopoly" of judicial wisdom. The Deep Falls citizen could, for example, call upon the local branch of the Prudential Judicial Company.

How would courts be financed in a free society? There are many possibilities. Possibly, each individual would subscribe to a court service, paying a monthly premium, and then calling upon the court if he is in need. Or, since courts will probably be needed much less frequently than policemen, he may pay a fee whenever he chooses to use the court, with the criminal or contract-breaker eventually recompensing the victim or plaintiff. Or, in still a third possibility, the courts may be hired by the police agencies to settle disputes, *or* there may even be "vertically integrated" firms supplying *both* police and judicial service: the Prudential Judicial Company might have a police and a judicial division. Only the market will be able to decide which of these methods will be most appropriate.

We should all be more familiar with the increasing use of private arbitration, even in our present society. The government courts have become so clogged, inefficient, and wasteful that more and more parties to disputes are turning to private arbitrators as a cheaper and far less time-consuming way of settling their disputes. In recent years, private arbitration has become a growing and highly successful profession. Being voluntary, furthermore, the rules of arbitration can be decided rapidly by the parties themselves, without the need for a ponderous, complex legal framework applicable to all citizens. Arbitration therefore permits judgments to be made by people expert in the trade or occupation concerned. Currently, the American Arbitration Association, whose motto is "The Handclasp is Mightier than the Fist," has 25 regional offices throughout the country, with 23,000 abitrators. In 1969, the Association conducted over 22,000 arbitrations. In addition, the insurance companies adjust over 50,000 claims a year through voluntary arbitration. There is also a growing and successful use of private arbitrators in automobile accident claim cases.

It might be protested that, while performing an ever greater proportion of judicial functions, the private arbitrators' decisions are still enforced by the courts, so that once the disputing parties agree on an arbitrator, his decision becomes legally binding. This is true, but it was *not* the case before 1920, and the arbitration profession grew at as rapid a rate from 1900 to 1920 as it has since. In fact, the modern arbitration movement began in full force in England during the time of the American Civil War, with merchants increasingly using the "private courts" provided by voluntary arbitrators, even though the decisions were not legally binding. By 1900, voluntary arbitration began to take hold in the United States. In fact, in medieval England, the entire structure of merchant law, which was handled clumsily and inefficiently by the government's courts, grew up in private merchants' courts. The merchants' courts were purely voluntary arbitrators, and the decisions were not legally binding. How, then, were they successful?

The answer is that the merchants, in the Middle Ages and down to 1920, relied solely on ostracism and boycott by the other merchants in the area. In other words, should a merchant refuse to submit to arbitration or ignore a decision, the other merchants would publish this fact in the trade, and would refuse to deal with the recalcitrant merchant, bringing him quickly to heel. Wooldridge mentions one medieval example:

Merchants made their courts work simply by agreeing to abide by the results. The merchant who broke the understanding would not be sent to jail, to be sure, but neither would he long continue to be a merchant, for the compliance exacted by his fellows, and their power over his goods, proved if anything more effective than physical coercion. Take John of Homing, who made his living marketing wholesale quantities of fish. When John sold a lot of herring on the representation that it conformed to a three-barrel sample, but which, his fellow merchants found, was actually mixed with "sticklebacks and putrid herring," he made good the deficiency on pain of economic ostracism.[2]

In modern times, ostracism became even more effective, and it included the knowledge that anyone who ignored an arbitrator's award could never again avail himself of an arbitrator's services. Industrialist Owen D. Young, head of General Electric, concluded that the moral censure of other businessmen was a far more effective sanction than legal enforcement. Nowadays, modern technology, computers, and credit ratings would make such nationwide ostracism even more effective than it has ever been in the past.

Even if purely voluntary arbitration is sufficient for commercial disputes, however, what of frankly criminal activities: the mugger, the rapist, the bank robber? In these cases, it must be admitted that ostracism would probably not be sufficient—even though it would also include, we must remember, refusal of private street owners to allow such criminals in their areas. For the criminal cases, then, courts and legal enforcement become necessary.

How, then, would the courts operate in the libertarian society? In particular, how could they *enforce* their decisions? In all their operations, furthermore, they must observe the critical libertarian rule that no physical force may be used against anyone who has not been convicted as a criminal—otherwise, the users of such force, whether police or courts, would be themselves liable to be convicted as aggressors if it turned out that the person they had used force against was innocent of crime. In contrast to statist systems, no policeman or judge could be granted special immunity to use coercion beyond what anyone else in society could use.

Let us now take the case we mentioned before. Mr. Jones is robbed, his hired detective agency decides that one Brown com-

---

[2] Wooldridge, *op. cit.*, p. 96. Also see *ibid.*, pp. 94–110.

mitted the crime, and Brown refuses to concede his guilt. What then? In the first place, we must recognize that there is at present no overall world court or world government enforcing its decrees; yet while we live in a state of "international anarchy" there is little or no problem in disputes between private citizens of two countries. Suppose that right now, for example, a citizen of Uruguay claims that he has been swindled by a citizen of Argentina. Which court does he go to? He goes to his own, i.e., the victim's or the plaintiff's court. The case proceeds in the Uruguayan court, and its decision is honored by the Argentinian court. The same is true if an American feels he has been swindled by a Canadian, and so on. In Europe after the Roman Empire, when German tribes lived side by side and in the same areas, if a Visigoth felt that he had been injured by a Frank, he took the case to his own court, and the decision was generally accepted by the Franks. Going to the plaintiff's court is the rational libertarian procedure as well, since the victim or plaintiff is the one who is aggrieved, and who naturally takes the case to his own court. So, in our case, Jones would go to the Prudential Court Company to charge Brown with theft.

It is possible, of course, that Brown is also a client of the Prudential Court, in which case there is no problem. The Prudential's decision covers both parties, and becomes binding. But one important stipulation is that no coercive subpoena power can be used against Brown, because he must be considered innocent until he is convicted. But Brown would be served with a voluntary subpoena, a notice that he is being tried on such and such a charge and inviting him or his legal representative to appear. If he does not appear, then he will be tried *in absentia*, and this will obviously be less favorable for Brown since his side of the case will not be pleaded in court. If Brown is declared guilty, then the court and its marshals will employ force to seize Brown and exact whatever punishment is decided upon—a punishment which obviously will focus first on restitution to the victim.

What, however, if Brown does not recognize the Prudential Court? What if he is a client of the Metropolitan Court Company? Here the case becomes more difficult. What will happen then? First, victim Jones pleads his case in the Prudential Court. If Brown is found innocent, this ends the controversy. Suppose, however, that defendant Brown is found guilty. If he does nothing, the court's judgment proceeds against him. Suppose, however, Brown then takes the case to the Metropolitan Court Company, pleading inefficiency or venality by Prudential. The case will then be heard by Metropolitan. If Metropolitan also finds Brown guilty, this too ends the controversy and Prudential will proceed against Brown with dispatch. Suppose, however, that Metropolitan finds Brown innocent of the charge. Then what? Will the two courts and their arms-wielding marshals shoot it out in the streets?

Once again, this would clearly be irrational and self-destructive behavior on the part of the courts. An essential part of their judicial service to their clients is the provision of just, objective, and peacefully functioning decisions—the best and most objective way of arriving at the truth of who committed the crime. Arriving at a decision and then allowing chaotic gunplay would scarcely be considered valuable judicial service by their customers. Thus, an essential part of any court's service to its clients would be an appeals procedure. In short, every court would agree to abide by an appeals trial, as decided by a voluntary arbitrator to whom Metropolitan and Prudential would now turn. The appeals judge would make his decision and the result of this third trial would be treated as binding on the guilty. The Prudential court would then proceed to enforcement.

An appeals court! But isn't this setting up a compulsory monopoly government once again? No, because there is nothing in the system that requires any one person or court to be the court of appeal. In short, in the United States at present the Supreme Court is established as *the* court of final appeal, so the Supreme Court judges become the final arbiters regard-

less of the wishes of plaintiff or defendant alike. In contrast, in
the libertarian society the various competing private courts
could go to *any* appeals judge they think fair, expert, and objective. No single appeals judge or set of judges would be foisted
upon society by coercion.

How would the appeals judges be financed? There are many
possible ways, but the most likely is that they will be paid by
the various original courts who would charge their customers
for appeals services in their premiums or fees.

But suppose Brown insists on another appeals judge, and yet
another? Couldn't he escape judgment by appealing ad infini-
tum? Obviously, in *any* society legal proceedings cannot continue indefinitely; there must be *some* cutoff point. In the
present statist society, where government monopolizes the judicial function, the Supreme Court is arbitrarily designated as
the cutoff point. In the libertarian society, there would also
have to be an agreed-upon cutoff point, and since there are only
two parties to any crime or dispute—the plaintiff and the defendant—it seems most sensible for the legal code to declare
that *a decision arrived at by any two courts* shall be binding.
This will cover the situation when both the plaintiff's and the
defendant's courts come to the same decision, as well as the
situation when an appeals court decides on a disagreement between the two original courts.

The Law and the Courts

It is now clear that there will have to be a legal code in the
libertarian society. How? How can there be a legal code, a system of law *without* a government to promulgate it, an appointed system of judges, or a legislature to vote on statutes?
To begin with, is a legal code consistent with libertarian principles?

To answer the last question first, it should be clear that a
legal code is necessary to lay down precise guidelines for the
private courts. If, for example, Court A decides that all red-

heads are inherently evil and must be punished, it is clear that such decisions are the reverse of libertarian, that such a law would constitute an invasion of the rights of redheads. Hence, any such decision would be *illegal* in terms of libertarian principle, and could not be upheld by the rest of society. It then becomes necessary to have a legal code which would be generally accepted, and which the courts would pledge themselves to follow. The legal code, simply, would insist on the libertarian principle of no aggression against person or property, define property rights in accordance with libertarian principle, set up rules of evidence (such as currently apply) in deciding who are the wrongdoers in any dispute, and set up a code of maximum punishment for any particular crime. Within the framework of such a code, the particular courts would compete on the most efficient procedures, and the market would then decide whether judges, juries, etc., are the most efficient methods of providing judicial services.

Are such stable and consistent law codes possible, with only competing judges to develop and apply them, and without government or legislature? Not only are they *possible*, but over the years the best and most successful parts of our legal system were developed precisely in this manner. Legislatures, as well as kings, have been capricious, invasive, and inconsistent. They have only introduced anomalies and despotism into the legal system. In fact, the government is no more qualified to develop and apply law than it is to provide any other service; and just as religion has been separated from the state, and the economy can be separated from the State, so can every other State function, including police, courts, *and* the law itself!

As indicated above, for example, the entire law merchant was developed, not by the State or in State courts, but by private merchant courts. It was only much later that government took over mercantile law from its development in merchants' courts. The same occurred with admiralty law, the entire structure of the law of the sea, shipping, salvages, etc. Here again, the State was not interested, and its jurisdiction did not apply to the high seas; so the shippers themselves took on the task of not only applying, but working out the whole structure of admiralty law in their own private courts. Again, it was only later that the government appropriated admiralty law into its own courts.

Finally, the major body of Anglo-Saxon law, the justly celebrated *common law,* was developed over the centuries by competing judges applying time-honored principles rather than the shifting decrees of the State. These principles were not decided upon arbitrarily by any king or legislature; they grew up over centuries by applying rational—and very often libertarian—principles to the cases before them. The idea of following precedent was developed, *not* as a blind service to the past, but because all the judges of the past had made their decisions in applying the generally accepted common law principles to specific cases and problems. For it was universally held that the judge did not *make* law (as he often does today); the judge's task, his expertise, was in *finding* the law in accepted common law principles, and then applying that law to specific cases or to new technological or institutional conditions. The glory of the centuries-long development of the common law is testimony to their success.

The common law judges, furthermore, functioned very much like private arbitrators, as experts in the law to whom private parties went with their disputes. There was no arbitrarily imposed "supreme court" whose decision would be binding, nor was precedent, though honored, considered as *automatically* binding either. Thus, the libertarian Italian jurist Bruno Leoni has written:

. . . courts of judicature could not easily enact arbitrary rules of their own in England, as they were never in a position to do so directly, that is to say, in the usual, sudden, widely ranging and imperious manner of legislators. Moreover, there were so many courts of justice in England and they were so jealous of one another that even the famous principle of the binding precedent was not openly recognized as valid by them until comparatively recent times. Besides, they could never decide anything that had not been previously brought before them by private persons. Finally, comparatively few people used to go before the courts to ask from them the rules deciding their cases.[3]

And on the absence of "supreme courts":

. . . it cannot be denied that the lawyers' law or the judiciary law may tend to acquire the characteristics of legislation, including its undesirable ones, whenever jurists or judges are entitled to decide ultimately on a case. . . . In our time the mechanism of the judiciary in certain countries where "supreme courts" are established results in the imposition of the personal views of the members of these courts, or of a majority of them, on all the other people concerned whenever there is a great deal of disagreement between the opinion of the former and the convictions of the latter. But . . . this possibility, far from being necessarily implied in the nature of lawyers' law or of judiciary law, is rather a deviation from it. . . .[4]

Apart from such aberrations, the imposed personal views of the judges were kept to a minimum: (a) by the fact that judges could only make decisions when private citizens brought cases to them; (b) each judge's decisions applied only to the particular case; and (c) because the decisions of the common-law judges and lawyers always considered the precedents of the centuries. Furthermore, as Leoni points out, in contrast to legislatures or the executive, where dominant majorities or pressure groups ride roughshod over minorities, judges, by their very position, are constrained to hear and weigh the arguments of the two contending parties in each dispute. "Parties are *equal* as regards the judge, in the sense that they are free to produce arguments and evidence. They do not constitute a group in which dissenting minorities give way to triumphant majorities. . . ." And Leoni points out the analogy between this process and the free-market economy: "Of course, arguments may be stronger or weaker, but the fact that every party can

[3] Bruno Leoni, *Freedom and the Law* (Los Angeles: Nash Publishing Co., 1972), p. 87.
[4] *Ibid.*, pp. 23–24.

produce them is comparable to the fact that everybody can individually compete with everybody else in the market in order
to buy and sell." [5]

Professor Leoni found that, in the *private law* area, the ancient Roman judges operated in the same way as the English
common law courts:

The Roman jurist was a sort of scientist; the objects of his research
were the solutions to cases that citizens submitted to him for study,
just as industrialists might today submit to a physicist or to an
engineer a technical problem concerning their plants or their production. Hence, private Roman law was something to be described
or to be discovered, not something to be enacted—a world of things
that were there, forming part of the common heritage of all Roman
citizens. Nobody enacted that law; nobody could change it by any
exercise of his personal will. . . . This is the long-run concept or,
if you prefer, the Roman concept, of the certainty of the law.[6]

Finally, Professor Leoni was able to use his knowledge of the
operations of ancient and common law to answer the vital
question: In a libertarian society, "who will appoint the judges
. . . to let them perform the task of defining the law?" His
answer is: the *people* themselves, people who would go to the
judges with the greatest reputation of expertise and wisdom in
knowing and applying the basic common legal principles of the
society:

In fact, it is rather immaterial to establish in advance who will appoint the judges, for, in a sense, everybody could do so, as happens
to a certain extent when people resort to private arbiters to settle
their own quarrels. . . . For the appointment of judges is not such
a special problem as would be, for example, that of "appointing"
physicists or doctors or other kinds of learned and experienced people. The emergence of good professional people in any society is
only apparently due to official appointments, if any. It is, in fact,
based on a widespread consent on the part of clients, colleagues,
and the public at large—a consent without which no appointment

[5] *Ibid.*, p. 188.
[6] *Ibid.*, pp.84–85.

is really effective. Of course, people can be wrong about the true value chosen as being worthy, but these difficulties in their choice are inescapable in any kind of choice.[7]

Of course, in the future libertarian society, the basic legal code would not rely on blind custom, much of which could well be antilibertarian. The code would have to be established on the basis of acknowledged libertarian principle, of nonaggression against the person or property of others; in short, on the basis of reason rather than on mere tradition, however sound its general outlines. Since we have a body of common law principles to draw on, however, the task of reason in correcting and amending the common law would be far easier than trying to construct a body of systematic legal principles *de novo* out of the thin air.

The most remarkable historical example of a society of libertarian law and courts, however, has been neglected by historians until very recently. And this was also a society where not only the courts and the law were largely libertarian, but where they operated within a purely *state-less* and libertarian society—in short, a society of virtual "free-market anarchism." This was ancient Ireland—an Ireland which persisted in this libertarian path for roughly a thousand years until its brutal conquest by England in the seventeenth century. And, in contrast to many similarly functioning primitive tribes (such as the Ibos in West Africa, and many European tribes), preconquest Ireland was not in any sense a "primitive" society: it was a highly complex society that was, for centuries, the most advanced, most scholarly, and most civilized in all of Western Europe.

For a thousand years, then, ancient Celtic Ireland had no State or anything like it. As the leading authority on ancient Irish law has written: "There was no legislature, no bailiffs, no police, no public enforcement of justice. . . . There was no trace of State-administered justice." [8]

---

[7] *Ibid.*, p. 183.

[8] Quoted in the best introduction to ancient, anarchistic Irish institutions, Joseph R. Peden, "Stateless Societies: Ancient Ireland," *The Liber-*

How then was justice secured? The basic political unit of ancient Ireland was the *tuath*. All "freemen" who owned land, all professionals, and all craftsmen, were entitled to become members of a *tuath*. Each *tuath*'s members formed an annual assembly which decided all common policies, declared war or peace on other *tuatha*, and elected or deposed their "kings." An important point is that, in contrast to primitive tribes, no one was stuck or bound to a given *tuath*, either because of kinship or of geographical location. Individual members were free to, and often did, secede from a *tuath* and join a competing *tuath*. Often, two or more *tuatha* decided to merge into a single, more efficient unit. As Professor Peden states, "the *tuath* is thus a body of persons voluntarily united for socially beneficial purposes and the sum total of the landed properties of its members constituted its territorial dimension." [9] In short, they did not have the modern State with its claim to sovereignty over a given (usually expanding) territorial area, divorced from the landed property rights of its subjects; on the contrary, *tuatha* were voluntary associations which only comprised the landed properties of its voluntary members. Historically, about 80 to 100 *tuatha* coexisted at any time throughout Ireland.

But what of the elected "king"? Did *he* constitute a form of State ruler? Chiefly, the king functioned as a religious high priest, presiding over the worship rites of the *tuath*, which functioned as a voluntary religious, as well as a social and political, organization. As in pagan, pre-Christian, priesthoods, the kingly function was hereditary, this practice carrying over to Christian times. The king was elected by the *tuath* from within a royal kin-group (the *derbfine*), which carried the hereditary priestly function. *Politically*, however, the king had strictly limited functions: he was the military leader of the *tuath*, and he

---

tarian Forum (April 1971), pp. 3ff. Also see Daniel A. Binchy, *Anglo-Saxon and Irish Kingship* (London: Oxford University Press, 1970); Myles Dillon, *The Celtic Realms* (London: George Weidenfeld & Nicolson, 1967), and *id., Early Irish Society* (Dublin, 1954).
    [9] Peden, *op. cit.*, p. 4.

presided over the *tuath* assemblies. But he could only conduct war or peace negotiations as agent of the assemblies; and he was in no sense sovereign and had no rights of administering justice over *tuath* members. He could not legislate, and when he himself was party to a lawsuit, he had to submit his case to an independent judicial arbiter.

Again, how, then, was law developed and justice maintained? In the first place, the law itself was based on a body of ancient and immemorial custom, passed down as oral and then written tradition through a class of professional jurists called the *filid*. The *filid* were in no sense public, or governmental, officials; they were simply selected by parties to disputes on the basis of their reputations for wisdom, knowledge of the customary law, and the integrity of their decisions. As Professor Peden states:

. . . the professional jurists were consulted by parties to disputes for advice as to what the law was in particular cases, and these same men often acted as arbitrators between suitors. They remained at all times private persons, not public officials; their functioning depended upon their knowledge of the law and the integrity of their judicial reputations.[10]

Furthermore, the *filid* jurists had *no connection whatsoever* with the individual *tuatha* or with their kings. They were completely private, national in scope, and were used by disputants throughout Ireland. Moreover, and this is a vital point, in contrast to the system of private Roman lawyers, the *filid* was all there was; there were no other judges, no "public" judges of any kind, in ancient Ireland.

It was the *filid* who were schooled in the law, and who added glosses and applications to the law to fit changing conditions. Furthermore, there was no monopoly, in any sense, of the *filid* jurists; instead, several competing schools of jurisprudence existed and competed for the custom of the Irish people.

How were the decisions of the *filid* enforced? Through an elaborate, voluntarily developed system of "insurance," or

---

[10] Peden, *op. cit.*, p. 4.

sureties. Men were linked together by a variety of surety rela-
tionships by which they guaranteed one another for the right-
ing of wrongs, and for the enforcement of justice and the decisions of the *filid*. In short, the *filid* themselves were not involved in the enforcement of decisions, which rested again with
private individuals linked through sureties. There were various
types of surety. For example, the surety would guarantee with
his own property the payment of a debt, and then join the
plaintiff in enforcing a debt judgment if the debtor refused to
pay. In that case, the debtor would have to pay double damages: one to the original creditor, and another as compensation
to his surety. And this system applied to all offences, aggressions and assaults as well as commercial contracts; in short, it
applied to all cases of what we would call "civil" and "criminal"
law. All criminals were considered to be "debtors" who owed
restitution and compensation to their victims, who thus became
their "creditors." The victim would gather his sureties around
him and proceed to apprehend the criminal or to proclaim his
suit publicly and demand that the defendant submit to adjudi-
cation of their dispute with the *filid*. The criminal might then
send his own sureties to negotiate a settlement or agree to submit the dispute to a *filid*. If he did not do so, he was considered an "outlaw" by the entire community; he could no longer
enforce any claim of his own in the courts, and he was treated
to the opprobrium of the entire community.[11]

There were occasional "wars," to be sure, in the thousand
years of Celtic Ireland, but they were minor brawls, negligible
compared to the devastating wars that racked the rest of
Europe. As Professor Peden points out, "without the coercive
apparatus of the State which can through taxation and con-

---

[11] Professor Charles Donahue of Fordham University has maintained
that the secular part of ancient Irish law was not simply haphazard tradition; that it was consciously rooted in the Stoic conception of *natural law*,
discoverable by man's reason. Charles Donahue, "Early Celtic Laws" (unpublished paper, delivered at the Columbia University Seminar in the History of Legal and Political Thought, Autumn, 1964), pp. 13ff.

scription mobilize large amounts of arms and manpower, the Irish were unable to sustain any large scale military force in the field for any length of time. Irish wars . . . were pitiful brawls and cattle raids by European standards." [12]

Thus, we have indicated that it is perfectly possible, in theory and historically, to have efficient and courteous police, competent and learned judges, and a body of systematic and socially accepted law—and none of these things being furnished by a coercive government. Government—claiming a compulsory monopoly of protection over a geographical area, and extracting its revenues by force—can be separated from the entire field of protection. Government is no more necessary for providing vital protection service than it is necessary for providing anything else. And we have not stressed a crucial fact about government: that its compulsory monopoly over the weapons of coercion has led it, over the centuries, to infinitely more butcheries and infinitely greater tyranny and oppression than any decentralized, private agencies could possibly have done. If we look at the black record of mass murder, exploitation, and tyranny levied on society by governments over the ages, we need not be loath to abandon the Leviathan State and . . . try freedom.

Outlaw Protectors

We have saved for the last this problem: What if police or judges and courts should be venal and biased—what if they should bias their decisions, for example, in favor of particularly wealthy clients? We have shown how a libertarian legal and judicial system could work on the purely free market, assuming honest differences of opinion—but what if one or more police or courts should become, in effect, outlaws? What then?

In the first place, libertarians do not flinch from such a question. In contrast to such utopians as Marxists or left-wing anarchists (anarcho-communists or anarcho-syndicalists), liber-

---

[12] Peden, *op. cit.*, p. 3.

tarians do *not* assume that the ushering in of the purely free society of their dreams will also bring with it a new, magically transformed Libertarian Man. We do not assume that the lion will lie down with the lamb, or that no one will have criminal or fraudulent designs upon his neighbor. The "better" that people will be, of course, the better *any* social system will work, in particular the less work *any* police or courts will have to do. But no such assumption is made by libertarians. What we assert is that, given any particular degree of "goodness" or "badness" among men, the purely libertarian society will be at once the most moral and the most efficient, the least criminal and the most secure of person or property.

Let us first consider the problem of the venal or crooked judge or court. What of the court which favors its own wealthy client in trouble? In the first place, any such favoritism will be highly unlikely, given the rewards and sanctions of the free market economy. The very life of the court, the very livelihood of a judge, will depend on his reputation for integrity, fair-mindedness, objectivity, and the quest for truth in every case. This is his "brand name." Should word of any venality leak out, he will immediately lose clients and the courts will no longer have customers; for even those clients who may be criminally inclined will scarcely sponsor a court whose decisions are no longer taken seriously by the rest of society, or who themselves may well be in jail for dishonest and fraudulent dealings. If, for example, Joe Zilch is accused of a crime or breach of contract, and he goes to a "court" headed by his brother-in-law, no one, least of all other, honest courts will take this "court's" decision seriously. It will no longer be considered a "court" in the eyes of anyone but Joe Zilch and his family.

Contrast this built-in corrective mechanism to the present-day government courts. Judges are appointed or elected for long terms, up to life, and they are accorded a monopoly of decision-making in their particular area. It is almost impossible, except in cases of gross corruption, to do anything about venal decisions of judges. Their power to make and to enforce their decisions continues unchecked year after year. Their salaries continue to be paid, furnished under coercion by the hapless taxpayer. But in the totally free society, any suspicion of a judge or court will cause their customers to melt away and their "decisions" to be ignored. This is a far more efficient system of keeping judges honest than the mechanism of government.

Furthermore, the temptation for venality and bias would be far less for another reason: business firms in the free market earn their keep, *not* from wealthy customers, but from a mass market by consumers. Macy's earns its income from the mass of the population, not from a few wealthy customers. The same is true of Metropolitan Life Insurance today, and the same would be true of any "Metropolitan" court system tomorrow. It would be folly indeed for the courts to risk the loss of favor by the bulk of its customers for the favors of a few wealthy clients. But contrast the present system, where judges, like all other politicians, may be beholden to wealthy contributors who finance the campaigns of their political parties.

There is a myth that the "American System" provides a superb set of "checks and balances," with the executive, the legislature, and the courts all balancing and checking one against the other, so that power cannot unduly accumulate in one set of hands. But the American "checks and balances" system is largely a fraud. For each one of these institutions is a coercive monopoly in its area, and all of them are part of one government, headed by one political party at any given time. Furthermore, at best there are only two parties, each one close to the other in ideology and personnel, often colluding, and the actual day-to-day business of government headed by a civil service bureaucracy that *cannot* be displaced by the voters. Contrast to these mythical checks and balances the *real* checks and balances provided by the free-market economy! What keeps A&P honest is the competition, actual and potential, of Safeway, Pioneer, and countless other grocery stores. What keeps them honest is the ability of the consumers to cut off their patronage. What would keep the free-market judges and courts honest is the lively possibility of heading down the block or down the road to *another* judge or court if suspicion should descend on any particular one. What would keep them honest is the lively possibility of their customers cutting off their business. These are the *real*, active checks and balances of the free-market economy and the free society.

The same analysis applies to the possibility of a private police force becoming outlaw, of using their coercive powers to exact tribute, set up a "protection racket" to shake down their victims, etc. Of course, such a thing *could* happen. But, in contrast to present-day society, there would be immediate checks and balances available; there would be *other* police forces who could use their weapons to band together to put down the aggressors against their clientele. If the Metropolitan Police Force should become gangsters and exact tribute, then the rest of society could flock to the Prudential, Equitable, etc., police forces who could band together to put them down. And this contrasts vividly with the State. If a group of gangsters should capture the State apparatus, with its monopoly of coercive weapons, there is nothing at present that can stop them—short of the immensely difficult process of revolution. In a libertarian society there would be no need for a massive revolution to stop the depredation of gangster-States; there would be a swift turning to the honest police forces to check and put down the force that had turned bandit.

And, indeed, what is the State anyway but organized banditry? What is taxation but theft on a gigantic, unchecked, scale? What is war but mass murder on a scale impossible by private police forces? What is conscription but mass enslavement? Can anyone envision a private police force getting away with a tiny fraction of what States get away with, and do habitually, year after year, century after century?

There is another vital consideration that would make it almost impossible for an outlaw police force to commit anything like the banditry that modern governments practice. One of the crucial factors that permits governments to do the monstrous things they habitually do is the sense of *legitimacy* on the part of the stupefied public. The average citizen may not like—may even strongly object to—the policies and exactions of his government. But he has been imbued with the idea—carefully indoctrinated by centuries of governmental propaganda—that the government is his legitimate sovereign, and that it would be wicked or mad to refuse to obey its dictates. It is this sense of legitimacy that the State's intellectuals have fostered over the ages, aided and abetted by all the trappings of legitimacy: flags, rituals, ceremonies, awards, constitutions, etc. A bandit gang— *even if all* the police forces conspired together into one vast gang—could never command such legitimacy. The public would consider them purely bandits; their extortions and tributes would never be considered legitimate though onerous "taxes," to be paid automatically. The public would quickly resist these illegitimate demands and the bandits would be resisted and overthrown. Once the public had tasted the joys, prosperity, freedom, and efficiency of a libertarian, State-less society, it would be almost impossible for a State to fasten itself upon them once again. Once freedom has been fully enjoyed, it is no easy task to force people to give it up.

But *suppose*—just suppose—that despite all these handicaps and obstacles, despite the love for their new-found freedom, despite the inherent checks and balances of the free market, suppose *anyway* that the State manages to reestablish itself. What then? Well, then, all that would have happened is that we would have a State once again. We would be no worse off than we are now, with our current State. *And,* as one libertarian philosopher has put it, "at least the world will have had a glorious holiday." Karl Marx's ringing promise applies far more to a libertarian society than to communism: In trying freedom, in abolishing the State, we have nothing to lose and everything to gain.

National Defense

We come now to what is usually the final argument against the libertarian position. Every libertarian has heard a sympathetic but critical listener say: "All right, I see how this system could be applied successfully to local police and courts. But how could a libertarian society defend us against the Russians?"

There are, of course, several dubious assumptions implied in such a question. There is the assumption that the Russians are bent upon military invasion of the United States, a doubtful assumption at best. There is the assumption that any such desire would still remain after the United States had become a purely libertarian, "free-market anarchist" society. This notion overlooks the lesson of history that wars result from conflicts between nation-states, each armed to the teeth, each direly suspicious of attack by the other. But a libertarian America would clearly not be a threat to anyone, not because it had no arms but because it would be dedicated to no aggression against anyone, or against any country. Being no longer a nation-state, which is inherently threatening, there would be little chance of any country attacking us. One of the great evils of the nation-state is that each State is able to identify all of its subjects with itself; hence in any inter-State war, the innocent civilians, the subjects of each country, are subject to aggression from the enemy State. But in a libertarian society there would be no such identification, and hence very little chance of such a devastating war. Suppose, for example, that our outlaw Metropolitan Police Force has initiated aggression not only against Americans but also against Mexicans. If Mexico had a government, then clearly the Mexican government would know full well that Americans in general were not implicated in the Metropolitan's crimes, and had no symbiotic relationship with it. If the Mexican police engaged in a punitive expedition to punish the Metropolitan force, they would not be at war with Americans in general—as they would be now. In fact, it is highly likely that other A erican forces would join the Mexicans in putting down the aggressor. Hence, the idea of inter-State war against a libertarian country or geographical area would most likely disappear.

There is, furthermore, a grave philosophical error in the very posing of this sort of question about the Russians. When we

The Public Sector, III: Police, Law, and the Courts 249

contemplate *any* sort of new system, whatever it may be, we must *first* decide whether we want to see it brought about. In order to decide whether we *want* libertarianism or communism, or left-wing anarchism, or theocracy, or any other system, we must first assume that it has been established, and *then* consider whether the system could work, whether it could remain in existence, and how efficient just such a system would be. We have shown, I believe, that a libertarian system, once instituted, could work, be viable, and be at once far more efficient, prosperous, moral, and free than any other social system. But we have said nothing about how to *get* from the present system to the ideal; for these are two totally separate questions: The question of what *is* our ideal goal, and of the strategy and tactics of how to get from the present system *to* that goal. The Russian question mixes these two levels of discourse. It assumes, *not* that libertarianism has been established everywhere throughout the globe, but that for some reason it has been established *only* in America and nowhere else. But why assume this? Why not first assume that it has been established *everywhere* and see whether we like it? After all, the libertarian philosophy is an eternal one, not bound to time or place. We advocate liberty for everyone, everywhere, not just in the United States. If someone agrees that a world libertarian society, once established, is the best that he can conceive, that it would be workable, efficient, and moral, then let him *become* a libertarian, let him join us in accepting liberty as our ideal goal, and *then* join us further in the separate—and obviously difficult— task of figuring out how to bring this ideal about.

If we do move on to strategy, it is obvious that the larger an area in which liberty is first established the *better* its chances for survival, and the better its chance to resist any violent overthrow that may be attempted. If liberty is established instantaneously throughout the world, then there will of course be *no* problem of "national defense." *All* problems will be local police problems. If, however, only Deep Falls, Wyoming, becomes libertarian while the rest of America and the world remain statist, its chances for survival will be very slim. If Deep Falls, Wyoming, declares its secession from the United States government and establishes a free society, the chances are great that the United States—given its historical ferocity toward secessionists—would quickly invade and crush the new free society, and there is little that *any* Deep Falls police force could do about it. Between these two polar cases, there is an infinite continuum of degrees, and obviously, the larger the area of freedom, the better it could withstand any outside threat. The "Russian question" is therefore a matter of strategy rather than a matter of deciding on basic principles and on the goal toward which we wish to direct our efforts.

But after all this is said and done, let us take up the Russian question anyway. Let us assume that the Soviet Union would really be hell-bent on attacking a libertarian population within the present boundaries of the United States (clearly, there would no longer be a United States government to form a single nation-state). In the first place, the form and quantity of defense expenditures would be decided upon by the American consumers themselves. Those Americans who favor Polaris submarines, and fear a Soviet threat, would subscribe toward the financing of such vessels. Those who prefer an ABM system would invest in such defensive missiles. Those who laugh at such a threat or those who are committed pacifists would not contribute to any "national" defense service at all. Different defense theories would be applied in proportion to those who agree with, and support, the various theories being offered. Given the enormous waste in all wars and defense preparations in all countries throughout history, it is certainly not beyond the bounds of reason to propose that private, voluntary defense efforts would be far more efficient than government boondoggles. Certainly these efforts would be infinitely more moral.

But let us assume the worst. Let us assume that the Soviet Union at last invades and conquers the territory of America. What then? We have to realize that the Soviet Union's difficulties will have only just begun. The main reason a conquering country can rule a defeated country is that the latter has an existing State apparatus to transmit and enforce the victor's orders onto a subject population. Britain, though far smaller in area and population, was able to rule India for centuries because it could transmit British orders to the ruling Indian princes, who in turn could enforce them on the subject population. But in those cases in history where the conquered *had* no government, the conquerors found rule over the conquered extremely difficult. When the British conquered West Africa, for example, they found it extremely difficult to govern the Ibo tribe (later to form Biafra) because that tribe was essentially anarchistic, and had no ruling government of tribal chiefs to transmit orders to the natives. And perhaps the major reason it took the English centuries to conquer ancient Ireland is that the Irish had no State, and that there was therefore no ruling governmental structure to keep treaties, transmit orders, etc. It is for this reason that the English kept denouncing the "wild" and "uncivilized" Irish as "faithless," because they would not keep treaties with the English conquerors. The English could never understand that, lacking any sort of State, the Irish warriors who concluded treaties with the English could *only* speak for themselves; they could never commit any other group of the Irish population.[13]

Furthermore, the occupying Russians' lives would be made even more difficult by the inevitable eruption of guerrilla warfare by the American population. It is surely a lesson of the twentieth century—a lesson first driven home by the successful American revolutionaries against the mighty British Empire—that no occupying force can long keep down a native population determined to resist. If the giant United States, armed with far greater productivity and firepower, could not succeed against a tiny and relatively unarmed Vietnamese population, how in the world could the Soviet Union succeed in keeping down the

[13] Peden, *op. cit.*, p. 3; also see Kathleen Hughes, introduction to A. Jocelyn Otway-Ruthven, *A History of Medieval Ireland* (New York: Barnes & Noble, 1968).

American people? No Russian occupation soldier's life would be safe from the wrath of a resisting American populace. Guerrilla warfare has proved to be an irresistible force precisely because it stems, not from a dictatorial central government, but from the people themselves, fighting for their liberty and independence against a foreign State. And surely the anticipation of this sea of troubles, of the enormous costs and losses that would inevitably follow, would stop well in advance even a hypothetical Soviet government bent on military conquest.

12

Conservation, Ecology, and Growth

Liberal Complaints

LEFT-LIBERAL INTELLECTUALS are often a wondrous group to behold. In the last three or four decades, not a very long time in human history, they have, like whirling dervishes, let loose a series of angry complaints against free-market capitalism. The curious thing is that each of these complaints has been contradictory to one or more of their predecessors. But contradictory complaints by liberal intellectuals do not seem to faze them or serve to abate their petulance—even though it is often the very same intellectuals who are reversing themselves so rapidly. And these reversals seem to make no dent whatever in their self-righteousness or in the self-confidence of their position.

Let us consider the record of recent decades:

1. In the late 1930s and early 1940s, the liberal intellectuals came to the conclusion that capitalism was suffering from inevitable "secular stagnation," a stagnation imposed by the slowing down of population growth, the end of the old Western frontier, and by the supposed fact that no further inven-

tions were possible. All this spelled eternal stagnation, permanent mass unemployment, and therefore the need for socialism, or thoroughgoing state planning, to replace free-market capitalism. This on the threshold of the greatest boom in American history!

2. During the 1950s, despite the great boom in postwar America, the liberal intellectuals kept raising their sights; the cult of "economic growth" now entered the scene. To be sure, capitalism was growing, but it was not growing fast enough. Therefore free-market capitalism must be abandoned, and socialism or government intervention must step in and force-feed the economy, must build investments and compel greater saving in order to maximize the rate of growth, even if we don't *want* to grow that fast. Conservative economists such as Colin Clark attacked this liberal program as "growthmanship."

3. Suddenly, John Kenneth Galbraith entered the liberal scene with his best-selling *The Affluent Society* in 1958. And just as suddenly, the liberal intellectuals reversed their indictments. The trouble with capitalism, it now appeared, was that it had grown *too much*; we were no longer stagnant, but *too well off*, and man had lost his spirituality amidst supermarkets and automobile tail fins. What was necessary, then, was for government to step in, either in massive intervention or as socialism, and tax the consumers heavily in order to reduce their bloated affluence.

4. The cult of excess affluence had its day, to be superseded by a contradictory worry about poverty, stimulated by Michael Harrington's *The Other America* in 1962. Suddenly, the problem with America was not excessive affluence, but increasing and grinding poverty—and, once again, the solution was for the government to step in, plan mightily, and tax the wealthy in order to lift up the poor. And so we had the War on Poverty for several years.

5. Stagnation; deficient growth; over-affluence; over-poverty; the intellectual fashions changed like ladies' hemlines. Then,

in 1964, the happily short-lived Ad Hoc Committee on the Triple Revolution issued its then-famous manifesto, which brought us and the liberal intellectuals full circle. For two or three frenetic years we were regaled with the idea that America's problem was not stagnation but the exact reverse: in a few short years all of America's production facilities would be automated and cybernated, incomes and production would be enormous and superabundant, *but* everyone would be automated out of a job. Once again, free-market capitalism would lead to permanent mass unemployment, which could *only* be remedied—you guessed it!—by massive state intervention or by outright socialism. For several years, in the mid-1960s, we thus suffered from what was justly named the "Automation Hysteria." [1]

6. By the late 1960s it was clear to everyone that the automation hysterics had been dead wrong, that automation was proceeding at no faster a pace than old-fashioned "mechanization," and indeed that the 1969 recession was causing a falling off in the rate of increase of productivity. One hears no more about automation dangers nowadays; we are now in the seventh phase of liberal economic flip-flops.

7. Affluence is again excessive, and, in the name of conservation, ecology, and the increasing scarcity of resources, free-market capitalism is growing much too fast. State planning, or socialism, must, of course, step in to abolish all growth and bring about a zero-growth society and economy—in order to avoid negative growth, or retrogression, sometime in the future! We are now back to a super-Galbraithian position, to which has been added scientific jargon about effluents, ecology, and "spaceship earth," as well as a bitter assault on technology itself as being an evil polluter. Capitalism has brought about technology, growth—including population growth, industry, and

[1] Ironically, the conservative economist Dr. George Terborgh, who had written the major refutation of the stagnation thesis a generation earlier (*The Bogey of Economic Maturity* [1945]), now wrote the leading refutation of the new wave, *The Automation Hysteria* (1966).

pollution—and government is supposed to step in and eradicate these evils.

It is not at all unusual, in fact, to find the same people now holding a contradictory blend of positions 5 and 7 and maintaining *at one and the same time* that (a) we are living in a "post-scarcity" age where we no longer need private property, capitalism, or material incentives to production; *and* (b) that capitalist greed is depleting our resources and bringing about imminent worldwide scarcity. The liberal answer to both, or indeed to all, of these problems turns out, of course, to be the same: socialism or state planning to replace free-market capitalism. The great economist Joseph Schumpeter put the whole shoddy performance of liberal intellectuals into a nutshell a generation ago: "Capitalism stands its trial before judges who have the sentence of death in their pockets. They are going to pass it, whatever the defense they may hear; the only success victorious defense can possibly produce is a change in the indictment." [2] And so, the charges, the indictments, may change and contradict previous charges—but the answer is always and wearily the same.

The Attack on Technology and Growth

The fashionable attack on growth and affluence is palpably an attack by comfortable, contented upper-class liberals. Enjoying a material contentment and a living standard undreamt of by even the wealthiest men of the past, it is easy for upper-class liberals to sneer at "materialism," and to call for a freeze on all further economic advance. For the mass of the world's population still living in squalor such a cry for the cessation of growth is truly obscene; but even in the United States, there is little evidence of satiety and superabundance. Even the upper-class liberals themselves have not been conspicuous for making

[2] Joseph A. Schumpeter, *Capitalism, Socialism, and Democracy* (New York: Harper & Bros., 1942), p. 144.

a bonfire of their salary checks as a contribution to their war on "materialism" and affluence.

The widespread attack on technology is even more irresponsible. If technology were to be rolled back to the "tribe" and to the preindustrial era, the result would be mass starvation and death on a universal scale. The vast majority of the world's population is dependent for its very survival on modern technology and industry. The North American continent was able to accommodate approximately one million Indians in the days before Columbus, all living on a subsistence level. It is now able to accommodate several hundred million people, all living at an infinitely higher living standard—and the reason is modern technology and industry. Abolish the latter and we will abolish the people as well. For all one knows, to our fanatical antipopulationists this "solution" to the population question may be a good thing, but for the great majority of us, this would be a draconian "final solution" indeed.

The irresponsible attack on technology is another liberal flip-flop: it comes from the same liberal intellectuals who, thirty-odd years ago, were denouncing capitalism for not putting modern technology to full use in the service of State planning and were calling for absolute rule by a modern "technocratic" elite. Yet now the very same intellectuals who not so long ago were yearning for a technocratic dictatorship over all of our lives are now trying to deprive us of the vital fruits of technology itself.

Yet the various contradictory phases of liberal thought never completely die; and many of the same antitechnologists, in a 180-degree reversal of the automation hysteria, are *also* confidently forecasting technological stagnation from now on. They cheerily predict a gloomy future for mankind by assuming that technology will stagnate, and not continue to improve and accelerate. This is the technique of pseudoscientific forecasting of the widely touted antigrowth Club of Rome Report. As Passell, Roberts, and Ross write in their critique of the report, "If the telephone company were restricted to turn-of-the-century technology 20 million operators would be needed to handle today's volume of calls. Or, as British editor Norman Macrae has observed, an extrapolation of the trends of the 1880s would show today's cities buried under horse manure." [3] Or, further:

While the team's [Club of Rome's] model hypothesizes exponential growth for industrial and agricultural needs, it places arbitrary, non-exponential, limits on the technical progress that might accommodate these needs. . . .

The Rev. Thomas Malthus made a similar point two centuries ago without benefit of computer printouts. . . . Malthus argued that people tend to multiply exponentially, while the food supply at best increases at a constant rate. He expected that starvation and war would periodically redress the balance. . . .

But there is no particular criterion beyond myopia on which to base that speculation. Malthus was wrong; food capacity has kept up with population. While no one knows for certain, technical progress shows no sign of slowing down. The best econometric estimates suggest that it is indeed growing exponentially.[4]

What we need is more economic growth, not less; more and better technology, and not the impossible and absurd attempt to scrap technology and return to the primitive tribe. Improved technology and greater capital investment will lead to higher living standards for all and provide greater material comforts, as well as the leisure to pursue and enjoy the "spiritual" side of life. There is precious little culture or civilization available for people who must work long hours to eke out a subsistence living. The real problem is that productive capital investment is being siphoned off by taxes, restrictions, and government contracts for unproductive and wasteful government expenditures, including military and space boondoggling. Furthermore, the precious technical resource of scientists and engineers is being ever more intensively diverted to government, instead of to

---

[3] D. Meadows, *et al.*, *The Limits to Growth* (New York: Universe Books, 1972); P. Passell, M. Roberts, and L. Ross, "Review of *The Limits to Growth*," *New York Times Book Review* (April 2, 1972), p. 10.

[4] Passell, Roberts, and Ross, *op. cit.*, p. 12.

"civilian" consumer production. What we need is for government to get out of the way, remove its incubus of taxation and expenditures from the economy, and allow productive and technical resources once again to devote themselves fully to increasing the well-being of the mass of consumers. We need growth, higher living standards, and a technology and capital equipment that meet consumer wants and demands; but we can only achieve these by removing the incubus of statism and allowing the energies of all of the population to express themselves in the free-market economy. We need an economic and technological growth that emerges freely, as Jane Jacobs has shown, from the free-market economy, and not the distortions and wastes imposed upon the world economy from the liberal force-feeding of the 1950s. We need, in short, a truly free-market, libertarian economy.

Conservation of Resources

As we have mentioned, the selfsame liberals who claim that we have entered the "postscarcity" age and are in no further need of economc growth, are in the forefront of the complaint that "capitalist greed" is destroying our scarce natural resources. The gloom-and-doom soothsayers of the Club of Rome, for example, by simply extrapolating current trends of resource use, confidently predict the exhaustion of vital raw materials within forty years. But confident—and completely faulty—predictions of exhaustion of raw materials have been made countless times in recent centuries.

What the soothsayers have overlooked is the vital role that the free-market economic mechanism plays in conserving, and adding to, natural resources. Let us consider, for example, a typical copper mine. Why has copper ore not been exhausted long before now by the inexorable demands of our industrial civilization? Why is it that copper miners, once they have found and opened a vein of ore, do not mine all the copper immediately; why, instead, do they conserve the copper mine, add to it, and extract the copper gradually, from year to year? Because the mine owners realize that, for example, if they triple *this year's* production of copper they may indeed triple this year's income, *but* they will also be depleting the mine, and therefore the *future* income they will be able to derive from it. On the market, this loss of future income is immediately reflected in the monetary value—the price—of the mine as a whole. This monetary value, reflected in the selling price of the mine, and then of individual shares of mining stock, is based on the expected future income to be earned from the production of the copper; any depletion of the mine, then, will lower the value of the mine and hence the price of the mining stock. Every mine owner, then, has to weigh the advantages of immediate income from copper production against the loss in the "capital value" of the mine as a whole, and hence against the loss in the value of his shares.

The mine owners' decisions are determined by their expectations of future copper yields and demands, the existing and expected rates of interest, etc. Suppose, for example, that copper is expected to be rendered obsolete in a few years by a new synthetic metal. In that case, copper mine owners will rush to produce more copper now when it is more highly valued, and save less for the future when it will have little value—thereby benefitting the consumers and the economy as a whole by producing copper now when it is more intensely needed. But, on the other hand, if a copper shortage is expected in the future, mine owners will produce less now and wait to produce more later when copper prices are higher—thereby benefitting society by producing more in the future when it will be needed more intensely. Thus, we see that the market economy contains a marvelous built-in mechanism whereby the decisions of resource owners on present as against future production will benefit not only their own income and wealth, but the mass of consumers and the economy as a whole.

But there is much more to this free-market mechanism: Suppose that a growing shortage of copper is now expected in the future. The result is that more copper will be withheld now and saved for future production. The price of copper now will rise. The increase in copper prices will have several "conserving" effects. In the first place, the higher price of copper is a signal to the users of copper that it is scarcer and more expensive; the copper users will then conserve the use of this more expensive metal. They will use less copper, substituting cheaper metals or plastics; and copper will be conserved more fully and saved for those uses for which there is no satisfactory substitute. Moreover, the greater cost of copper will stimulate (a) a rush to find new copper ores; and (b) a search for less expensive substitutes, perhaps by new technological discoveries. Higher prices for copper will also stimulate campaigns for saving and recycling the metal. This price mechanism of the free market is precisely the reason that copper, and other natural resources, have not disappeared long ago. As Passell, Roberts, and Ross say in their critique of the Club of Rome:

Natural resource reserves and needs in the model are calculated [in] . . . the absence of prices as a variable in the "Limits" projection of how resources will be used. In the real world, rising prices act as an economic signal to conserve scarce resources, providing incentives to use cheaper materials in their place, stimulating research efforts on new ways to save on resource inputs, and making renewed exploration attempts more profitable.[5]

In fact, in contrast to the gloom-and-doomers, raw material and natural resource prices have remained low, and have generally declined relative to other prices. To liberal and Marxist intellectuals, this is usually a sign of capitalist "exploitation" of the underdeveloped countries which are often the producers of the raw materials. But it is a sign of something completely different, of the fact that natural resources have not been growing scarcer but more abundant; hence their relatively lower cost. The development of cheap substitutes, e.g., plastics, synthetic fibers, has kept natural resources cheap and abundant. And in

[5] Passell, Roberts, and Ross, *op. cit.*, p. 12.

a few decades we can expect that modern technology will develop a remarkably cheap source of energy—nuclear fusion—a development which will automatically yield a great abundance of raw materials for the work that will be needed.

The development of synthetic materials and of cheaper energy highlights a vital aspect of modern technology the doomsayers overlook: that technology and industrial production *create* resources which had never existed as effective resources. For example, before the development of the kerosene lamp and especially the automobile, petroleum was not a resource but an unwanted waste, a giant liquid black "weed." It was only the development of modern industry that converted petroleum *into* a useful resource. Furthermore, modern technology, through improved geological techniques and through the incentives of the market, has been *finding* new petroleum reserves at a rapid rate.

Predictions of imminent exhaustion of resources, as we have noted, are nothing new. In 1908, President Theodore Roosevelt, calling a Governors' Conference on natural resources, warned of their "imminent exhaustion." At the same conference, steel industrialist Andrew Carnegie predicted the exhaustion of the Lake Superior iron range by 1940, while railroad magnate James J. Hill forecast the exhaustion of much of our timber resources in ten years. Not only that: Hill even predicted an imminent shortage of wheat production in the United States, in a country where we are still grappling with the wheat *surpluses* generated by our farm subsidy program. Current forecasts of doom are made on the same basis: a grievous underweighting of the prospects of modern technology and an ignorance of the workings of the market economy.[6]

It is true that several particular natural resources have suffered, in the past and now, from depletion. But in each case the reason has not been "capitalist greed"; on the contrary, the reason has been the *failure* of government to allow private prop-

[6] On these mistaken forecasts, see Thomas B. Nolan, "The Inexhaustible Resource of Technology," in H. Jarrett, ed., *Perspectives on Conservation* (Baltimore: Johns Hopkins Press, 1958), pp. 49–66.

erty in the resource—in short, a failure to pursue the logic of private property rights far enough.

One example has been timber resources. In the American West and in Canada, most of the forests are owned, not by private owners but by the federal (or provincial) government. The government then *leases* their use to private timber companies. In short, private property is permitted only in the annual *use* of the resource, but not in the forest, the resource, itself. In this situation, the private timber company does not own the capital value, and therefore does not have to worry about depletion of the resource itself. The timber company has no economic incentive to conserve the resource, replant trees, etc. Its only incentive is to cut as many trees as quickly as possible, since there is no economic value to the timber company in maintaining the capital value of the forest. In Europe, where private ownership of forests is far more common, there is little complaint of destruction of timber resources. For wherever private property is allowed in the forest itself, it is to the benefit of the owner to preserve and restore tree growth while he is cutting timber, so as to avoid depletion of the forest's capital value.[7]

Thus, in the United States, a major culprit has been the Forest Service of the U.S. Department of Agriculture, which owns forests and leases annual rights to cut timber, with resulting devastation of the trees. In contrast, private forests such as those owned by large lumber firms like Georgia-Pacific and U.S. Plywood scientifically cut and reforest their trees in order to maintain their future supply.[8]

---

[7] On timber, and on conservation generally, see Anthony Scott, *Natural Resources: The Economics of Conservation* (Toronto: University of Toronto Press, 1955), pp. 121–25 and *passim*.

On ways in which the federal government itself has been destroying rather than conserving timber resources, from highway building to the indiscriminate dams and other projects of the Army Corps of Engineers, see Edwin G. Dolan, TANSTAAFL (New York: Holt, Rinehart & Winston, 1971), p. 96.

[8] See Robert Poole, Jr., "Reason and Ecology," in D. James, ed., *Outside, Looking In* (New York: Harper & Row, 1972), pp. 250–51.

Another unhappy consequence of the American government's failure to allow private property in a resource was the destruction of the Western grasslands in the late nineteenth century. Every viewer of "Western" movies is familiar with the mystique of the "open range" and the often violent "wars" among cattlemen, sheepmen, and farmers over parcels of ranch land. The "open range" was the failure of the federal government to apply the policy of homesteading to the changed conditions of the drier climate west of the Mississippi. In the East, the 160 acres granted free to homesteading farmers on government land constituted a viable technological unit for farming in a wetter climate. But in the dry climate of the West, no successful cattle or sheep ranch could be organized on a mere 160 acres. But the federal government refused to expand the 160-acre unit to allow the "homesteading" of larger cattle ranches. Hence, the "open range," on which private cattle and sheep owners were able to roam unchecked on government-owned pasture land. But this meant that no one owned the pasture, the land itself; it was therefore to the economic advantage of every cattle or sheep owner to graze the land and use up the grass as quickly as possible, otherwise the grass would be grazed by some other sheep or cattle owner. The result of this tragically shortsighted refusal to allow private property in grazing land itself was an overgrazing of the land, the ruining of the grassland by grazing too early in the season, and the failure of anyone to restore or replant the grass—anyone who bothered to restore the grass would have had to look on helplessly while someone else grazed his cattle or sheep. Hence the overgrazing of the West, and the onset of the "dust bowl." Hence also the illegal attempts by numerous cattlemen, farmers, and sheepmen to take the law into their own hands and fence off the land into private property—and the range wars that often followed.

Professor Samuel P. Hays, in his authoritative account of the conservation movement in America, writes of the range problem:

Much of the Western livestock industry depended for its forage upon the "open" range, owned by the federal government, but free for anyone to use. . . . Congress had never provided legislation regulating grazing or permitting stockmen to acquire range lands. Cattle and sheepmen roamed the public domain. . . . Cattlemen fenced range for their exclusive use, but competitors cut the wire. Resorting to force and violence, sheepherders and cowboys "solved" their disputes over grazing lands by slaughtering rival livestock and murdering rival stockmen. . . . Absence of the most elementary institutions of property law created confusion, bitterness, and destruction.

Amid this turmoil the public range rapidly deteriorated. Originally plentiful and lush, the forage supply was subjected to intense pressure by increasing use. . . . The public domain became stocked with more animals than the range could support. Since each stockman feared that others would beat him to the available forage, he grazed early in the year and did not permit the young grass to mature and reseed. Under such conditions the quality and quantity of available forage rapidly decreased; vigorous perennials gave way to annuals and annuals to weeds.[9]

Hays concludes that public-domain range lands may have been depleted by over two-thirds by this process, as compared to their virgin condition.

There is a vitally important area in which the absence of private property in the resource has been and is causing, not only depletion of resources, but also a complete failure to develop vast potential resources. This is the potentially enormously productive *ocean* resource. The oceans are in the international public domain, i.e., no person, company, or even national government is allowed property rights in parts of the ocean. As a result, the oceans have remained in the same primitive state as was the land in the precivilized days before the development of agriculture. The way of production for primitive man was "hunting-and-gathering": the hunting of wild animals and the gathering of fruits, berries, nuts, and wild seeds and vegetables. Primitive man worked passively *within* his en-

---

[9] Samuel P. Hays, *Conservation and the Gospel of Efficiency* (Cambridge: Harvard University Press, 1959), pp. 50–51. See also E. Louise Peffer, *The Closing of the Public Domain* (Stanford: Stanford University Press, 1951), pp. 22–31, and *passim*.

vironment instead of acting to transform it; hence he just lived off the land without attempting to remould it. As a result, the land was unproductive, and only a relatively few tribesmen could exist at a bare subsistence level. It was only with the development of agriculture, the farming of the soil, and the transformation of the land through farming that productivity and living standards could take giant leaps forward. And it was only with agriculture that civilization could begin. But to permit the development of agriculture there had to be private property rights, first in the fields and crops, and then in the land itself.

With respect to the ocean, however, we are still in the primitive, unproductive hunting and gathering stage. Anyone can capture fish in the ocean, or extract its resources, but only on the run, only as hunters and gatherers. No one can *farm* the ocean, no one can engage in *aquaculture*. In this way we are deprived of the use of the immense fish and mineral resources of the seas. For example, if anyone tried to farm the sea and to increase the productivity of the fisheries by fertilizers, he would immediately be deprived of the fruits of his efforts because he could not keep other fishermen from rushing in and seizing the fish. And so no one tries to fertilize the oceans as the land is fertilized. Furthermore, there is no economic incentive —in fact, there is every *dis*incentive—for anyone to engage in technological research in the ways and means of improving the productivity of the fisheries, or in extracting the mineral resources of the oceans. There will only be such incentive when property rights in parts of the ocean are as fully allowed as property rights in the land. Even now there is a simple but effective technique that could be used for increasing fish productivity: parts of the ocean could be fenced off electronically, and through this readily available electronic fencing, fish could be segregated by size. By preventing big fish from eating smaller fish, the production of fish could be increased enormously. And if private property in parts of the ocean were permitted, a vast flowering of *aquaculture* would create and multiply ocean resources in numerous ways we cannot now even foresee.

National governments have tried vainly to cope with the problem of fish depletion by placing irrational and uneconomic restrictions on the total size of the catch, or on the length of the allowable season. In the cases of salmon, tuna, and halibut, technological methods of fishing have thereby been kept primitive and unproductive by unduly shortening the season and injuring the quality of the catch and by stimulating overproduction—and underuse during the year—of the fishing fleets. And of course such governmental restrictions do nothing at all to stimulate the growth of aquaculture. As Professors North and Miller write:

Fishermen are poor because they are forced to use inefficient equipment and to fish only a small fraction of the time [by the governmental regulations] and of course there are far too many of them. The consumer pays a much higher price for red salmon than would be necessary if efficient methods were used. Despite the ever-growing intertwining bonds of regulations, the preservation of the salmon run is still not assured.

The root of the problem lies in the current non-ownership arrangement. It is not in the interests of any individual fisherman to concern himself with perpetuation of the salmon run. Quite the contrary: It is rather in his interests to catch as many fish as he can during the season.[10]

In contrast, North and Miller point out that private property rights in the ocean, under which the owner would use the least costly and most efficient technology *and* preserve and make productive the resource itself, is now more feasible than ever: "The invention of modern electronic sensing equipment has now made the policing of large bodies of water relatively cheap and easy." [11]

---

[10] Douglass C. North and Roger LeRoy Miller, *The Economics of Public Issues* (New York: Harper & Row, 1971), p. 107.

[11] *Ibid.*, p. 108. Also see James A. Crutchfield and Giulio Pontecorvo, *The Pacific Salmon Fisheries: A Study of Irrational Conservation* (Baltimore: Johns Hopkins Press, 1969). On a similar situation in the tuna industry, see Francis T. Christy, Jr., "New Dimensions for Transnational Marine Resources," *American Economic Review, Papers and Proceedings*

The growing international conflicts over parts of the ocean only further highlight the importance of private property rights in this vital area. For as Ecuador asserts its sovereignty over the Pacific Ocean 200 miles from her shores, and as private companies and governments squabble over areas of the ocean; and as trawlers, fishing nets, oil drillers, and mineral diggers war over the same areas of the ocean—property rights become increasingly and patently more important. As Francis Christy writes:

. . . coal is mined in shafts below the sea floor, oil is drilled from platforms fixed to the bottom rising above the water, minerals can be dredged from the surface of the ocean bed . . . sedentary animals are scraped from the bed on which telephone cables may lie, bottom feeding animals are caught in traps or trawls, mid-water species may be taken by hook and line or by trawls which occasionally interfere with submarines, surface species are taken by net and harpoon, and the surface itself is used for shipping as well as the vessels engaged in extracting resources.[12]

This growing conflict leads Christy to predict that "the seas are in a stage of transition. They are moving from a condition in which property rights are almost nonexistent to a condition in which property rights of some form will become appropriated or made available." Eventually, concludes Christy, "as the sea's resources become more valuable, exclusive rights will be acquired." [13]

(May 1970), p. 112; and on the Pacific halibut industry, see James A. Crutchfield and Arnold Zellner, *Economic Aspects of the Pacific Halibut Industry* (Washington, D.C.: U.S. Dept. of the Interior, 1961). For an imaginative proposal for private property in parts of the ocean even before the advent of electronic fencing, see Gordon Tullock, *The Fisheries—Some Radical Proposals* (Columbia, S.C.: University of South Carolina Bureau of Business and Economic Research, 1962).

[12] Christy, *loc. cit.*, p. 112.

[13] *Ibid.*, pp. 112–113. For a definitive discussion, economic, technological, and legal, of the entire problem of the ocean and ocean fisheries, see Francis T. Christy, Jr., and Anthony Scott, *The Common Wealth in Ocean Fisheries* (Baltimore: Johns Hopkins Press, 1965).

Pollution

All right: Even if we concede that full private property in resources and the free market will conserve and create resources, and do it far better than government regulation, what of the problem of pollution? Wouldn't we be suffering aggravated pollution from unchecked "capitalist greed"?

There is, first of all, this stark empirical fact: Government ownership, even socialism, has proved to be no solution to the problem of pollution. Even the most starry-eyed proponents of government planning concede that the poisoning of Lake Baikal in the Soviet Union is a monument to heedless industrial pollution of a valuable natural resource. But there is far more to the problem than that. Note, for example, the two crucial areas in which pollution has become an important problem: the air and the waterways, particularly the rivers. But these are precisely two of the vital areas in society in which private property has not been permitted to function.

First, the rivers. The rivers, and the oceans too, are generally owned by the government; private property, certainlv complete private property, has not been permitted in the water. In essence, then, government owns the rivers. But government ownership is not true ownership, because the government officials, while able to control the resource, cannot themselves reap their capital value on the market. Government officials cannot sell the rivers or sell stock in them. Hence, they have no economic incentive to preserve the purity and value of the rivers. Rivers are, then, in the economic sense, "unowned"; therefore government officials have permitted their corruption and pollution. Anyone has been able to dump polluting garbage and wastes in the waters. But consider what would happen if private firms were able to own the rivers and the lakes. If a private firm owned Lake Erie, for example, then anyone dumping garbage in the lake would be promptly sued in the courts for their aggression against private property and would be forced by the courts to pay damages and to cease and desist from any further aggression. Thus, only private property rights will insure an end to pollution-invasion of resources. Only because the rivers are unowned is there no owner to rise up and defend his precious resource from attack. If, in contrast, anyone should dump garbage or pollutants into a lake which is privately owned (as are many smaller lakes), he would not be permitted to do so for very long—the owner would come roaring to its defense.[14] As Professor Dolan writes:

> With a General Motors owning the Mississippi River, you can be sure that tiff effluent charges would be assessed on industries and municipalities along its banks, and that the water would be kept clean enough to maximize revenues from leases granted to firms seeking rights to drinking water, recreation, and commercial fishing.[15]

If government as owner has allowed the pollution of the rivers, government has also been the single major active polluter, especially in its role as municipal sewage disposer. There already exist low-cost chemical toilets which can burn off sewage without polluting air, ground, or water; but who will invest in chemical toilets when local governments will dispose of sewage free to their customers?

This example points up a problem similar to the case of the stunting of aquaculture technology by the absence of private property: if governments as owners of the rivers permit pollution of water, then industrial technology will—and has—become a water-polluting technology. If production processes are allowed to pollute the rivers unchecked by their owners, then that is the sort of production technology we will have.

If the problem of water pollution can be cured by private

---

[14] Existing "appropriation" law in the Western states already provides the basis for full "homesteading" private property rights in the rivers. For a full discussion, see Jack Hirshleifer, James C. DeHaven, and Jerome W. Milliman, *Water Supply; Economics, Technology, and Policy* (Chicago: University of Chicago Press, 1960), Chapter IX.

[15] Edwin G. Dolan, "Capitalism and the Environment," *Individualist* (March 1971), p. 3.

property rights in water, how about air pollution? How can libertarians possibly come up with a solution for this grievous problem? Surely, there can't be private property in the *air*? But the answer is: yes, there can. We have already seen how radio and TV frequencies can be privately owned. So could channels for airlines. Commercial airline routes, for example, could be privately owned; there is no need for a Civil Aeronautics Board to parcel out—and restrict—routes between various cities. But in the case of air pollution we are dealing, not so much with private property *in the air* as with protecting private property in one's lungs, fields, and orchards. The vital fact about air pollution is that the polluter sends unwanted and unbidden pollutants—from smoke to nuclear radiation to sulfur oxides— *through* the air and into the lungs of innocent victims, as well as onto their material property. All such emanations which injure person or property constitute aggression against the private property of the victims. Air pollution, after all, is just as much aggression as committing arson against another's property or injuring him physically. Air pollution that injures others is aggression pure and simple. The major function of government—of courts and police—is to stop aggression; instead, the government has failed in this task and has failed grievously to exercise its defense function against air pollution.

It is important to realize that this failure has *not* been a question purely of ignorance, a simple time lag between recognizing a new technological problem and facing up to it. For if some of the modern pollutants have only recently become known, factory smoke and many of its bad effects have been known ever since the Industrial Revolution, known to the extent that the American courts, during the late—and as far back as the early—nineteenth century made the deliberate decision to allow property rights to be violated by industrial smoke. To do so, the courts had to—and did—systematically change and weaken the defenses of property right embedded in Anglo-Saxon common law. Before the mid and late nineteenth century, any injurious air pollution was considered a tort, a nuisance against which the victim could sue for damages and against which he could take out an injunction to cease and desist from any further invasion of his property rights. But during the nineteenth century, the courts systematically altered the law of negligence and the law of nuisance to *permit* any air pollution which was not unusually greater than any similar manufacturing firm, one that was not more extensive than the customary practice of fellow polluters.

As factories began to arise and emit smoke, blighting the orchards of neighboring farmers, the farmers would take the manufacturers to court, asking for damages and injunctions against further invasion of their property. But the judges said, in effect, "Sorry. We *know* that industrial smoke (i.e., air pollution) invades and interferes with your property rights. But there is something *more important* than mere property rights: and that is public policy, the 'common good.' And the common good decrees that industry is a good thing, industrial progress is a good thing, and therefore your mere private property rights must be overridden on behalf of the general welfare." And now all of us are paying the bitter price for this overriding of private property, in the form of lung disease and countless other ailments. And all for the "common good"! [16]

That this principle has guided the courts during the air age as well may be seen by a decision of the Ohio courts in *Antonik v. Chamberlain* (1947). The residents of a suburban area near Akron sued to enjoin the defendants from operating a privately owned airport. The grounds were invasion of property rights through excessive noise. Refusing the injunction, the court declared:

In our business of judging in this case, while sitting as a court of equity, we must not only weigh the conflict of interests between the airport owner and the nearby landowners, but we must further recognize the public policy of the generation in which we live. We must recognize that the establishment of an airport . . . is of great

16 See E. F. Roberts, "Plead the Ninth Amendment!," *Natural History* (August–September 1970), pp. 18ff.

concern to the public, and if such an airport is abated, or its establishment prevented, the consequences will be not only a serious injury to the owner of the port property but may be a serious loss of a valuable asset to the entire community.[17]

To cap the crimes of the judges, legislatures, federal and state, moved in to cement the aggression by prohibiting victims of air pollution from engaging in "class action" suits against polluters. Obviously, if a factory pollutes the atmosphere of a city where there are tens of thousands of victims, it is impractical for each victim to sue to collect his particular damages from the polluter (although an *injunction* could be used effectively by one small victim). The common law, therefore, recognizes the validity of "class action" suits, in which one or a few victims can sue the aggressor not only on their own behalf, but on behalf of the entire *class* of similar victims. But the legislatures systematically outlawed such class action suits in pollution cases. For this reason, a victim may successfully sue a polluter who injures him individually, in a one-to-one "private nuisance" suit. But he is prohibited by law from acting against a mass polluter who is injuring a large number of people in a given area! As Frank Bubb writes, "It is as if the government were to tell you that it will (attempt to) protect you from a thief who steals only from you, but it will not protect you if the thief also steals from everyone else in the neighborhood . . ."[18]

Noise, too, is a form of air pollution. Noise is the creation of sound waves which go through the air and then bombard and invade the property and persons of others. Only recently have physicians begun to investigate the damaging effects of noise on the human physiology. Again, a libertarian legal system would permit damage and class action suits and injunctions against excessive and damaging noise: against "noise pollution."

[17] Quoted in Milton Katz, *The Function of Tort Liability in Technology Assessment* (Cambridge: Harvard University Program on Technology and Society, 1969), p. 610.
[18] Frank Bubb, "The Cure for Air Pollution," *The Libertarian Forum* (April 15, 1970), p. 1. Also see Dolan, *TANSTAAFL*, pp. 37–39.

The remedy against air pollution is therefore crystal clear, and it has nothing to do with multibillion-dollar palliative government programs at the expense of the taxpayers which do not even meet the real issue. The remedy is simply for the courts to return to their function of defending person and property rights against invasion, and therefore to enjoin anyone from injecting pollutants into the air. But what of the propollution defenders of industrial progress? And what of the increased costs that would have to be borne by the consumer? And what of our present polluting technology?

The argument that such an injunctive prohibition against pollution would add to the costs of industrial production is as reprehensible as the pre-Civil War argument that the abolition of slavery would add to the costs of growing cotton, and that therefore abolition, however morally correct, was "impractical." For this means that the polluters are able to impose all of the high costs of pollution upon those whose lungs and property rights they have been allowed to invade with impunity.

Furthermore, the cost and technology argument overlooks the vital fact that if air pollution is allowed to proceed with impunity, there continues to be no economic incentive to develop a technology that will *not* pollute. On the contrary, the incentive would continue to cut, as it has for a century, precisely the other way. Suppose, for example, that in the days when automobiles and trucks were first being used, the courts had ruled as follows: "Ordinarily, we would be opposed to trucks invading people's lawns as an invasion of private property, and we would insist that trucks confine themselves to the roads, regardless of traffic congestion. But trucks are vitally important to the public welfare, and therefore we decree that trucks should be allowed to cross any lawns they wish provided they believe that this would ease their traffic problems." If the courts had ruled in this way, then we would now have a transportation system in which lawns would be systematically desecrated by trucks. And any attempt to stop this would be decried in the name of modern transportation needs! The point is that this is precisely the way that the courts ruled on air pollution—pollution which is far more damaging to all of us than trampling on lawns. In this way, the government gave the green light, from the very start, to a polluting technology. It is no wonder then that this is precisely the kind of technology we have. The only remedy is to force the polluting invaders to stop their invasion, and thereby to redirect technology into nonpolluting or even antipolluting channels.

Already, even at our necessarily primitive stage in antipollution technology, techniques have been developed to combat air and noise pollution. Mufflers can be installed on noisy machines that emit sound waves precisely contra-cyclical to the waves of the machines, and thereby can cancel out these racking sounds. Air wastes can even now be recaptured as they leave the chimney and be recycled to yield products useful to industry. Thus, sulfur dioxide, a major noxious air pollutant, can be captured and recycled to produce economically valuable sulfuric acid.[19] The highly polluting spark ignition engine will either have to be "cured" by new devices or replaced altogether by such nonpolluting engines as diesel, gas turbine, or steam, or by an electric car. And, as libertarian systems engineer Robert Poole, Jr., points out, the costs of installing the non or antipolluting technology would then "ultimately be borne by the consumers of the firms' products, i.e., by those who *choose* to associate with the firm, rather than being passed on to innocent third parties in the form of pollution (or as taxes)." [20]

Robert Poole cogently defines pollution "as the transfer of harmful matter or energy to the person or property of another, without the latter's consent." [21] The libertarian—and the only complete—solution to the problem of air pollution is to use the courts and the legal structure to combat and prevent such in-

[19] See Jane Jacobs, *The Economy of Cities* (New York: Random House, 1969), pp. 109ff.; and Jerome Tuccille, *This Desecrated Earth*: A *Libertarian Analysis of the Air Pollution Problem* (unpublished MS.).

[20] Poole, *op. cit.*, pp. 251–52.

[21] Poole, *op. cit.*, p. 245.

vasion. There are recent signs that the legal system is beginning to change in this direction: new judicial decisions and repeal of laws disallowing class action suits. But this is only a beginning.[22]

Among conservatives—in contrast to libertarians—there are two ultimately similar responses to the problem of air pollution. One response, by Ayn Rand and Robert Moses among others, is to deny that the problem exists, and to attribute the entire agitation to leftists who want to destroy capitalism and technology on behalf of a tribal form of socialism. While part of this charge may be correct, denial of the very existence of the problem is to deny science itself and to give a vital hostage to the leftist charge that defenders of capitalism "place property rights above human rights." Moreover, a defense of air pollution does *not even* defend property rights; on the contrary, it puts these conservatives' stamp of approval on those industrialists who are trampling upon the property rights of the mass of the citizenry.

A second, and more sophisticated, conservative response is by such free-market economists as Milton Friedman. The Friedmanites concede the existence of air pollution but propose to meet it, *not* by a defense of property rights, but rather by a supposedly utilitarian "cost-benefit" calculation by government, which will then make and enforce a "social decision" on *how much* pollution to allow. This decision would then be enforced either by licensing a given amount of pollution (the granting of "pollution rights"), by a graded scale of taxes against it, or by the taxpayers paying firms *not* to pollute. Not only would these proposals grant an enormous amount of bureaucratic power to government in the name of safeguarding the "free market"; they would continue to override property rights in the name of a collective decision enforced by the State. This is far from any genuine "free market," and reveals that, as in many other economic areas, it is impossible to *really* defend freedom and the free market without insisting on defending the rights of private property. Friedman's grotesque dictum that those urban inhabi-

[22] Thus, See Dolan, TANSTAAFL, p. 39, and Katz, *passim*.

tants who don't wish to contract emphysema should move to the country is starkly reminiscent of Marie Antoinette's famous "Let them eat cake"—and reveals a lack of sensitivity to human or property rights. Friedman's statement, in fact, is of a piece with the typically conservative, "If you don't like it here, leave," a statement that implies that the government rightly owns the entire land area of "here," and that anyone who objects to its rule must therefore leave the area. Robert Poole's libertarian critique of the Friedmanite proposals offers a refreshing contrast:

Unfortunately, it is an example of the most serious failing of the conservative economists: nowhere in the proposal is there any mention of *rights*. This is the same failing that has undercut advocates of capitalism for 200 years. Even today, the term "laissez-faire" is apt to bring forth images of eighteenth century English factory towns engulfed in smoke and grimy with soot. The early capitalists agreed with the courts that smoke and soot were the "price" that must be paid for the benefits of industry. . . . Yet laissez-faire without rights is a contradiction in terms; the laissez-faire position is based on and derived from man's rights, and can endure only when rights are held inviolable. Now, in an age of increasing awareness of the environment, this old contradiction is coming back to haunt capitalism.

It is *true* that air is a scarce resource [as the Friedmanites say], but one must then ask *why* it is scarce. If it is scarce because of a systematic violation of rights, then the solution is not to raise the price of the status quo, thereby sanctioning the rights-violations, but to assert the rights and demand that they be protected. . . . When a factory discharges a great quantity of sulfur dioxide molecules that enter someone's lungs and cause pulmonary edema, the factory owners have aggressed against him as much as if they had broken his leg. The point must be emphasized because it is vital to the libertarian laissez-faire position. A laissez-faire polluter is a contradiction in terms and must be identified as such. A libertarian society would be a *full-liability* society, where everyone is fully responsible for his actions and any harmful consequences they might cause.[23]

[23] Poole, *op. cit.*, pp. 252–53. Friedman's dictum can be found in Peter Maiken, "Hysterics Won't Clean Up Pollution," *Human Events* (April 25,

In addition to betraying its presumed function of defending private property, government has contributed to air pollution in a more positive sense. It was not so long ago that the Department of Agriculture conducted mass sprayings of DDT by helicopter over large areas, overriding the wishes of individual objecting farmers. And the Atomic Energy Commission has poured radioactive wastes into the air and into the ground by means of its nuclear power plants, and through atomic testing. Municipal power and water plants, and the plants of licensed monopoly utility companies, mightily pollute the atmosphere. One of the major tasks of the State in this area is therefore to stop its *own* poisoning of the atmosphere.

Thus, when we peel away the confusions and the unsound philosophy of the modern ecologists, we find an important bedrock case against the existing system; but the case turns out to be not against capitalism, private property, growth, or technology per se. It is a case against the failure of government to allow and to defend the rights of private property against invasion. If property rights were to be defended fully, against private and governmental invasion alike, we would find here, as in other areas of our economy and society, that private enterprise and modern technology would come to mankind not as a curse but as its salvation.

1970), pp. 13, 21–23. A fuller presentation of the Friedmanite position may be found in Thomas D. Crocker and A. J. Rogers III, *Environmental Economics* (Hinsdale, Ill.: Dryden Press, 1971); and similar views may be found in J. H. Dales, *Pollution, Property, and Prices* (Toronto: University or Toronto Press, 1968), and Larry E. Ruff, "The Economic Common Sense of Pollution," *Public Interest* (Spring, 1970), pp. 69–85.

13

War and Foreign Policy

"Isolationism," Left and Right

"ISOLATIONISM" WAS COINED as a smear term to apply to opponents of American entry into World War II. Since the word was often applied through guilt-by-association to mean pro-Nazi, "isolationist" took on a "right-wing" as well as a generally negative flavor. If not actively pro-Nazi, "isolationists" were at the very least narrow-minded ignoramuses ignorant of the world around them, in contrast to the sophisticated, worldly, *caring* "internationalists" who favored American crusading around the globe. In the last decade, of course, antiwar forces have been considered "leftists," and interventionists from Lyndon Johnson to Richard Nixon and their followers have constantly tried to pin the "isolationist" or at least "neoisolationist" label on today's left-wing.

Left or right? During World War I, opponents of the war were bitterly attacked, just as now, as "leftists," even though they included in their ranks libertarians and advocates of laissez-faire capitalism. In fact, the major center of opposition to the American war with Spain and the American war to crush the

Philippine rebellion at the turn of the century was laissez-faire liberals, men like the sociologist and economist William Graham Sumner, and the Boston merchant Edward Atkinson, who founded the "Anti-Imperialist League." Furthermore, Atkinson and Sumner were squarely in the great tradition of the classical English liberals of the eighteenth and nineteenth centuries, and in particular such laissez-faire "extremists" as Richard Cobden and John Bright of the "Manchester School." Cobden and Bright took the lead in vigorously opposing every British war and foreign political intervention of their era, and for his pains Cobden was known not as an "isolationist" but as the "International Man." [1] Until the smear campaign of the late 1930s, opponents of war were considered the true "internationalists," men who opposed the aggrandizement of the nation-state and favored peace, free trade, free migration, and peaceful cultural exchanges among peoples of all nations. Foreign intervention is "international" only in the sense that war is international: coercion, whether the threat of force or the outright movement of troops, will always cross frontiers between one nation and another.

"Isolationism" has a right-wing sound; "neutralism" and "peaceful coexistence" sound leftish. But their essence is the same: opposition to war and political intervention between countries. This has been the position of antiwar forces for two centuries, whether they were the classical liberals of the eighteenth and nineteenth centuries, the "leftists" of World War I and the Cold War, or the "rightists" of World War II. In very few cases have these antiinterventionists favored literal "isolation": what they have generally favored is political nonintervention in the affairs of other countries, coupled with economic and cultural internationalism in the sense of peaceful freedom of trade, investment, and interchange between the citizens of all countries. And this is the essence of the libertarian position as well.

[1] See William H. Dawson, *Richard Cobden and Foreign Policy* (London: George Allen and Unwin, 1926).

Limiting Government

Libertarians favor the abolition of all States everywhere, and the provision of legitimate functions now supplied poorly by governments (police, courts, etc.) by means of the free market. Libertarians favor liberty as a natural human right, and advocate it not only for Americans but for all peoples. In a purely libertarian world, therefore, there would *be no* "foreign policy" because there would be no States, no governments with a monopoly of coercion over particular territorial areas. But since we live in a world of nation-states, and since this system is hardly likely to disappear in the near future, what is the attitude of libertarians toward foreign policy in the current State-ridden world?

Pending the dissolution of States, libertarians desire to *limit*, to whittle down, the area of government power in all directions and as much as possible. We have already demonstrated how this principle of "de-statizing" might work in various important "domestic" problems, where the goal is to push back the role of government and to allow the voluntary and spontaneous energies of free persons full scope through peaceful interaction, notably in the free-market economy. In foreign affairs, the goal is the same: to keep government from interfering in the affairs of other governments or other countries. Political "isolationism" and peaceful coexistence—refraining from acting upon other countries—is, then, the libertarian counterpart to agitating for laissez-faire policies at home. The idea is to shackle government from acting abroad just as we try to shackle government at home. Isolationism or peaceful coexistence is the foreign policy counterpart of severely limiting government at home.

Specifically, the entire land area of the world is now parcelled out among various States, and each land area is ruled by a central government with monopoly of violence over that area. In relations between States, then, the libertarian goal is to keep each of these States from extending their violence to other countries, so that each State's tyranny is *at least* confined to its own bailiwick.

Let us assume, for the moment, a world with two hypothetical countries: Graustark and Belgravia. Each is ruled by its own State. What happens if the government of Graustark invades the territory of Belgravia? From the libertarian point of view two evils immediately occur. First, the Graustark Army begins to slaughter innocent Belgravian civilians, persons who are not implicated in whatever crimes the Belgravian government might have committed. War, then, is mass murder, and this massive invasion of the right to life, of self-ownership, of numbers of people is not only a crime but, for the libertarian, the ultimate crime. Second, since all governments obtain their revenue from the thievery of coercive taxation, any mobilization and launching of troops inevitably involve an increase in tax-coercion in Graustark. For both reasons—because inter-State wars inevitably involve both mass murder and an increase in tax-coercion, the libertarian opposes war. Period.

It was not always thus. During the Middle Ages, the scope of wars was far more limited. Before the rise of modern weapons, armaments were so limited that governments could—and often *did*—strictly confine their violence to the *armies* of the rival governments. It is true that tax-coercion increased, but at least there was no mass murder of the innocents. Not only was firepower low enough to confine violence to the armies of the contending sides, but in the premodern era there was no central nation-state that spoke inevitably in the name of all inhabitants of a given land area. If one set of kings or barons fought another, it was not felt that everyone in the area must be a dedicated partisan. Moreover, instead of mass conscript armies enslaved to their respective rulers, armies were small bands of hired mercenaries. Often, a favorite sport for the populace was to observe a battle from the safety of the town ramparts, and war was regarded as something of a sporting match. But with the rise of the centralizing State and of modern weapons of mass destruction, the slaughter of civilians, as well as conscript armies, have become a vital part of inter-State war-fare.

Suppose that Graustark has invaded Belgravia, and that a third government, Walldavia, now leaps into the war in order to defend Belgravia against "Graustarkian aggression." Is this action justifiable? Here, indeed, is the germ of the pernicious twentieth-century theory of "collective security"—the idea that when one government "aggresses" against another, it is the moral obligation of the other governments of the world to band together to defend the "victimized" state.

There are several fatal flaws in this concept of collective security against "aggression." One is that when Walldavia, or any other states, leap into the fray they are themselves expanding and compounding the extent of the aggression, because they are (1) unjustly slaughtering masses of Graustarkian civilians, and (2) increasing tax-coercion over Walldavian citizens. Furthermore, (3) in this age when States and subjects are closely identifiable, Walldavia is thereby leaving Walldavian civilians open to retaliation by Graustarkian bombers or missiles. Thus, entry into the war by the Walldavian government puts into jeopardy the very lives and properties of Walldavian citizens which the government is *supposed* to be protecting. Finally, (4) conscription-enslavement of Walldavian citizens will usually intensify.

If this kind of "collective security" should really be applied on a worldwide scale, with all the "Walldavias" rushing into every local conflict and escalating them, every local skirmish would soon be raised into a global conflagration.

There is another crucial flaw in the collective security concept. The idea of entering a war in order to stop "aggression" is clearly an analogy from aggression by one *individual* upon another. Smith is seen to be beating up Jones—aggressing against him. Nearby police then rush to the defense of the victim Jones; they are using "police action" to stop aggression. It was in pursuit of this myth, for example, that President Truman persisted in referring to American entry into the

Korean war as a "police action," a collective UN effort to repel "aggression."

But "aggression" only makes sense on the individual Smith-Jones level, as does the very term "police action." These terms make no sense whatever on an inter-State level. First, we have seen that governments entering a war thereby become aggressors themselves against innocent civilians; indeed, become mass murderers. The *correct* analogy to individual action would be: Smith beats up Jones, the police rush in to help Jones, and in the course of trying to apprehend Smith, the police bomb a city block and murder thousands of people, or spray machine-gun fire into an innocent crowd. *This* is a far more accurate analogy, for that is what a warring government does, and in the twentieth century it does so on a monumental scale. But any police agency that behaves this way *itself* becomes a criminal aggressor, often far more so than the original Smith who began the affair.

But there is yet another fatal flaw in the analogy with individual aggression. When Smith beats up Jones or steals his property we can identify Smith as an aggressor upon the personal or property right of his victim. But when the Graustarkian State invades the territory of the Belgravian State, it is impermissible to refer to "aggression" in an analogous way. For the libertarian, no government has a just claim to any property or "sovereignty" right in a given territorial area. The Belgravian State's claim to its territory is therefore totally different from Mr. Jones' claim to his property (although the latter might also, on investigation, turn out to be the illegitimate result of theft). No State has any legitimate property; all of its territory is the result of some kind of aggression and violent conquest. Hence the Graustarkian State's invasion is necessarily a battle between two sets of thieves and aggressors: the only problem is that innocent civilians on both sides are being trampled upon.

Aside from this general caveat on governments, the so-called "aggressor" State often has a quite plausible claim on its "victim"; plausible, that is, within the context of the nation-state system. Suppose that Graustark has crossed the Belgravian border because Belgravia had, a century earlier, invaded Graustark and seized its northeastern provinces. The inhabitants of these provinces are culturally, ethnically, and linguistically Graustarkian. Graustark now invades in order to be reunited at last with its fellow Graustarkians. In this situation, by the way, the libertarian, while condemning both governments for making war and killing civilians, would have to side with Graustark as having the more just, or the less unjust, claim. Let us put it this way: In the unlikely event that the two countries could return to premodern warfare, with (a) weapons limited so that no civilians were injured in their persons or property; (b) volunteer rather than conscript armies; and also (c) financing by voluntary methods instead of taxation; the libertarian could then, given our context, side unreservedly with Graustark.

Of all the recent wars, none has come closer—though not completely so—to satisfying these three criteria for a "just war" than the Indian war of late 1971 for the liberation of Bangla Desh. The government of Pakistan had been created as a last terrible legacy of Imperial Britain to the Indian subcontinent. In particular, the nation of Pakistan consisted of imperial rule by the Punjabis of West Pakistan over the more numerous and productive Bengalis of East Pakistan (and also over the Pathans of the North-West Frontier). The Bengalis had long been yearning for independence from their imperial oppressors; in early 1971, parliament was suspended as a result of Bengali victory in the elections; from then on, Punjabi troops systematically slaughtered the civilian Bengal population. Indian entry into the conflict aided the popular Bengali resistance forces of the Mukhti Bahini. While taxes and conscription were, of course, involved, the Indian armies did not use their weapons against Bengali civilians; on the contrary, here was a genuine revolutionary war of the Bengali public *against* a Punjabi occupying State. Only Punjabi soldiers were on the receiving end of Indian bullets.

This example points up another characteristic of warfare:

that revolutionary guerrilla war *can be* far more consistent with libertarian principles than any inter-State war. By the very nature of their activities, guerrillas defend the civilian population *against* the depredations of a State; hence, guerrillas, inhabiting as they do the same country as the enemy State, *cannot* use nuclear or other weapons of mass destruction. Further: since guerrillas rely for victory on the support and aid of the civilian population, they *must*, as a basic part of their strategy, spare civilians from harm and pinpoint their activities solely against the State apparatus and its armed forces. Hence, guerrilla war returns us to the ancient and honorable virtue of pinpointing the enemy and sparing innocent civilians. And guerrillas, as part of their quest for enthusiastic civilian support, often refrain from conscription and taxation and rely on voluntary support for men and materiel.

The libertarian qualities of guerrilla warfare reside only on the revolutionary side; for the counterrevolutionary forces of the State, it is quite a different story. While the State cannot go to the length of "nuking" their own subjects, they do, of necessity, rely primarily on campaigns of mass terror: killing, terrorizing, and rounding up the mass of civilians. Since guerrillas, to be successful, must be supported by the bulk of the population, the State, in order to wage its war, must concentrate on destroying that population, or must herd masses of civilians into concentration camps in order to separate them from their guerrilla allies. This tactic was used by the Spanish general, "Butcher" Weyler, against the Cuban rebels in the 1890s, was continued by the American troops in the Philippines, and by the British in the Boer War, and continues to be used down to the current ill-fated "strategic hamlet" policy in South Vietnam.

Apart from the small band of Tolstoyan anarchists, then, the libertarian foreign policy is *not* a pacifist policy. We do not hold, as do the pacifists, that no individual has the right to use violence in defending himself against violent attack. What we *do* hold is that no one has the right to conscript, tax, or murder others, or to use violence against others in order to defend himself. Since all States exist and have their being in aggression against their subjects and in the acquiring of their present territory, and since inter-State wars slaughter innocent civilians, such wars are always unjust—although some may be more unjust than others. Guerrilla warfare against States at least has the potential for meeting libertarian requirements by pinpointing the guerrilla's battle against State officials and armies, and by their use of voluntary methods to staff and finance their struggle.

American Foreign Policy

Libertarians have as their prime responsibility focussing on the invasions and aggressions of their *own* State. The libertarians of Graustark must center their attentions on attempting to limit and whittle down the Graustark State, the Walldavian libertarians must try to check the Walldavian State, and so on. In foreign affairs, then, the libertarians of every country must press their government to refrain from war and foreign intervention, and to withdraw from any war in which they may be engaged. If for no other reason, then, the libertarians in the United States must center their critical attention on the imperial and warlike activities of their own government.

But there are still other reasons for libertarians to focus upon the United States. Empirically, the *most* warlike, *most* interventionist, *most* imperial government throughout the twentieth century has been the United States. The expansionist impulse of the American State began to take increasing hold in the late nineteenth century; but it reached its full flower during and after World War I. It was wartime President Woodrow Wilson who set the lineaments of American foreign policy for the rest of this century. Wilson's particular genius was to supply a pietistic and moralistic cloak around a policy of worldwide intervention and domination. In the name of "national self-determination" and collective security against aggression the American government has pursued a goal and a policy of world domination and forcible suppression of any rebellion against the *status quo* anywhere in the world.[2] In the name of combatting "aggression" everywhere—of being the world's "policeman"—it has itself become the great and permanent aggressor.

Our monstrous—and seemingly permanent—butchery in Vietnam is but a particularly glaring example of this worldwide policy. American intervention in Vietnam did not begin, as many journalists believe, with Kennedy or Eisenhower or even with Truman. It began certainly no later than the date when the American government, on November 26, 1941, delivered a sharp and insulting ultimatum to Japan to get its armed forces out of "China"—and specifically, Camranh Bay in Indochina. This Cordell Hull ultimatum set the stage inevitably for Pearl Harbor. Engaged in a war in the Pacific to oust Japan from the Asian continent, the United States favored Ho Chi Minh's national resistance movement against the Japanese. But after the end of the war, the United States helped Great Britain and France double-cross their agreement with Ho and reinstall unwelcome French imperialism in Indochina. When the French lost to the reconstituted Viet Minh guerrilla movement under Ho, the United States endorsed, and then proceeded to break, the Geneva agreement of 1954. Having by trickery managed to oust the Communist-led Viet Minh forces from the southern half of Vietnam, the United States proceeded to replace the French, installing Ngo Dinh Diem and his family in power in Saigon. When Diem became an embarrassment, the CIA engineered a coup to assassinate Diem and replace him with another dictatorial regime. The war still continues; and despite the glaring failure of President Nixon's concept of "Vietnamization," it has become all too clear that the conflict in Viet-

[2] The view of America as a world imperial and counterrevolutionary power has taken hold among historians in recent years as the result of the compelling and scholarly work of the new revisionist historians such as William Appleman Williams, Gabriel Kolko, Lloyd Gardner, N. Gordon Levin, Jr., Walter LaFeber, Robert F. Smith, and Barton Bernstein. Many of the conservative isolationists of World War II foresaw these consequences, notably John T. Flynn and Garet Garrett.

nam is not so much a "civil war" as it is a doomed but continuing attempt by the United States to flout and suppress the wishes of the great bulk of the Vietnamese population, and to maintain unpopular counterrevolutionary regimes in Indochina by genocide, if necessary.

Since the United States is the great global aggressor, intervener, and war-maker, a libertarian concentration on foreign policy takes on decisive importance. In particular, the primary plank of a libertarian foreign policy program is to call upon the United States for a massive worldwide withdrawal: to withdraw immediately and completely from Vietnam, Indochina, Southeast Asia, Europe, Latin America, the Middle East, to withdraw from *everywhere*. The cry here should be for the United States to "get out now," militarily and politically, in every way that involves the United States government. The United States should dismantle its bases, withdraw its troops, stop its political meddling, and abolish the CIA, which is a pure instrument for meddling with and suborning politicians and intellectuals overseas. It should also end all foreign aid—a device for the American taxpayer to subsidize American export industries and foreign governments, all in the name of "helping the starving peoples of the world." In short, to withdraw the United States totally within its own boundaries, and to maintain a policy of strict "isolation" or neutrality everywhere.

The spirit of this ultraisolationist, libertarian foreign policy was expressed during the 1930s by retired Marine Corps Maj. Gen. Smedley D. Butler. In the fall of 1936, General Butler proposed a now-forgotten constitutional amendment, an amendment which would delight libertarian hearts if it once again were to be taken seriously. Here is Butler's proposed constitutional amendment in its entirety:

1. The removal of members of the land armed forces from within the continental limits of the United States and the Panama Canal Zone for any cause whatsoever is hereby prohibited.
2. The vessels of the United States Navy, or of the other branches of the armed service, are hereby prohibited from steaming, for any

reason whatsoever except on an errand of mercy, more than five hundred miles from our coast.

3. Aircraft of the Army, Navy and Marine Corps is hereby prohibited from flying, for any reason whatsoever, more than seven hundred and fifty miles beyond the coast of the United States.[3]

Many libertarians are uncomfortable with foreign policy matters, and prefer to spend their energies either on fundamental questions of libertarian theory, or on such "domestic" concerns as the free market or private postal service or garbage disposal. Yet an attack on war and a warlike foreign policy is of crucial importance to libertarians. There are two critical reasons. One has become a cliché, but is all too true nevertheless: the overriding importance of preventing a nuclear holocaust. To all the long-standing reasons, moral and economic, against an interventionist foreign policy has now been added the imminent, ever-present threat of world destruction. If the world should be destroyed, all the other problems and all the other isms—socialism, capitalism, liberalism, or libertarianism—would be of no importance whatsoever. Hence the prime importance of a peaceful foreign policy and of ending the nuclear threat.

Secondly, and apart from the nuclear menace, war, in the words of the libertarian Randolph Bourne, "is the health of the State." War has always been the occasion of a great—and usually permanent—acceleration and intensification of State power over society. War is the great excuse for mobilizing all the energies and resources of the nation, in the name of patriotic rhetoric, under the aegis and dictation of the State apparatus. It is particularly ironic that war always enables the State to rally the energies of its citizens under the slogan of helping the State to defend the country against some bestial outside menace. What the State is *really* doing is calling upon its subjects to defend not themselves, but *its* existence from outside rivals.

In the history of the United States, war has generally been

[3] *The Woman's Home Companion* (September 1936), p. 4. Reprinted in Mauritz A. Hallgren, *The Tragic Fallacy* (New York: Knopf, 1937), p. 194n.

the occasion for the often permanent intensification of the power of the State over society. In the War of 1812 against Great Britain, the modern inflationary banking system first came into being on a large scale, as did protective tariffs, internal federal taxation, and a standing army and navy. Virtually all of these statist policies and institutions continued permanently after the war was over. The Civil War and its virtual one-party system led to the permanent establishment of a neo-mercantilist policy of Big Government and the subsidizing of various Big Business interests through protective tariffs, huge land grants to railroads, federal excise taxation, and a federally controlled banking system. It also brought the first imposition of federal conscription and an income tax, setting a dangerous precedent for the future. World War I brought the decisive and fateful turn from a relatively free and laissez-faire economy to the present system of corporate state monopoly at home and permanent global intervention abroad. The collectivist economic mobilization during the war, headed by War Industries Board Chairman Bernard Baruch, fulfilled the emerging dream of big business leaders and progressive intellectuals for a cartelized and monopolized economy planned by the federal government in cozy collaboration with big business leadership. And it was precisely this wartime collectivism that nurtured and developed a nationwide labor movement that would eagerly take its place as junior partner in the new corporate state economy. The wartime collectivism, furthermore, remained as the permanent beacon and model for big business leaders and corporatist politicians for the kind of permanent peacetime economy they would like to impose on the United States. As Secretary of Commerce and later as President, Herbert C. Hoover helped bring this permanent monopolized statist economy into being, and the vision was fulfilled—by a recrudescence of wartime agencies and even wartime personnel—in Franklin D. Roosevelt's New Deal.[4] World War I also brought with it

---

[4] Numerous revisionist historians have recently informed us of this interpretation of twentieth-century American history. In particular, see the works, among others, of Gabriel Kolko, James Weinstein, Robert D. Cuff,

a permanent Wilsonian global intervention abroad, the fastening of the newly imposed Federal Reserve System and a permanent income tax on society, high federal budgets, mass conscription, and intimate connections between economic boom, war and defense contracts, and loans to Western nations.

World War II was the culmination and fulfillment of all these trends: Franklin D. Roosevelt then finally fastened on American life the heady promise of the Wilsonian domestic and foreign program: permanent partnership of Big Government, Big Business, and Big Unions, a continuing and ever-expanding military-industrial complex, permanent conscription, continuing inflation, and an endless and costly role as counterrevolutionary "policeman" for the entire world. The Roosevelt-Truman-Eisenhower-Kennedy-Johnson-Nixon world (and there is little substantive difference among any of these administrations), is "corporate liberalism," the corporate state, fulfilled.

It is particularly ironic that conservatives, at least in rhetoric supporters of a free-market economy, should be so complacent and even admiring of our vast military-industrial complex. There is no greater single distortion in the present-day America of the free market. The great bulk of our scientists and engineers have been diverted from basic research for civilian ends, for increasing productivity and the standard of living, into wasteful, inefficient and nonproductive military and space boondoggles, boondoggles that are every bit as wasteful but infinitely more destructive than the vast pyramid-building of the Pharaohs. It is no accident that Lord Keynes' economics has proved to be the economics par excellence of the corporate liberal state. The Keynesian economists place equal approval upon all forms of government spending, whether on pyramids, missiles, or steel plants; by definition all of these expenditures swell the Gross

---

William E. Leuchtenburg, Melvin I. Urofsky, Joan Hoff Wilson, Ronald Radosh, and Paul Conkin—again, as in foreign policy revisionism, under the inspiration of William Appleman Williams. A recent series of essays on this approach may be found in Ronald Radosh and Murray N. Rothbard, eds., A New History of Leviathan (New York: Dutton, 1972).

National Product, regardless of how wasteful they may be. It is only recently that many liberals have begun to awaken to the evils of the waste, inflation, and militarism that Keynesian corporate liberalism has brought to America.

As the scope of government spending—military and civilian alike—has widened, science and industry have been skewed more and more into unproductive goals and into highly inefficient processes. Satisfying the consumer as efficiently as possible has been increasingly replaced by the currying of favors by government contractors, many in the form of wasteful "cost-plus" contracts. Politics, in field after field, has replaced economics in guiding the activities of industry. Furthermore, as entire industries and regions of the country have come to depend upon government and military contracts, an enormous vested interest has been created in continuing the programs, heedless of whether they remain within the most threadbare excuse of military necessity. Senator Hubert Humphrey's campaign warnings that jobs and contracts would vanish in California if military spending were reduced is just one surface manifestation of the sorry fact that our economic prosperity has been made to depend on continuing the narcotic of unproductive and antiproductive spending.[5]

We have already dealt theoretically with the standard and supposedly crushing argument against establishing anarcho-capitalism: what if the Soviet Union should attack? But there is more to be said empirically; American military and foreign policy since World War II has postulated an imminent threat of Soviet attack against which American energies were supposed to be mobilized. But in contrast, if we take a sober look at Soviet Russian foreign policy since the Bolshevik Revolution, we find a continuing passion for peace which has sometimes bordered on the suicidal. Poland attacked Soviet Russia after World War I, and gained a large chunk of White Russia and the

[5] On the economic distortions imposed by the military-industrial program, see Seymour Melman, ed., *The War Economy of the United States* (New York: St. Martin's Press, 1971).

294 For a New Liberty

Ukraine as a result. Before World War II, so devoted was Stalin to peace that he failed to make adequate provision against the Nazi attack. The much vaunted "expansion" of the Soviet Union occurred only and solely in response to the un-provoked German attack; in defeating Germany, the Soviet Union of course had to roll over Germany's military allies in Eastern Europe. Not only was there no Russian expansion whatever apart from the exigencies of defeating Germany, but the Soviet Union time and again leaned over backward to avoid any cold or hot war with the West. It pulled its troops out of Azerbaijan and Austria; pressured the Communist guerrillas of France and Italy into *not* taking power as the German armies withdrew and instead forced them into ruinous coalitions with centrist parties; abandoned the Greek Communist guerrillas and turned Greece over to Great Britain; *tried* to pressure Tito into subordinating himself into a coalition with Mihailovich and Mao Tse-tung into a coalition with Chiang Kai-shek; and it did *not* impose communism in Eastern Europe until after several years of a Western-launched Cold War. Thus, Stalin, far from being expansionist, did his best to accede to American demands in the name of peaceful coexistence, but the United States, in *its* global expansionism, proved implacable.[6]

Disarmament

Strict isolationism and neutrality, then, is the first plank of a libertarian foreign policy, in addition to recognizing the chief responsibility of Imperial America for the Cold War and for

[6] On this analysis, see Kolko and the other revisionist works mentioned in footnote 2 of this chapter. Neither has Communist China been the aggressive bugbear of American propaganda. If we examine Chinese deeds since the inception of the Communist regime, we find no territorial expansion, a passive acquiescence in virtual American occupation of Chinese territory (Taiwan, Quemoy, Matsu) as well as British and Portuguese occupation (Hong Kong, Macao), and a *unilateral* cease-fire and withdrawal to its border after India had aggressed against China in border skirmishes. On the last, see Neville Maxwell, *India's China War* (New York: Pantheon Books, 1970).

its entry into all the other conflicts of this century. Given isolation, however, what sort of arms policy should the United States pursue? Many of the original isolationists also advocated a policy of "arming to the teeth"; but such a program, in a nuclear age, continues the grave risk of global holocaust, a mightily armed State, and the enormous waste and distortions that unproductive government spending imposes on the economy.

Even from a purely military point of view, the United States and the Soviet Union have the power to annihilate each other many times over; and the United States could easily preserve all of its nuclear retaliatory power by scrapping every armament except Polaris submarines, which are invulnerable and armed with nuclear missiles with multi-targeted warheads. But for the libertarian, or indeed for anyone worried about massive nuclear destruction of human life, even disarming down to Polaris submarines is hardly a satisfactory settlement. World peace would continue to rest on a shaky "balance of terror," a balance that could always be upset by accident or by the actions of madmen in power. No; for anyone to become secure from the nuclear menace it is vital to achieve worldwide nuclear disarmament, a disarmament toward which the SALT agreement of 1972 is only a very hesitant beginning.

American pacifists have long advocated unilateral disarmament of nuclear and other weapons of mass destruction by the United States. But while such disarmament would be vastly preferable to the present balance of terror, there is another solution which would be far more preferable: joint, worldwide nuclear disarmament. Such joint "general and complete" disarmament of nuclear and other massive weapons has been feasible ever since the Soviet Union accepted Western proposals to this effect on May 10, 1955—an acceptance which only gained a total and panicky Western abandonment of their own proposals! [7]

[7] On the details of the shameful Western record in these negotiations, and as a corrective to the portrayals in the American press, see Philip Noel-Baker, *The Arms Race* (New York: Oceana Publications, 1958).

The American version has long held that while we have wanted disarmament plus inspection, the Soviets persist in wanting only disarmament without inspection. The actual picture is very different: since May 1955, the Soviet Union has favored any and all disarmament and unlimited inspection of whatever has been disarmed; whereas the Americans have advocated unlimited inspection but accompanied by little or no disarmament! This was the burden of President Eisenhower's spectacular but basically dishonest "open skies" proposal, which replaced the disarmament proposals we quickly withdrew after the Soviet acceptance of May 1955. Even now that open skies have been essentially achieved through American and Russian space satellites, President Nixon's controversial SALT agreement involves no actual disarmament, only limitations on further nuclear expansion. Furthermore, since American strategic might throughout the world rests on nuclear and air power, there is good reason to believe in Soviet sincerity in any agreement to liquidate nuclear missiles or offensive bombers.

Not only should there be joint disarmament of nuclear weapons, but also of all weapons capable of being fired massively across national borders; in particular bombers. It is precisely such weapons of mass destruction as the missile and the bomber which can never be pinpoint-targeted to avoid their use against innocent civilians. In addition, the total abandonment of missiles and bombers would *enforce* upon every government, especially including the American, a policy of isolation and neutrality. Only if governments are deprived of weapons of offensive warfare will they be forced to pursue a policy of isolation and peace. Surely, in view of the black record of all governments, including the American, it would be folly to leave these harbingers of mass murder and destruction in their hands, and to trust them never to employ those monstrous weapons. If it is illegitimate for government ever to employ such weapons, why should they be allowed to remain, fully loaded, in their none-too-clean hands?

The contrast between the conservative and the libertarian po-

sitions on war and American foreign policy was starkly expressed in an interchange between William F. Buckley, Jr., and
the libertarian Ronald Hamowy in the early days of the contemporary libertarian movement. Scorning the libertarian critique of conservative foreign policy postures, Buckley wrote:
"There is room in any society for those whose only concern is
for tablet-keeping; but let them realize that it is only because
of the conservatives' disposition to sacrifice in order to withstand the [Soviet] enemy, that they are able to enjoy their mo-
nasticism, and pursue their busy little seminars on whether or
not to demuncipalize the garbage collectors." To which Hamowy trenchantly replied:

It might appear ungrateful of me, but I must decline to thank Mr.
Buckley for saving my life. It is, further, my belief that if his viewpoint prevails and that if he persists in his unsolicited aid the result
will almost certainly be my death (and that of tens of millions of
others) in nuclear war or my imminent imprisonment as an "un-
American.". . .

I hold strongly to my personal liberty and it is precisely because
of this that I insist that no one has the right to force his decisions
on another. Mr. Buckley chooses to be dead rather than Red. So do
I. But I insist that all men be allowed to make that decision for
themselves. A nuclear holocaust will make it for them.[8]

To which we might add that anyone who wishes is entitled to
make the personal decision of "better dead than Red" or "give
me liberty or give me death." What he is *not* entitled to do is
to make these decisions *for* others, as the prowar policy of conservatism would do. What conservatives are really saying is:
"Better *them* dead than Red," and "give me liberty or give
them death"—which are the battle cries not of noble heroes but
of mass murderers.

In one sense alone is Mr. Buckley correct: in the nuclear
age it *is* more important to worry about war and foreign policy
than about demunicipalizing garbage disposal, as important as

[8] Ronald Hamowy and William F. Buckley, Jr., *"National Review:* Criticism and Reply," *New Individualist Review* (November 1961), pp. 9, 11.

the latter may be. But if we do so, we come ineluctably to the reverse of the Buckleyite conclusion. We come to the view that since modern air and missile weapons *cannot* be pinpoint-targeted to avoid harming civilians, their very existence must be condemned. And nuclear and air disarmament becomes a great and overriding good to be pursued for its own sake, more avidly even than the demunicipalization of garbage.

PART III:
Epilogue

14

A Strategy for Liberty

Education: Theory and Movement

AND SO WE HAVE IT: a body of truth, sound in theory and capable of application to our political problems—the new libertarianism. But now that we have the truth, how can we achieve victory? We face the great strategic problem of all "radical" creeds throughout history: How can we get from here to there, from our current State-ridden and imperfect world to the great goal of liberty?

There is no magic formula for strategy; any strategy for social change, resting as it does on persuasion and conversion, can only be an art rather than an exact science. But having said this, we are still not bereft of wisdom in the pursuit of our goals. There *can* be a fruitful theory, or at the very least, theoretical discussion, of the proper strategy for change.

On one point there can scarcely be disagreement: a prime and necessary condition for libertarian victory (or, indeed, for victory for *any* social movement, from Buddhism to vegetarianism) is *education*: the persuasion and conversion of large numbers of people to the cause. Education, in turn, has two vital aspects: *calling people's attention* to the existence of such a system, and converting people to the libertarian system. If our movement consisted only of slogans, publicity, and other attention-getting devices, then we might be *heard* by many people, but it would soon be discovered that we had nothing to say—and so the hearing would be fitful and ephemeral. Libertarians must, therefore, engage in hard thinking and scholarship, put forth theoretical and systematic books, articles, and journals, and engage in conferences and seminars. On the other hand, a mere elaboration of the theory will get nowhere if no one has ever heard of the books and articles; hence the need for publicity, slogans, student activism, lectures, radio and TV spots, etc. True education cannot proceed without theory *and* activism, without an ideology and people to carry that ideology forward.

Thus, just as the theory needs to be carried to the attention of the public, so does the theory need *people* to hold the banner, discuss, agitate, and carry the message forward and outward to the public. Once again, both theory and movement become futile and sterile without each other; the theory will die on the vine without a self-conscious movement which dedicates itself to advancing the theory and the goal. The movement will become mere pointless motion if it loses sight of the ideology and the goal in view. Some libertarian theorists feel that there is something impure or disreputable about a living movement with acting individuals; but how can liberty be achieved without libertarians to advance the cause? On the other hand, some militant activists, in their haste for action— *any* action—scorn what seems to be parlor discussions of theory; yet their action becomes futile and wasted energy if they have only a dim idea of what they are being active *about*.

Furthermore, one often hears libertarians (as well as members of other social movements) bewail that they are "only talking to themselves" with their books and journals and conferences; that few people of the "outside world" are listening. But this frequent charge gravely misconceives the many-sided purpose of "education" in the broadest sense. It is not only necessary to educate *others;* continual self-education is also (and equally) necessary. The corps of libertarians must always try to recruit others to their ranks, to be sure; but they must *also* keep their own ranks vibrant and healthy. Education of "ourselves" accomplishes two vital goals. One is the refining and advancing of the libertarian "theory"—the goal and purpose of our whole enterprise. Libertarianism, while vital and true, cannot be merely graven in stone tablets; it must be a living theory, advancing through writing and discussion, and through refuting and combatting errors as they arise. The libertarian movement has dozens of small newsletters and magazines, ranging from mimeographed sheets to slick publications, constantly emerging and dying. This is a sign of a healthy, growing movement, a movement that consists of countless individuals thinking, arguing, and contributing. But there is another critical reason for "talking to ourselves," *even if* that were all the talking that was going on. And that is *reinforcement*—the psychologically necessary knowledge that there are other people of like mind to talk to, argue with, and generally communicate and interact with. At present, the libertarian creed is that of a small minority, and, furthermore, it proposes radical changes in the *status quo.* Hence, it is bound to be a lonely creed, and the reinforcement of having a movement, of "talking to ourselves," can combat and overcome that isolation. The contemporary movement is now old enough to have had a host of defectors; analysis of these defections shows that, in almost every case, the libertarian has been isolated, cut off from fellowship and interaction with his colleagues. A flourishing movement with a sense of community and *esprit de corps* is the best antidote for giving up liberty as a hopeless or "impractical" cause.

Are We "Utopians"?

All right, we are to have education through both theory and a movement. But what then should be the *content* of that education? Every "radical" creed has been subjected to the charge of being "utopian," and the libertarian movement is no exception. Some libertarians themselves maintain that we should not frighten people off by being "too radical," and that therefore the full libertarian ideology and program should be kept hidden from view. These people counsel a "Fabian" program of gradualism, concentrating solely on a gradual whittling away of State power. An example would be in the field of taxation: Instead of advocating the "radical" measure of abolition of all taxation, or even of abolishing income taxation, we should confine ourselves to a call for tiny improvements; say, for a two percent cut in income tax.

In the field of strategic thinking, it behooves libertarians to heed the lessons of the Marxists, because they have been thinking about strategy for radical social change longer than any other group. Thus, the Marxists see two critically important strategic fallacies that "deviate" from the proper path: one they call "ultra-left sectarianism"; the other, and opposing, deviation is "right-wing opportunism." The critics of libertarian "extremist" principles are the analog of the Marxian "right-wing opportunists." The major problem with the opportunists is that by confining themselves strictly to gradual and "practical" programs, programs that stand a good chance of immediate adoption, they are in grave danger of completely losing sight of the ultimate objective, the libertarian goal. He who confines himself to calling for a two percent reduction in taxes helps to bury the ultimate goal of abolition of taxation altogether. By concentrating on the immediate means, he helps liquidate the ultimate goal, and therefore the point of being a libertarian in the first place. If libertarians refuse to hold aloft the banner of the pure principle, of the ultimate goal, *who will?* The answer is no one, hence another major source of defection from the ranks in recent years has been the erroneous path of opportunism.

A prominent case of defection through opportunism is someone we shall call "Robert," who became a dedicated anarcho-capitalist back in the early 1950s. Reaching quickly for activism and immediate gains, Robert concluded that the proper strategic path was to play down all talk of the libertarian goal, and in particular to play down libertarian hostility to government. His aim was to stress only the "positive" and the accomplishments that people could achieve through voluntary action. As his career advanced, Robert began to find uncompromising libertarians an encumbrance; so he began systematically to fire anyone in his organization caught being "negative" about government. It did not take very long for Robert to abandon the libertarian ideology openly and explicitly, and to call for a "partnership" between government and private enterprise—between coercion and the voluntary—in short, to take his place openly in the Establishment. Yet, in his cups, Robert will often continue to refer to himself as an "anarchist," but only in some abstract cloudland totally unrelated to the world as it is.

The free-market economist F. A. Hayek, himself in no sense an "extremist," has written eloquently of the vital importance for the success of liberty of holding the pure and "extreme" ideology aloft as a never-to-be-forgotten creed. Hayek has written that one of the great attractions of socialism has always been the continuing stress on its "ideal" goal, an ideal that permeates, informs, and guides the actions of all those striving to attain it. Hayek then adds:

We must make the building of a free society once more an intellectual adventure, a deed of courage. What we lack is a liberal Utopia, a programme which seems neither a mere defence of things as they are nor a diluted kind of socialism, but a truly liberal radicalism which does not spare the susceptibility of the mighty (including the trade unions), which is not too severely practical and which does not confine itself to what appears today as politically possible. We need intellectual leaders who are prepared to resist the blandishments of power and influence and who are willing to work for an ideal, however small may be the prospects of its early realization. They must be men who are willing to stick to principles and to fight for their full realization, however remote. . . . Free trade and freedom of opportunity are ideals which still may rouse the imaginations of large numbers, but a mere "reasonable freedom of trade"

or a mere "relaxation of controls" is neither intellectually respectable nor likely to inspire any enthusiasm. The main lesson which the
true liberal must learn from the success of the socialists is that it
was their courage to be Utopian which gained them the support of
the intellectuals and thereby an influence on public opinion which
is daily making possible what only recently seemed utterly remote.
Those who have concerned themselves exclusively with what seemed
practicable in the existing state of opinion have constantly found
that even this has rapidly become politically impossible as the result of changes in a public opinion which they have done nothing
to guide. Unless we can make the philosophic foundations of a free
society once more a living intellectual issue, and its implementation
a task which challenges the ingenuity and imagination of our liveli-
est minds, the prospects of freedom are indeed dark. But if we can
regain that belief in the power of ideas which was the mark of liberalism at its best, the battle is not lost.[1]

Hayek is here highlighting an important truth, and an important reason for stressing the ultimate goal: the excitement
and enthusiasm that a logically consistent system can inspire.
Who, in contrast, will go to the barricades for a two percent
tax reduction?

There is another vital tactical reason for cleaving to pure
principle. It is true that day-to-day social and political events
are the resultants of many pressures, the often unsatisfactory
outcome of the push-and-pull of conflicting ideologies and interests. But if only for that reason, it is all the more important
for the libertarian to keep upping the ante. The call for a two
percent tax reduction may achieve only the slight moderation
of a projected tax *increase*; a call for a drastic tax cut may indeed achieve a substantial reduction. And, over the years, it is
precisely the strategic role of the "extremist" to keep pushing
the matrix of day-to-day action further and further in his direction. The socialists have been particularly adept at this strategy. If we look at the socialist program advanced sixty, or even

[1] F. A. Hayek, "The Intellectuals and Socialism," in *Studies in Philosophy, Politics, and Economics* (Chicago: University of Chicago Press, 1967),
p. 194.

thirty years ago, it will be evident that measures considered dangerously socialistic a generation or two ago are now considered an indispensable part of the "mainstream" of the American heritage. In this way, the day-to-day compromises of supposedly "practical" politics get pulled inexorably in the collectivist direction. There is no reason why the libertarian cannot accomplish the same result. In fact, one of the reasons that the conservative opposition to collectivism has been so weak is that conservatism, by its very nature, offers not a consistent political philosophy but only a "practical" defense of the existing *status quo*, enshrined as embodiments of the American "tradition." Yet, as statism grows and accretes, it becomes, by definition, increasingly entrenched and therefore "traditional"; conservatism can then find no intellectual weapons to accomplish its overthrow.

While it is vital for the libertarian to hold his ultimate and "extreme" ideal aloft, this does not, contrary to Hayek, make him a "utopian." The true utopian is one who advocates a system that is contrary to the natural law of human beings and of the real world. A utopian system is one that could not work even if everyone were persuaded to try to put it into practice. The utopian system could not work, i.e., could not sustain itself in operation. The utopian goal of the left: communism— the abolition of specialization and the adoption of uniformity— could not work even if everyone were willing to adopt it immediately. It could not work because it violates the very nature of man and the world, especially the uniqueness and individuality of every person, of his abilities and interests, and because it would mean a drastic decline in the production of wealth, so much so as to doom the great bulk of the human race to rapid starvation and extinction.

In short, the term "utopian" in popular parlance confuses two kinds of obstacles in the path of a program radically different from the *status quo*. One is that it violates the nature of man and of the world and therefore could not work once it was put into effect. This is the utopianism of communism. The second is the difficulty in *convincing* enough people that the program should be adopted. The former is a bad theory because it violates the nature of man; the latter is simply a problem of human *will*, of convincing enough people of the rightness of the doctrine. "Utopian" in its common pejorative sense applies only to the former. In the deepest sense, then, the libertarian doctrine is not utopian but eminently realistic, because it is the only theory that is really consistent with the nature of man and the world. The libertarian does not deny the variety and diversity of man, he glories in it and seeks to give that diversity full expression in a world of complete freedom. And in doing so, he also brings about an enormous increase in productivity and in the living standards of everyone, an eminently "practical" result generally scorned by true utopians as evil "materialism."

The libertarian is also eminently realistic because he alone understands fully the nature of the State and its thrust for power. In contrast, it is the seemingly far more realistic conservative believer in "limited government" who is the truly impractical utopian. This conservative keeps repeating the litany that the central government should be severely limited by a constitution. Yet, at the same time that he rails against the corruption of the original Constitution and the widening of federal power since 1789, the conservative fails to draw the proper lesson from that degeneration. The idea of a strictly limited constitutional State was a noble experiment that failed, even under the most favorable and propitious circumstances. If it failed then, why should a similar experiment fare any better now? No, it is the conservative laissez-fairist, the man who puts all the guns and all the decision-making power into the hands of the central government and *then* says, "Limit yourself"; it is *he* who is truly the impractical utopian.

There is another deep sense in which libertarians scorn the broader utopianism of the left. The left utopians invariably postulate a drastic change in the nature of man; to the left, man *has* no nature. The individual is supposed to be infinitely malleable by his institutions, and so the communist ideal (or the transitional socialist system) is supposed to bring about the New Communist Man. The libertarian believes that, in the ultimate analysis, every individual has free will and moulds himself; it is therefore folly to put one's hope in a uniform and drastic change in people brought about by the projected New Order. The libertarian would *like* to see a moral improvement in everyone, although his moral goals scarcely coincide with those of the socialists. He would, for example, be overjoyed to see all desire for aggression by one man against another disappear from the face of the earth. But he is far too much of a realist to put his trust in this sort of change. Instead, the libertarian system is one that will at once be far more moral and work much better than any other, *given* any existing human values and attitudes. The more the desire for aggression disappears, of course, the better *any* social system will work, including the libertarian; the less need will there be, for example, for any resort to police or to the courts. But the libertarian system places no reliance on any such change.

If libertarians must always hold high the banner of their ultimate ideal, this does not mean that they should scorn any and all advances made toward that ideal. If we should not wax ecstatic about a two percent tax cut, we should *at least* recognize that this would be a step in the right direction. If libertarians have too often been opportunists who have lost sight of their ultimate goal, some have erred in the opposite direction: fearing and condemning any *advances* toward the ideal as sell-outs of the goal itself. The tragedy is that these sectarians, in condemning all advances that fall short of the goal, serve to render vain and futile the cherished goal itself. Much as all of us would be overjoyed to arrive at total liberty at a single bound, the realistic prospects for such a mighty leap are negligible. If social change is not always tiny and gradual neither does it ever occur in a single great leap. In rejecting any approaches to the goal, then, these sectarian libertarians make it impossible for that goal ever to be reached. Thus, in the long run, they can be as fully "liquidationist" of the pure goal as the opportunists themselves.

How, then, can we know whether any halfway measure should be hailed as a step forward or condemned as an opportunist betrayal? There are two guides to the proper libertarian strategy on this question. One is that the libertarian, while hailing, say, a two percent tax cut, should always keep in mind the ultimate goal of tax abolition. It is not incumbent on a libertarian to proclaim continually his ultimate objective; but he must never rest content short of that goal. He must never express his total satisfaction with the new, and marginally better, *status quo*. He must always press on to greater fulfillment; achievement of partial goals must be treated, not as a soporific or with a sigh of relief, but as stepping stones for still more advanced demands. Secondly, no short-run strategy must ever, ever *contradict* the ultimate goal. A short-run demand may never go as far as we would like, but it should always be *consistent* with the pure end; if it is not, the short-run goal will work against the long-run purpose, and opportunist liquidation of libertarian principle will be at hand.

An example of such counter-productive strategy can be taken from the tax system. The libertarian, who looks forward to eventual tax abolition, should always, on any concrete issue, support a tax *cut*, but never support a new tax or a tax increase. Advocating a two percent tax cut, as piddling as it may be, is at least a step in the right direction and it does not *cut against* the ultimate goal. On the other hand, consider the Milton Friedman proposal for a new negative income tax to replace the welfare system. By advocating a new form of taxation, Friedman, if for that reason alone, vitiates and destroys the basic libertarian principle and goal of a taxless society. The basic tax program of the Henry Georgists, for another example, is to remove all tax on land improvements while instituting a confiscatory tax on *un*improved land. The libertarian should not become trapped into such a program in the name of immediate practicality; instead, he should point out the enormous benefits from the former part of the program, while *also* attacking the unfortunate effects of the proposed tax on unimproved land. The libertarian should never allow himself to be trapped into any sort of proposal for "positive" government action; in his perspective the role of government should be to remove itself from all spheres of society as rapidly as it can be pressured to do so.

Neither must there be any contradictions in rhetoric. The libertarian should not indulge in any rhetoric, let alone any policy conclusions, which work against the eventual goal. Thus, suppose that a libertarian is asked to give his views on a specific tax cut. He can perfectly properly speak in favor of such a cut without at the moment pressing on to tax abolition. But it is also incumbent upon him never to violate that goal by rhetoric such as, "Well, of course *some* taxation is essential . . . ," etc. Only harm to the ultimate objective can be achieved by rhetorical flourishes which contradict principle.

Is Education Enough?

All libertarians, of whatever faction or persuasion, lay great stress on education, on convincing an ever larger number of people to become libertarians, and hopefully, highly dedicated ones. The problem, however, is that the great bulk of libertarians hold a very simplistic view of the role and scope of such education. They do not, in short, even attempt to answer the question: After education, what? What then? What happens after X number of people are convinced? And how many need to be convinced to press on to the next stage? *Everyone?* A majority? Many people?

The implicit view of many libertarians is that only education is needed because everyone is an equally likely prospect for conversion. *Everyone* can be converted. While logically, of course, this is true, *sociologically* this is a feeble strategy indeed. Libertarians, of all people, should recognize that the State is a parasitic enemy of society, and that the State creates an elite of rulers who dominate the rest of us and extract their income by coercion. *Convincing* the ruling groups of their own iniquity, while logically possible (and perhaps even feasible in one or two instances), is almost impossible in practice. How much chance is there, for example, of convincing the executives of General Dynamics or of Lockheed that they should not take government largesse? How much likelihood is there that the President of the United States will read this book, or any other piece of libertarian literature, and then exclaim: "They're right. I've been wrong. I resign"? Clearly the chances of converting those who are waxing fat by means of State exploitation are negligible, to say the least. Our hope is to convert the mass of the people who are being victimized by State power, not those who are gaining by it.

But when we say this, we are also saying that beyond the problem of education lies the problem of power. After a substantial number of people have been converted, there will be the additional task of finding ways and means to romove State power from our society. Since the State will not gracefully convert itself out of power, other means than education, means of pressure, will have to be used. What particular means or what combination of means—whether by voting, alternative institutions untouched by the State or massive failure to cooperate with the State—depends on the conditions of the time and what will be found to work or not to work. In contrast to matters of theory and principle, the particular tactics to be used—so long as they are consistent with the ultimate goal of a purely free society—are a matter of pragmatism, judgment, and the inexact "art" of the tactician.

Which Groups?

But education is the current strategic problem for the foreseeable and indefinite future. An important strategic question is *who*: If we cannot hope to convert our rulers in substantial numbers, *who* are the most likely prospects for conversion? which social, occupational, economic, or ethnic classes?

Conservatives and libertarians have often placed their central hopes in big businessmen. This view of big business was most starkly expressed in Ayn Rand's *dictum* that "Big Business is America's most persecuted minority." Persecuted? With a few honorable exceptions, big business jostles one another eagerly to line up at the public trough. Does Lockheed, or General Dynamics, or AT&T or Nelson Rockefeller feel persecuted?

Big business support for the Corporate Welfare-Warfare State is so blatant and so far-ranging, on all levels from the local to the federal, that even many conservatives have had to acknowledge it, at least to some extent. How then explain such fervent support from "America's most persecuted minority"? The only way out for conservatives is to assume (a) that these businessmen are dumb, and don't understand their own economic interests, and/or (b) that they have been brainwashed by left-liberal intellectuals, who have poisoned their souls with guilt and misguided altruism. Neither of these explanations will wash, however, as only a glance at AT&T or Lockheed will amply show. Big businessmen tend to be admirers of statism, to be "corporate liberals," not because their souls have been poisoned by intellectuals, but because a good thing has thereby been coming their way. Ever since the acceleration of statism at the turn of the twentieth century, big businessmen have been using the great powers of State contracts, subsidies and cartellization to carve out privileges for themselves at the expense of the rest of the society. It is not too farfetched to assume that Nelson Rockefeller is guided far more by self-interest than he is by woolly-headed altruism. It is generally admitted even by liberals, for example, that the vast network of government regulatory agencies is being used to cartellize each industry on behalf of the large firms and at the expense of the public. But to salvage their New Deal world-view, liberals have to console themselves with the thought that these agencies and similar "reforms," enacted during the Progressive, Wilson, or Rooseveltian periods, were launched in good faith, with the "public weal" grandly in view. The idea and genesis of the agencies and other liberal reforms were therefore "good"; it was only in prac-

tice that the agencies somehow slipped into sin and into sub-
servience to private, corporate interests. But what Kolko, Weinstein, Domhoff and other revisionist historians have shown,
clearly and thoroughly, is that this is a piece of liberal mythol-
ogy. In reality, all of these reforms, on the national and local
levels alike, were conceived, written, and lobbied for by these
very privileged groups themselves. The work of these historians
reveals conclusively that there *was* no Golden Age of Reform
before sin crept in; sin was there from the beginning, from the
moment of conception. The liberal reforms of the Progressive-
New Deal-Welfare State were designed to create what they did
in fact create: a world of centralized statism, of "partnership"
between government and industry, a world which subsists in
granting subsidies and monopoly privileges to business and
other favored groups.

Expecting the Rockefellers or the legion of other favored big
businessmen to convert to a libertarian or even a laissez-faire
view is a vain and empty hope. But this is not to say that *all*
big businessmen, or businessmen in general, must be written off.
Contrary to the Marxists, not all businessmen, or even big businessmen, constitute a homogeneous economic class with iden-
tical class interests. On the contrary, when the CAB confers
monopoly privileges on a few large airlines, or when the FCC
confers a monopoly on AT&T, there are numerous other firms
and businessmen, small and large, who are injured and *excluded*
from the privileges. The conferring of a monopoly of communications on AT&T by the FCC, for example, for a long
while kept the now rapidly growing data communications industry stagnating in infancy; it was only an FCC decision to
allow competition that enabled the industry to grow by leaps
and bounds. Privilege implies exclusion, so there will always be
a host of businesses and businessmen, large and small, who will
have a solid economic interest in ending State control over
their industry. There are therefore a host of businessmen, especially those remote from the privileged "Eastern Establishment," who are potentially receptive to free-market and libertarian ideas.

Which groups, then, could we expect to be particularly receptive to libertarian ideas? Where, as the Marxists would put it, is our proposed "agency for social change"? This, of course, is an important strategic question for libertarians, since it gives us leads on where to direct our educational energies.

Campus youth is one group that has already been prominent in the rising libertarian movement; in fact, the great bulk of its members are college students and activists in college chapters. This is not surprising: college is the time when people are most open to reflection and to considering basic questions of our society. As youth enamored of consistency and unvarnished truth, as collegians accustomed to a world of scholarship and abstract ideas, and not yet burdened with the care and the often narrower vision of adult employment, these youngsters provide a fertile field for libertarian conversion. Libertarianism has already taken hold on the nation's campuses, and we can expect more of this growth in the future, a growth that is already being matched by the adherence of an expanding number of young scholars, professors, and graduate students. The libertarian upsurge among campus youth gives at least the hope of an increased carryover into the adult world of tomorrow.

Youth in general should also be attracted by the libertarian position on subjects that are often closest to their concerns: specifically, our call for ab lition of the draft, withdrawal from Indochina and the Cold War, civil liberties for everyone, and legalization of drugs and other victimless crimes.

What of "Middle America"—that vast middle class and working class that constitute the bulk of the American population and which is often at polar opposites from campus youth? Do we have any appeal for them? Logically, our appeal to Middle America should be even greater. We direct ourselves squarely to the aggravated and chronic discontentments that afflict the mass of the American people: rising taxes, inflation, urban congestion, crime, welfare scandals. Only libertarians have concrete and consistent solutions to these pressing ills: solutions that center on getting them out from under government in all these areas and turning them over to private and voluntary action. We can show that government and statism have been responsible for these evils, and that getting coercive government off of our backs will provide the remedies.

To small businessmen we can promise a truly free-enterprise world, shorn of monopoly privilege, cartels, and subsidies engineered by the State and the Establishment. And to them and to the big businessmen outside the monopoly Establishment we can promise a world where their individual talents and energies can at last have full room to expand and to provide improved technology and increased productivity for them and for us all. To various ethnic and minority groups we can show that only under liberty is there full freedom for each group to cultivate its concerns and to run its own institutions, unimpeded and uncoerced by majority rule.

In short, the potential appeal of libertarianism is a multi-class appeal; it is an appeal that cuts across race, occupation, economic class, and the generations; any and all people not directly in the ruling elite are potentially receptive to our message. Every person or group that values its liberty or prosperity is a potential adherent to the libertarian creed.

Toward a Free America

The libertarian creed, finally, offers the fulfillment of the best of the American past along with the promise of a far better future. Even more than conservatives, who are often attached to the monarchical traditions of a happily obsolete European past, libertarians are squarely in the great classical liberal tradition that built the United States and bestowed on us the American heritage of individual liberty, a peaceful foreign policy, minimal government, and a free-market economy. Libertarians are the only genuine current heirs of Jefferson, Paine, Jackson, and the abolitionists.

And yet, while we are more truly traditional and more rootedly American than the conservatives, we are in some ways more radical than the radicals. Not in the sense that we have either the desire or the hope of remoulding human nature by the path of politics; but in the sense that only we provide the really sharp and genuine break with the encroaching statism of the twentieth century. The Old Left wants only more of what we are suffering from now; the New Left, in the last analysis, proposes only still more aggravated statism or compulsory egalitarianism and uniformity. Libertarianism is the logical culmination of the now forgotten "Old Right" (of the 1930s and '40s) opposition to the New Deal, war, centralization, and State intervention. Only we wish to break with *all* aspects of the liberal State: with its welfare *and* its warfare, its monopoly privileges *and* its egalitarianism, its repression of victimless crimes whether personal *or* economic. Only we offer technology without technocracy, growth without pollution, liberty without chaos, law without tyranny, the defense of property rights in one's person *and* in one's material possessions.

Strands and remnants of libertarian doctrines are, indeed, all around us, in large parts of our glorious past and in values and ideas in the confused present. But only libertarianism takes these strands and remnants and integrates them into a mighty, logical, and consistent system. The enormous success of Karl Marx and Marxism has been due not to the validity of his ideas —all of which, indeed, are fallacious—but to the fact that he dared to weave socialist theory into a mighty system. Liberty cannot succeed without an equivalent and contrasting systematic theory; and until the last few years, despite our great heritage of economic and political thought and practice, we have not had a fully integrated and consistent theory of liberty. We now have that systematic theory; we come, fully armed with our knowledge, prepared to bring our message and to capture the imagination of all groups and strands in the population. All other theories and systems have clearly failed: socialism is in retreat everywhere, and notably in Eastern Europe; liberalism has bogged us down in a host of insoluble problems; conservatism has nothing to offer but sterile defense of the *status quo*. Liberty has never been fully tried in the modern world; libertarians now propose to fulfill the American dream and the world dream of liberty and prosperity for all mankind.

Index